POLAR BEARS

POLAR BEARS

The Natural History of a Threatened Species

IAN STIRLING

Fitzhenry & Whiteside
www.fitzhenry.ca

Published in Canada by Fitzhenry & Whiteside, 195 Allstate Parkway,
Markham, Ontario L3R 4T8
Published in the United States by Fitzhenry & Whiteside, 311 Washington Street,
Brighton, Massachusetts 02135

www.fitzhenry.ca   godwit@fitzhenry.ca
10 9 8 7 6 5 4 3 2 1

Library and Archives Canada Cataloguing in Publication
Stirling, Ian
Polar bears : the natural history of an endangered species / Ian Stirling.
Includes bibliographical references and index.
ISBN 978-1-55455-155-2
1. Polar bear. 2. Polar bear--Pictorial works. I. Title.
QL737.C27S755 2011   599.786   C2011-902618-X

Publisher Cataloging-in-Publication Data (U.S.)
Stirling, Ian.
Polar bears : the natural history of a threatened species / Ian Stirling.
[352] p. : col. photos. ;   cm.
Includes index.
Summary: Comprehensive study of the polar bear: their evolution, life history, behavior,
how they are researched, and the current threat to their very existence.
ISBN-13: 978-1-55455-155-2 (pbk.)
1. Polar bear. I. Title.
599.786 dc22   QL737.C27S7575 2011

Fitzhenry & Whiteside acknowledges with thanks the Canada Council for the Arts,
and the Ontario Arts Council for their support of our publishing program. We acknowledge
the financial support of the Government of Canada through the Canada Book Fund for
our publishing activities

Design by Kerry Designs
Cover images courtesy of Stefan Lundgren
Printed in Canada by Friesens

To my grandchildren

Sophie, William, Maggie, Hazel, and Sam,

in the hope that their world, and that of their grandchildren, will still include
wild polar bears roaming the sea ice of the Arctic

CONTENTS

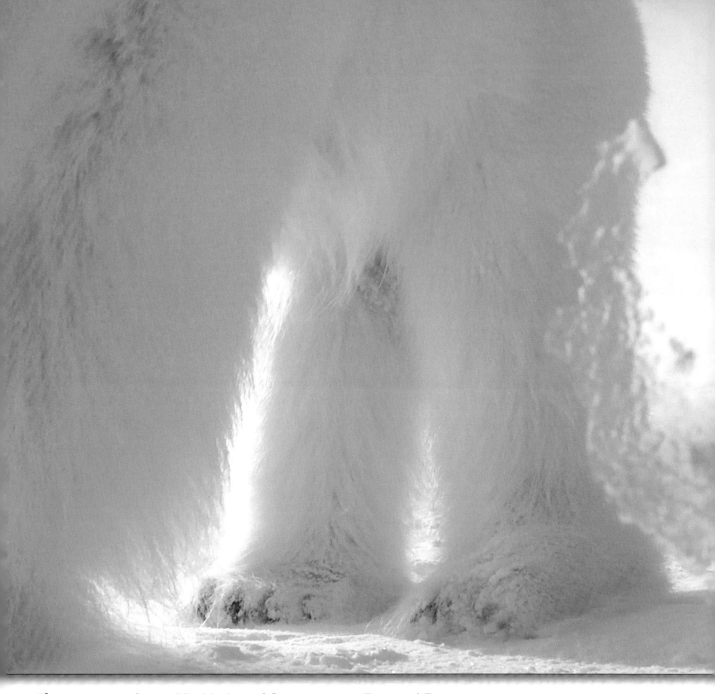

An adult female polar bear with her 4-month-old cub searches for seals along the edge of an ice floe. The cub stays close to its mother for safety but also to learn how to hunt by constantly observing her behaviour at close range.
(© Philip Dalton/John Downer Productions)

A 4-month-old cub takes its first tentative steps outside the maternity den as its mother leads it to the ocean to hunt seals. Note the ice that formed on the lens of the Spycam while it waited for days in bitter cold for the family to emerge (see pp. 152-153). (© Philip Dalton/John Downer Productions)
(© Philip Dalton/John Downer Productions)

ACKNOWLEDGEMENTS

When I began working with polar bears, seals, and their relationships to sea ice in the fall of 1970, basic research to understand species and ecosystems was a priority in Federal Government science departments. It was a truly exciting time when a person with ideas, initiative, and a willingness to work hard was primarily limited only by how hard he or she wished to work. The Canadian Wildlife Service of those days provided me with the freedom to ask ecological questions large and small, and to follow them up. As well, for 30 years, I have been an adjunct professor at the University of Alberta. That appointment provided me with a stimulating academic environment, made me eligible to apply for research funds I could not apply for as a civil servant and, most importantly, to take on a number of truly exceptional graduate students who wanted to conduct research on the ecology and conservation of polar bears and seals. To my great personal satisfaction, most of them are still working and contributing in the field.

I owe an enormous debt of gratitude to a very large number of organizations and individuals who have supported my research or participated in it in many ways. The Polar Continental Shelf Project, which for many years was probably the single most cost-effective organization that has ever operated in the Arctic, supported several of my projects, most of which would never have been completed without them. The Natural Sciences and Engineering Research Council supported me through the university for 25 years and helped make it possible for many graduate students to complete their degrees and move on to independent careers in arctic research. Several other organizations also provided significant long-term support, including the Canadian Wildlife Service, the Department of Biological Sciences at the University of Alberta, Manitoba Department of Natural Resources, Northwest Territories Wildlife Service, Department of Fisheries and Oceans, Department of Indian and Northern Affairs, Churchill Northern Studies Centre, Dome Petroleum, Esso Resources Canada Limited, Nunavut Wildlife Management Board, and World Wildlife Fund (Canada and International).

No one has the good fortune to work on so many projects for so many years without owing an enormous amount to many individuals. Dennis Andriashek worked with me and provided incredible support for almost 35 years in both the field and the lab. I also owe a special debt of thanks to my friend and colleague, Dr. Tom Smith, with whom I have shared research on polar bears and seals all over the Arctic for a couple of decades and from whom I learned a tremendous amount in many discussions over too many cups of coffee on bad-weather days. Wendy Calvert ran the lab, designed our computerised data base, and assisted on many field projects for over twenty years.

One of the things that makes me realize the decades have gone by is how many of the people to whom I owe thanks are no longer with us. On the one hand, that makes me quite sad. On the other, I am enormously grateful I was privileged to know them and work with them. I would like to thank the following for all the good company they provided in the field and in the lab and the invaluable feedback they contributed to my thinking about polar bears, seals, and their ecological interrelationships. These include Steve Amstrup, Stephen Atkinson, Erik Born, Holly Cleator, Corey Davis, Doug DeMaster, Andy Derocher, Mike Hammill, Lois Harwood, Lisa Hiruki, V.A. Hughey, Sara Iverson, Thor Larsen, Nick Lunn, the late Ralph Nelson, the late Nils Øritsland, Alana Phillips, the late Malcolm Ramsay, Evan Richardson, Ray Schweinsburg, Merlin Shoesmith, Don Siniff, Becky Sjare, Pauline Smith, Cheryl Spencer, Mitch Taylor, Greg Thiemann, the late Savva Uspenski, the late Christian Vibe, and Øystein Wiig. A very long list of pilots contributed to the success of various research projects but S.I. Kobiyashi, Steve Miller, and John Innes deserve particular recognition and thanks.

I am grateful to the following Inuk hunters from whom I learned a great deal over the years: the late Andy Carpenter, the late Fred Carpenter, Albert Elias, Peter Esau, Ipeelie Inookie, John Lucas, the late Wallace Lucas, the late Jimmy Memorana, David Nasogaluak, the late Henry Nasogaluak, Fred Wolkie, Geddes Wolkie, and the late Fred Wolkie Sr.

I also thank Sharon Fitzhenry, President of Fitzhenry and Whiteside Publishing, for encouraging me to write this book and for giving me the freedom to develop it as I saw fit. A large number of professional photographers and colleagues provided access to a stunning array of images which, collectively, provide the broadest visual coverage of the ecology of the polar bear that has ever been in a single book anywhere. To all those individuals, thank you so much for your contributions to this project. Dave Vasicek of Color Space Photographics in Edmonton, AB, provided excellent technical support for scanning slides, and re-finishing many images. I also thank Philip Dalton and John Downer of John Downer Productions for their generosity and willingness to allow the use of the unique and innovative photos taken with their "Spycams," as recently featured in the BBC documentary, "Polar Bear: Spy on the Ice." The National Aeronautics and Space Administration (NASA), the National Snow and Ice Data Centre (NSIDC), and the University Corporation for Atmospheric Research (UCAR) kindly allowed use of figures from their research reports. I also thank Evan Richardson for producing many of the figures as well as providing invaluable feedback on how they could best be presented.

Last, but not least, I would particularly like to thank my wife, Stella, and my children Lea, Claire, and Ross, for their constant support. In the course of doing the research described in this book, I was away a great deal. Even so, they were always supportive. We enjoyed a hugely rich life together, and still do, especially now with the addition of their spouses and our grandchildren. I thank them enormously for everything.

INTRODUCTION

"And from my heart I bless the fate that allowed me to be born at a time
when Arctic exploration by dog sledge was not yet a thing of the past."

Those words were written by the famous Danish ethnologist and explorer Knud Rasmussen after he completed an 18-month trip from Danish Island in Foxe Basin (Canada) to East Cape in Alaska in 1923-24 as part of the Fifth Thule Expedition. During that trip, he noted how fast things were changing for Inuit people all across North America and how much more rapidly the changes were apparent the farther he got from Greenland and the closer to Alaska. He realized that change was happening incredibly quickly and the window of opportunity to study the things he was most interested in was closing rapidly. I first read those words late one night near the end of March as a blizzard was building in Churchill, Manitoba. I had just settled down for a long read, knowing I wouldn't have to get up early, when that sentence simply electrified me. In that moment, I realized that I too had been fortunate enough to conduct the majority of my research in the Canadian Arctic during a similarly blessed period of opportunity.

The polar bear, more than any other animal, symbolizes the Arctic. People all around the world who will never see one know what it looks like. Like the vastness of the polar sea ice it has evolved to be at home on, the sheer size of an adult polar bear is impressive. Its pristine whiteness mat-

(© Mark Freedman)

ches the backdrop of snow and ice that we all associate with the Arctic.

At special moments when I have time to watch an undisturbed polar bear, I am often struck by an overwhelming sense that it is simply where it belongs. A wild polar bear is the Arctic incarnate. The Arctic is not a forsaken wasteland to a polar bear; it is home, and a comfortable home at that. For thousands of years, the climate, the ice, and the seals upon which it feeds have shaped and finely tuned the evolution of this predator so exquisitely that it has become not just a symbol but the very embodiment of life in the Arctic. While it is easy to understand why the polar bear became such an powerful icon, it is difficult even now to comprehend its vulnerability to a changing environment.

Although the polar bear is a true marine mammal in the sense that it depends on the sea for existence, the fact that it walks about on the sea ice like a regular land bear, and periodically comes ashore confuses some. For example, in the United States, the polar bear is considered a marine mammal for legal purposes. In Canada it is a land mammal. Ecologically, however, the polar bear is clearly an integral part of the marine ecosystem, and that is the context in which I will treat it.

I began my research on polar bears forty years ago, in

1970, after spending several years studying seals in Antarctica, Australia, and elsewhere. International concern for polar bears was high and the Polar Bear Specialist Group of the International Union for the Conservation of Nature (IUCN) had already begun holding biennial meetings that led to the Agreement on the Conservation of Polar Bears. Research was focused on determining the sizes of polar bear populations in different parts of the Arctic and on identifying where the core maternity denning areas were. Polar bears were still being hunted in Canada, Greenland, Norway, and the United States, though they were protected in the Soviet Union. Management and conservation plans were needed, but before they could be developed, a great deal of new information was needed.

Fairly early on, it became clear the polar bear was not threatened with extinction because of excessive hunting. However, because of their low reproductive rate, they were still vulnerable to overharvest if not properly managed. In recognition of this, the Polar Bear Specialist Group began to recommend more fundamental research and stressed the importance of broadly based fundamental studies on the ecology of the bears. With the support of the Canadian Wildlife Service and the Department of Biological Sciences at the University of Alberta, several long-time colleagues, and a number of outstanding graduate students, we undertook a wide variety of studies of polar bears, including population ecology, behaviour, physiology, genetics, interspecific relationships with seals and sea ice, the biological importance of polynyas (areas of open water surrounded by ice), and denning habitat. In this book, I have tried to boil down and integrate the results of that research, as well as studies by many of my colleagues, to provide a broad understanding of the ecology and natural history of polar bears in accessible non-technical language.

In writing the book, I have followed a couple of general themes. The first of these is that the polar bear does not exist in isolation. It is both a product and a part of the polar marine ecosystem. It is constantly influenced by a changing environment and it interacts with other species on a daily basis. One of my primary goals is to try to pass on an understanding of that concept. The polar bear has also been a significant factor in the evolution of the behaviour and ecology of the arctic seals and vice versa. More than anything else, a polar bear's life revolves around energy: the obtaining of as much energy as efficiently as possible when there is an opportunity, and then expending that energy as parsimoniously as possible because it

is often uncertain when or where the next meal will come from. Because their success as predators determines their very existence, and this is the aspect that most people have the greatest interest in, I have written the longest chapter on how they hunt and how diverse their techniques are. In part, I have also expanded that chapter because so many people are now observing polar bears hunting on the sea ice from expedition ships in Svalbard, Greenland, and Canada during the arctic spring and summer. As a part-time guide on some of those trips, I have seen the total excitement and fascination of ecotourists watching bears on the sea ice, and heard how many questions they have. Thus, I hope the chapter, "Hunters of the Northern Ice", will help future travellers interpret some of what they see and understand a bit about the bears as part of the arctic marine ecosystem. Similarly, because so many ecotourists also go to see and appreciate the famous polar bears of Churchill, Manitoba, I have also written a separate chapter ("The Polar Bear Capital of the World") to explain more about why the bears are there, what they are doing, and some of the truly special aspects of their ecology and behaviour.

A second theme is that each polar bear is an individual. A solitary predator in an extreme environment like the Arctic must live by its wits. Thus the behaviour of one bear may or may not be representative of the behaviour of all bears. A single solution for one bear will not answer all situations for others—often they need to invent their own. Conditions for hunting or other environmental factors may change quickly. Consequently, polar bears are highly inquisitive. They often contemplate a situation before they act, and they learn quickly from new experiences. It is also clear they remember a lot, although we do not know how much. As a result, each bear is unique because of its individual combination of experiences and knowledge.

At the risk of seeming too professorial, I have tried to supply enough background for readers to understand the basic material covered in each chapter. Over the years, I have given a lot of talks and have kept a record of the kinds of questions people asked so as to include as many of the answers as possible in the text, along with new things the reader may not have thought about before. Because so many students have asked me questions about how to study a polar bear, there is a short, separate chapter devoted to that topic. Because I wrote the book as a nontechnical reference, I have not put all the references into the text as one might in a scientific paper.

However, much of the specific and general source material is given in the Bibliography to provide some initial direction for those who may wish to go further in some areas. Also, I highly recommend the web site of the IUCN Polar Bear Specialist Group (http://pbsg.nopolar.no/en) which has a large reference section (click on "Library"). There are three sections: past proceedings of the PBSG (which can be downloaded as PDF files for free), English language polar bear literature, and Russian language polar bear references. This data base is being added to constantly so it is one of the most thorough sources of easily available information. The PBSG web site also provides a great deal of other information about polar bears in considerable depth. Because science operates on the metric system, numerical values are stated metrically, with English equivalents in parentheses.

Polar bears, the seals they eat, and the arctic marine environment in general have dominated most of my working life. As our knowledge of their behaviour and ecology has grown each year, so has my continuing fascination with them. Even so, there is still so much new to learn that in many ways, each additional trip is as revealing and exciting as the first. Yet, for all that, there is something special about the polar bear that takes me beyond science and objective description. That special sense is also at the heart of my concern about the effects of climate warming on the Arctic, and the world in general, as symbolised by the polar bear. It is also why I am so especially appreciative of the hugely important leadership that is being so ambitiously led by the non-governmental organizations, Polar Bears International, and the World Wildlife Fund, on behalf of both the polar bears and the ice-based arctic marine ecosystem, to combat climate warming.

After 40 years of studying polar bears, I am still overwhelmed by a feeling of privilege when I watch an undisturbed wild bear. I hope through the text that follows, you will come to understand a bit more about how they hunt, travel, eat, den, and live. More simply, I hope this book will help you understand what it means to be a wild polar bear in the Arctic.

The opinions expressed in the book are my own however, and do not necessarily reflect those of Environment Canada, the University of Alberta, or any of the agencies that have supported my research. And, of course, whatever mistakes of fact or interpretation may be in the book are completely my responsibility.

Chapter 1

An adult female with two yearling cubs crossing a section of multiyear ice, where conditions for hunting seals are poor
(© Stefan Lundgren).

PRESENT DAY DISTRIBUTION AND ABUNDANCE

Polar bears are found throughout the ice-covered waters of the circumpolar Arctic (Figure 1). Sea ice is a tough environment for any animal to survive in, let alone prosper, and polar bears depend on the ice for everything that matters to their survival, including hunting, seasonal movements, finding mates, and breeding. To the uninitiated observer looking down from a commercial jet flying over the north polar route, the seemingly endless sea ice on the Arctic Ocean may appear much the same, and all appears to be good for polar bears. However, there is as much variety in types of ice and the relative abundance of life associated with each ice type as there

An adult male walking on pack ice
(© Jenny E. Ross)

might be if you were to compare a coastal Douglas fir forest with the Great Plains of central North America. To hunt the seals they eat to survive, polar bears depend on the sea ice throughout the Arctic to provide the critical platform they need in order to be able to access their prey. Although the occasional bear has been known to kill a seal in open water near the shoreline, successful hunting in open-water is very uncommon. Seals are far more agile swimmers than bears, which makes expending energy trying to hunt by swimming in open water both inefficient and ineffective, especially in comparison to hunting from the surface of the ice. Not surprisingly, some types of ice are more important to polar bears than others, and brief descriptions of these will follow.

Some personal thoughts about the sea ice home of polar bears

I have paused to marvel at the very existence of the polar bear countless times, and in many places in the Arctic. While standing on annual ice several feet thick, at the edge of an ice floe, beside an open lead (a crack in the ice with water in it), or on a vast unbroken expanse of frozen ice in early April, there is nothing living in sight. In fact, there is not much of anything at all in sight but ice, snow, sometimes a bit of ice-cold blue water between nearby floes, or a few wisps of mist rising up from a lead. The ice occasionally cracks and creaks beneath your feet as the currents or winds make it shift slightly, possibly causing floes to grind against each other. The temperature may be -30°C (-22°F), sometimes with a wind of 30-50 kph (19-31 mph) with drifting snow.

In these conditions, the dry snow squeaks with even the slightest movement of your mukluks, as if you were walking over hundreds of mice with each step. Gusts of wind may batter you back and forth as you stand there. For as far as you can see, everything is white until the white eventually blends with the blue sky on a distant horizon. If you climb to the top of a pressure ridge of buckled ice, you can see slightly farther, but the view is the same.

At such special moments, I am often overwhelmed by several things, but especially by how tiny and ineffectual my presence is in the vastness of the frozen Arctic Ocean. While I watch a distant polar bear striding purposefully across the sea ice in such circumstances, oblivious to me or anything else, it is easy to under-

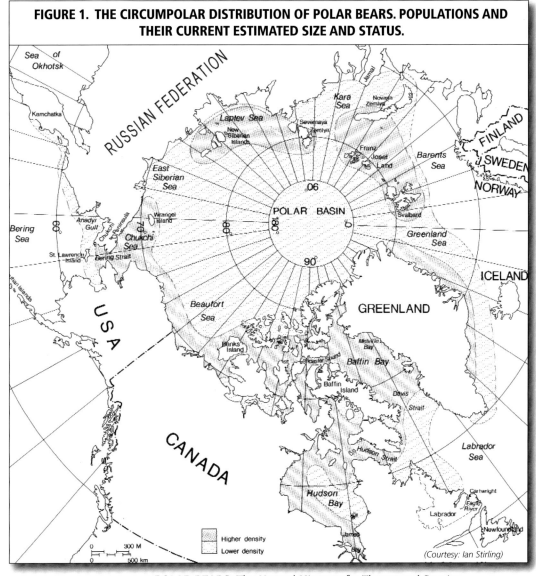

FIGURE 1. THE CIRCUMPOLAR DISTRIBUTION OF POLAR BEARS. POPULATIONS AND THEIR CURRENT ESTIMATED SIZE AND STATUS.

(Courtesy: Ian Stirling)

A polar bear drags a seal it has caught on a floe in the pack ice. An ivory gull looks on, waiting for an opportunity to scavenge.
(© Stefan Lundgren)

stand why it became the powerful iconic animal of the arctic sea ice in the first place, yet difficult even now to comprehend its vulnerability because of climate warming.

Types of sea ice

Two kinds of sea ice have the greatest influence on the ecology of polar bears, mainly because of how these influence the abundance and accessibility of their primary prey, the ubiquitous ringed seal. *Multiyear ice* may be several years old and is typically 2-5 m (6.5-16 ft) thick. It partially melts in summer but refreezes, replacing the melted portion, and thickening as more ice grows through the following winter. It is snow-covered, thus allowing a limited amount of sunlight to pass through it to stimulate biological productivity. Multiyear ice is predominantly found offshore in the central Arctic Ocean and near the coastlines

of the northern Canadian Arctic Islands and northern Greenland. A large portion of the multiyear ice lies over very deep and generally unproductive water with low densities of seals.

Annual ice forms in winter, melts completely in summer, and occurs mainly along the southern coastlines of the Arctic Ocean, in channels between the islands of various arctic archipelagos, and in more southerly areas such as Hudson Bay, Davis Strait, and Baffin Bay. Annual ice rarely exceeds about 2 m (6.5 ft) in thickness and is more easily penetrated by sunlight in the spring, thus stimulating algal growth on its underside. Most annual ice lies over the shallower and more biologically productive waters of the continental shelf where seal densities are highest. Consequently, that is where polar bears do most of their hunting. There are two main categories of annual ice: *land-fast ice*, is attached to the land, while *pack ice* is

POLAR BEARS: The Natural History of a Threatened Species

made up of moving ice floes not attached to land. Within these categories are several subcategories of ice types, but three are of greatest importance for seals, and thus for the bears that hunt them: stable landfast areas with snow drifts deep enough for seals to make their birth lairs (usually in bays, near the coast, or in channels between islands); the floe edge, which is the outer edge of the landfast ice with associated leads; and drifting pack ice dense enough to cover 75% or more of the surface of the ocean.

A few years ago, we did an analysis of observations of polar bears and their tracks collected in surveys over about 75,000 linear km in the Beaufort Sea to determine more specifically what kinds of sea ice habitat polar bears preferred. Although we identified seven general categories, the great majority of the bears we found (514 of 627) were along the floe edge and near the edges of leads in the ice, or in areas where the pack ice regularly cracked open because of wind and currents and then refroze. Bearded seals and young ringed seals are more abundant in these areas. Adult bearded seals are several times larger than ringed seals and consequently are mainly killed by adult male polar bears. Although bearded seals are capable of maintaining breathing holes with the claws on their foreflippers, like ringed seals, they tend not to. Seals are most vulnerable to capture by bears when they

An adult male jumping between floes in the pack ice.
(© Stefan Lundgren)

surface to breathe in narrow cracks or at breathing holes in patches of thin ice that have just frozen over. In newly re-frozen leads, the breathing holes have not yet become hidden or deeply buried and protected by the drifted snow. Subadult ringed seals also occur more frequently there, are less experienced than adults, and probably easier for bears to catch. Consequently, anywhere that younger seals are more abundant is especially attractive to polar bears.

The importance of these cracks in frozen ice to polar bears was rather dramatically illustrated one spring, in early March, when one of the most experienced of our research team members, Dennis Andriashek, travelled off to the Beaufort Sea to put radio collars on female bears. The weather had been calm and very cold for some time before he arrived and the ice was solidly frozen. There were no fresh cracks and the bears were widely dispersed at very low density. After searching over 2,500 km (1,550 mi) of ice, he saw only six bears. Then the weather changed and strong winds blew for several days, opening up a single new lead about 150 km (95 mi) offshore. In the next six days, he sighted 90 polar bears in the vicinity of the lead. Even allowing for possible duplicate sightings, that is a remarkable and immediate difference. The importance of the lead was further underlined by the fact that almost all the tracks recorded were in a corridor about 1 km (0.6 mi) wide on either side.

In stable ice areas where snow drifts accumulate along the pressure ridges, adult ringed seals maintain breathing holes in the ice below the drifts. In spring, the pregnant females dig out lairs in which they give birth to their pups. About 100 of the 627 polar bears were found in this kind of habitat, including a majority of adult female bears accompanied by their cubs-of-the-year. In most areas of the Arctic, this habitat tends to be along the coastlines, in large bays with islands in fiords such as those along the east coast of Baffin Island or Svalbard, and the inter-island channels of the various arctic archipelagos.

The least preferred areas are those where the ice is very rough, in part probably because it is difficult and expensive energetically to travel through such areas, but also because the seals' breathing holes are difficult to access beneath the ice blocks and pressure ridges. Nor do they like vast areas of smooth ice with little drifted snow on the surface to hide the breathing holes of seals, probably because the seals don't much like these areas either. Bears also tend to avoid areas of multiyear ice such as that which characterizes much of the polar basin, probably because of the low

density of seals. For these reasons, polar bears concentrate on the annual ice in coastal areas over the continental shelf where the biological productivity is higher than in deep-water areas.

The ecology of sea ice

Arctic sea ice is a tough environment for any animal to survive in, let alone prosper. The enormous variability, both predictable and unpredictable, in the distribution and abundance of the ice itself requires animals living there to be able to make large adjustments to their movements on a regular basis. The timing of spring break-up or freeze-up in the fall can fluctuate greatly between years. The extent of the ice cover or the distribution of leads and pressure ridges may also vary enormously between seasons or years. On a smaller scale, ice may be either absent or abundant locally through summer or fall, sometimes changing overnight because of wind or currents. When the ice is relatively thin during fall freeze-up, a storm may compress 80 km or more (50+ mi) of newly frozen ice stretching offshore into the ocean into a virtually impassable

The floe edge in the Southern Beaufort Sea. The ice to the left is still attached to the land. To the right of the open water lies pack ice. (© Ian Stirling)

A subadult ringed seal hauled out onto a large ice pan. The blood spots on its chest are from being attacked by a more dominant seal.
(© Ian Stirling)

rubble field only 20 or 30 km (12.5-18.5 mi) across, near the coast. Because of the large degree of interannual variability in distribution of types of ice, the location of the best habitat for over-wintering seals or the reproductive productivity of the seals themselves may vary greatly between years for reasons that are not currently under-stood. Such extreme variability exists in few other habitats. On a large scale, in the Beaufort and Chukchi Seas, stretching from the western Cana-dian Arctic, across Alaska, and eastern Russia, an individual ice floe may move hundreds of km in various directions throughout the year in response to wind and currents.

Both the surface and the underside of sea ice are vital to polar bears. The surface provides the critical platform on which bears travel and from which they are able to hunt seals. Less apparent, on the underside of the ice, is a unique and bio-logically rich, if transient, seasonal community of algae and marine organisms. This is the epontic,

or "under-ice," community. In response to the sunlight penetrating the ice in spring, a flourish-ing community of algae and single-cell organisms becomes established on the underside and within the ice itself. The rapid increase in day length and intensity of sunlight in spring stimulate a bloom in phytoplankton (plant cells) that support small invertebrates, which in turn are fed upon by larger invertebrates and small fish that live in cracks and on the underside of the ice, thus providing food for the ringed seals.

It has been estimated that in some areas, up to a third of the primary productivity of the ocean in ice-covered waters over the continental shelf is produced on the underside of the sea ice. Most importantly however, because the epontic com-munity is anchored in and beneath the ice, its bio-mass remains near the surface for several months until the ice eventually melts, after which most of the biomass sinks to the seafloor. It is the reten-tion of an abundant and accessible food source on

POLAR BEARS: The Natural History of a Threatened Species

the underside of the ice that attracts seals and keeps them there. In areas without ice cover, or after the ice melts, epontic nutrients fall to the ocean floor where they and the food chain that depend on them are less accessible to animals that feed near the surface.

Because seals hunted from the ice surface are mammals, they must regularly return to the surface to breathe. During winter and early spring, when most of the ice is frozen, they breathe at open cracks in the ice or in breathing holes they maintain themselves by abrading the ever-freezing ice with the heavy claws on their foreflippers. However, when seals surface to breathe, they are vulnerable to capture by the bears, especially in the late spring and early summer when the protective snow cover over the holes melts. Later in the summer, the annual ice over the continental shelf, the most important polar bear habitat, simply melts and disappears. At this point, the bears must either retreat onto land and survive on their stored fat reserves until freeze-up in the fall, or they may migrate north into the multiyear ice of the central Arctic Ocean, where they probably also mainly live on stored fat but are still able to hunt a certain amount. Bears in both these ecological circumstances are simply waiting until freeze-up allows them back to their preferred ice habitat in the fall: the annual ice over the continental shelf.

The "Arctic Ring of Life"

Parallel to the coastline of the polar basin, and around the various archipelagos, there is a system of leads and areas of open water surrounded by ice, called polynyas, which remains open through

An adult bearded seal in the pack ice.
(© Ian Stirling)

A breathing hole in landfast ice being maintained by a bearded seal using the claws on its foreflippers. It is twice the diametre of a ringed seal breathing hole.
(© Ian Stirling)

For many years, there was little research done on the biology of the ocean in shore lead and polynya areas, largely because they are often difficult to get to and dangerous to travel in. It is also very expensive to maintain a research project in such areas on a scale large enough to be worthwhile, in part because these regions are difficult to access without an icebreaker. Explorers, arctic biologists, and Inuit hunters alike have known for many years that there are substantial numbers of marine mammals and birds to be found along the edge of the ice pack and in the shore leads and polynyas that parallel the Arctic Basin. The wind and currents that maintain the polynyas physically also function to mix nutrients throughout the water column. The thinner and less complete ice cover around the shore lead polynya system allows more light into the water to stimulate photosynthesis and primary biological productivity. Over the last fifteen years or so, there have been several large, multi-disciplinary research projects in some of the most important arctic polynya areas such as in northern Baffin Bay. Although there is considerable variability between polynya areas, these studies have confirmed their importance in enhancing both biological production and biodiversity in the waters over the continental shelves around the southern coastlines of the Arctic Ocean.

Seasonal movements and home range sizes

In the early 1960s, it was thought that all the polar bears might be part of one circumpolar population nomadically roaming over the arctic wastes. This notion of the cosmopolitan arctic citizen randomly visiting a variety of polar countries through its lifetime was in vogue for a time and had a certain romantic attraction. However, that concept basically ignores most of what we know about the distribution and movements of mammals in general. In particular, when you think about it in evolutionary context, or even simple survival, it just doesn't make sense for an

the winter. Wind, upwellings, and tidal currents prevent permanent ice from forming. Recurring polynyas (ones that occur in the same place each year) are of the greatest biological importance because wintering or migrating marine mammals and birds can rely on them being there to facilitate breathing and feeding. Because of the biological significance of this circumpolar system of leads and polynyas, the late Russian biologist Savva Uspenski gave this phenomenon the somewhat romantic sounding, though quite accurate term, the "Arctic ring of life" (Figure 2).

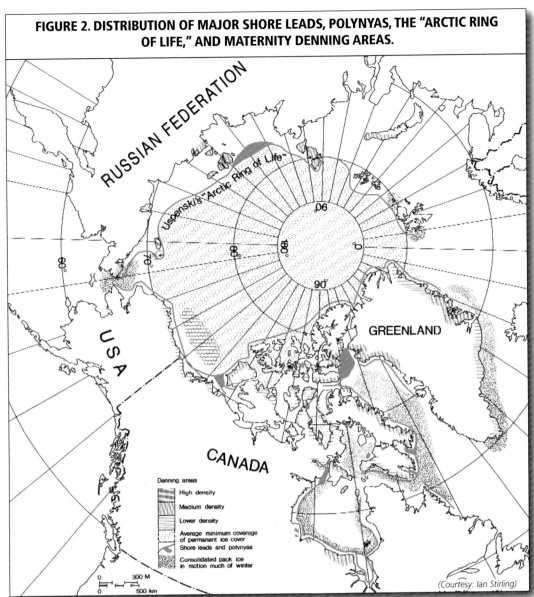

FIGURE 2. DISTRIBUTION OF MAJOR SHORE LEADS, POLYNYAS, THE "ARCTIC RING OF LIFE," AND MATERNITY DENNING AREAS.

RUSSIAN FEDERATION

Uspenski's "Arctic Ring of Life"

GREENLAND

USA

CANADA

Denning areas
- High density
- Medium density
- Lower density
- Average minimum coverage of permanent ice cover
- Shore leads and polynyas
- Consolidated pack ice in motion much of winter

0   300 M
0   500 km

(Courtesy: Ian Stirling)

animal to wander off in a random direction on the chance that food, mates, denning habitat, and other necessities will automatically be found when needed. A few arctic explorers who pursued this naive assumption met with a variety of disasters, including starvation. In earlier times, even Inuit who were resident and knowledgeable about the wildlife in their areas periodically suffered disastrous bouts of starvation. The risks of travel into areas where the availability of critical resources is unknown are unacceptably high for the majority of any population of animals to undertake. How-

ever, the theory that all polar bears were part of a single population persisted, so it was essential to test it. In particular, the circumpolar arctic countries needed to determine to what degree they might share populations, and thus be jointly responsible for their conservation.

By the mid-1980s, several thousand individual polar bears had been tagged by scientists from all five arctic countries with polar bears (Canada, Denmark/Greenland, Norway, Russia, USA). From the locations where these animals were recaptured by scientists in the years after tagging, and the return of ear tags from animals shot by Inuk and Indian hunters, the overall patterns of seasonal distribution and the extent of polar bears' movements in different areas quickly became apparent. Even at the beginning of this research, when sample sizes were still small, the locations where individually tagged polar bears were recaptured by scientists or shot by hunters consistently showed the animals had a strong tendency to return to the same areas, and in the same seasons, of subsequent years. For example, even though bears captured in the Beaufort Sea undertook substantial movements within that region during the year, very few were caught in the High Arctic Islands of the Canadian Arctic Archipelago, or Siberia, or vice versa. Clearly, the bears were not roaming at random throughout the Arctic. In places as disparate as northern Alaska, Hudson Bay, Greenland, and Svalbard, the pattern of being re-captured or shot in the same general area where they were first tagged, at the same time of year, was the same.

This behaviour, called seasonal fidelity, means an animal is faithful to the same part of its home range at the same season of subsequent years. It is, however, the exact opposite of what the theory of a single population roaming the entire Arctic would predict. After more than 40 years of tagging polar bears all over the Arctic, we have a lot more detail but the overall patterns are the same.

Once it had been established that polar bears showed strong seasonal fidelity, the next objective was to determine where they travelled throughout the year, not just where they were during a particular season. Sustained tracking of bears by aircraft throughout the year was hugely expensive, darkness precluded safe descent to secure visual confirmations on the bears and the survival of their cubs through the winter, and the vagaries of weather in the Arctic added a constant element of additional risk at the best of times, let alone when the scientist was hundreds of kilometres offshore. The hazards involved with tracking polar bears from an aircraft were underlined in

October 1990 by the tragic loss of two young biologists from the US Fish and Wildlife Service when their plane disappeared over the Beaufort Sea. Clearly, before the development of satellite radios, this was a problem that could not be adequately approached on a circumpolar basis.

Although several biologists were involved with the use and development of satellite radio collars over the years, none contributed more to the successful development of this technology on polar bears than Steve Amstrup, then with the US Fish and Wildlife Service. In a landmark study of the

movements of female polar bears in the Beaufort Sea through the late 1980s and 1990s, Amstrup and colleagues radio-tracked several dozen individual female polar bears for several consecutive years. His early results showed more clearly than any other studies up to that time that the bears know where they are and where they want to go; they are not just wandering aimlessly. Amstrup found that some bears had huge home ranges (i.e., the areas in which the animals spend their time and obtain all the resources they require to survive and reproduce) encompassing large sec- tions of the whole Beaufort Sea, while others, curiously, remained pretty much in the same place. The average annual home range of 75 radio-collared females was 149,000 km² (57,529 mi), although bears did not necessarily use all of their individual home ranges each year. There was also a large degree of individual variation, with the smallest home range being about 3,000 km² (1,158 mi²) while the largest was an incredible 597,000 km² (230,502 mi²). In the adjacent Chukchi Sea, the average home range for a sample of only six bears was 244,463 km²

A new crack that has just opened in a broad expanse of solidly frozen sea ice. Seals will soon start using it for breathing and it will quickly attract polar bears. (© Ian Stirling)

(94,388 mi²). The total distance travelled in a year, if one was to calculate it as a straight line, averaged 3,415 km (2,122 mi) and ranged up to 6,200 km (3,853 mi).

These are huge areas and represent a great deal of travel, but the movements of the bears need to be understood in the context of the dynamics of sea ice in the area of the Beaufort and Chukchi seas. During April and May, sea ice in the Beaufort Sea becomes a continuous sheet for hundreds of km, broken only by occasional leads, mainly along the coast but also far offshore. In most places, once the bears are more than a few km offshore, there are no landmarks to navigate by, or at least none that are readily apparent to humans. In the summer, when the annual ice in the southern Beaufort Sea melts, the bears must move several hundred km to the north for a few months in order to remain on the pack ice. In the late fall, after the ice refreezes, they return to the better

ward the pole again to begin another circuit. Within the gyre itself, the sea ice circulates constantly, varying with the season.

In spring it can travel from east to west at speeds in excess of 20 km/day.

In a similar study around the Svalbard Archipelago and in the adjacent Barents and Laptev seas, north of Norway and Russia, Mette Mauritzen and Andy Derocher, along with several colleagues, tracked 105 female polar bears for an average of 28 months each, between 1988 and 1999. They too found an enormous degree of variation in home range size, from 201 km² - 964,264 km² (78 mi² - 372,304 mi²). There was also a significant difference in the average size of the home ranges of bears that were associated with the Svalbard archipelago (70,027 km²/27,038 mi²) and those that favoured the more open ice areas of the Barents Sea (262,465 km²/101,338 mi²). In other studies, including some of mine in the area of the Labrador Sea and Davis Strait, scientists have found that bears spending a significant amount of time in large areas with a lot of ice movement, such as Davis Strait or Baffin Bay, have much larger home ranges than those that live primarily around the coastal areas with deep bays or in the inter-island channels of the Canadian Arctic Archipelago. A small number of females have even been shown to almost never leave a single large bay for years.

Figure 3 illustrates how different the strategies for using habitat of two successful adult females in the same population (Davis Strait) can be. One had a large home range, averaging about 156,000 km² (60,200 mi²) and travelled back and forth between southeastern Baffin Island and the Labrador coast, each year, including on pack ice well offshore from land. In contrast, the second female had a home range of only about 4,000 km² (about 1500 mi²), and simply remained in a few bays along a very short section of the northern Labrador coast, venturing offshore to only a very limited degree. Each maintained individually similar patterns of movement between years and

seal hunting areas closer to the coast over the shallower and more biologically productive waters of the continental shelf. In addition to this basically north-south pattern of ice movement between summer and winter, the pack ice circulates in a gigantic clockwise pattern called the Beaufort Gyre. Starting in the central polar basin, it drifts south along the west coast of Banks Island, then west along the Canadian and Alaskan coast to past Point Barrow before it heads back north to-

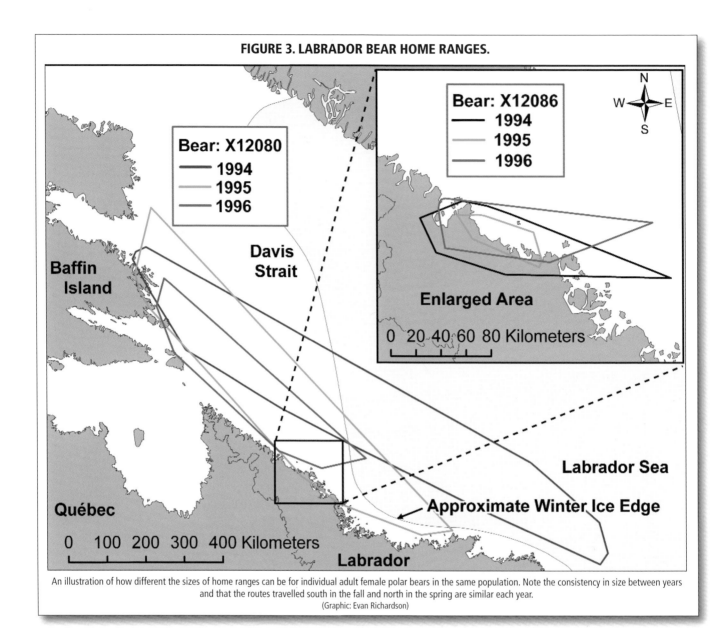

FIGURE 3. LABRADOR BEAR HOME RANGES.

Bear: X12080
1994
1995
1996

Baffin
Island

Davis
Strait

Bear: X12086
1994
1995
1996

Enlarged Area

0 20 40 60 80 Kilometers

Labrador Sea

Approximate Winter Ice Edge

Québec

0   100 200 300 400 Kilometers

Labrador

An illustration of how different the sizes of home ranges can be for individual adult female polar bears in the same population. Note the consistency in size between years and that the routes travelled south in the fall and north in the spring are similar each year.
(Graphic: Evan Richardson)

a high degree of seasonal fidelity. How such large differences in strategies developed in two adult females with similar demands for reproduction and cub-rearing in the same population is not well understood. It is likely they were both influenced strongly by learning the annual patterns of movements and hunting preferences of their mothers; that does not answer the question of why their mothers (or maybe grandmothers) might have done things so differently in the first place. Part of the answer also lies in the way these two individual bears balance their energy needs to facilitate the travel necessary to hunt for their preferred prey species. Prime fast ice habitat for ringed seals along the coast of northern Labrador is limited, so it is likely that the resident population is not large. From analyses of the fatty acids in a sample taken from the female with the small home range, the bulk of her diet was made up of ringed seal, augmented by harbour seals, a small, non-abundant coastal species. A possible interpretation of the data on her movements and diet could be that she has chosen to remain where prey species may be small and less abundant but, even if captured at a lower rate, still provide enough energy to meet her energetic needs if she travels only short distances and remains relatively local. In contrast, an analysis of the fat sample collected from the female with the large home range showed that roughly 55% of her diet was made up of harp seal (a larger and very abundant seal, but one that occurs further offshore in the pack ice in winter and spring) and beluga, a whale that winters in the offshore pack ice within her home range but also occurs near the coast. It is of course unknown whether this bear was able to kill a small whale herself (possibly a calf), or scavenged from those killed by adult males, which is more likely. However, it does appear that the greater energetic needs of this female's more extensive travel may be met by feeding on larger species.

It is likely that individual bears in other populations showing such large differences in home range size are making similar choices to balance how much travel is needed in relation to the relative availability of different prey. Overall however, given that bears with very small home ranges are much less common than those with much larger ones, it seems likely that overall, the strategy of searching more widely might be the more successful strategy for most bears over the longer term.

The southern limits

The southern boundaries of polar bear ranges are determined largely by the distribution of pack ice during the winter, but have also been significantly influenced by human hunting and habitation. During the winter, huge areas of sea ice freeze in the northern Bering Sea and then drift several hundred kilometres to the south so that polar bears are annual visitors at St. Lawrence Island (Figure 4). Today, most bears retreat back to the north when the ice melts during summer, but such was not always the case in earlier times.

When H.W. Elliot visited St. Matthew and Hall islands in the southern Bering Sea in August 1874, as part of a US Government survey of the potential for commercial harvesting of fur seals, he reported seeing an astonishing 250-300 polar bears. Because the commercial value of hunting fur seals was the primary interest of the survey, Elliott noted that even with the "scourge of polar bears" on the islands, late snow on the beaches rendered them unsuitable for fur seals. However, hunting polar bears for their hides was common at the time and the islands were regularly visited by Russian hunters for that purpose. By the time of the Harriman Expedition in 1899, there was no evidence of living bears on the islands, though the old, well-worn polar bear trails described in early reports were still plainly visible on the tundra adjacent to the beaches. Bears must have been summering there and mainly living on their stored fat reserves in much the same way that polar bears do today on the Hudson Bay coast or eastern Baffin Island, although some bears also hunted walruses which were sometimes available on the beaches.

On the southwestern side of the Bering Sea, along the coast of Siberia, polar bears have occasionally been carried on the drifting ice floes as far south as Kamchatka. On rare occasions, in particularly heavy ice years, bears have even shown up on the north coast of Hokkaido, Japan. According to the late Savva Uspenski, the lead Russian polar bear scientist for many years, it was once quite common for bears to be stranded on the south side of the Chukchi Peninsula when the ice melted in the northwestern Bering Sea during summer. Once on land, apparently some of these bears walked cross-country, up to several hundred km inland, as they travelled from the Anadyr Gulf back to the Chukchi Sea to the north.

In the Labrador Sea, in the northwestern Atlantic Ocean (Figure 1), polar bears live in the pack ice from fall freeze-up through to break-up in the following spring. Most spend the summer and fall on land along the northern Labrador coast or on southeastern Baffin. Polar bears arrive with the pack ice along the coast of southern Labrador and northern Newfoundland each winter. In most years several make it as far as the famous pupping grounds of the harp and hooded seals in March. The presence of a few hundred thousand harp seals and their whitecoat pups must be about as close to polar bear heaven as it is possible to get. The bears sometimes kill large numbers of pups, yet do not eat them all. In the heavy ice year of 1973, four bears (two males and two females) came ashore along the northeast coast and were subsequently shot. Historically however, polar bears were frequent visitors to Newfoundland, (as is evidenced by locations along the coast with names like White Bear Bay), and even into the Gulf of St. Lawrence. In July 1778, the explorer Captain George Cartwright reported variable numbers of polar bears hunting migrating Atlantic salmon, mainly in the Eagle River, but some in the White Bear River as well, in southern Labrador. At the Eagle River falls, he counted 32 polar bears and three black bears hunting in the river, noting there was an additional unknown number of animals in the adjacent bush. He also commented on the abundance of salmon killed and partially eaten by the bears. Sadly, apart from reporting whatever he killed every day, Cartwright was not much of a naturalist. Consequently, he recorded almost no other useful observations about this unique, but now extinct, behaviour. He did, however, report shooting several polar bears and a black bear, and noted his frustration at running out of ammunition which prevented him from killing even more animals. Today, although occasional bears are still reported in southern Labrador and Newfoundland, most are either removed or shot because of perceived danger. The possibility of resident, or seasonally abundant polar bears there is now a thing of the past.

In the Barents and Greenland seas, which lie along the northeastern perimetre of the Atlantic Ocean (Figure 1), the distribution of polar bears is largely governed by the seasonally changing distribution of sea ice. Norwegian polar bear trappers in Svalbard know that the number of bears present each year is largely determined by the presence of pack ice around the various islands. The bears arrive with the floes as they drift south from the Arctic Ocean in the fall and left with them again in the late spring. In most years, probably less than a quarter of the Barents Sea polar bear population remains on land in the islands of Svalbard in summer because, given a choice, most prefer the ice floes where they can still hunt seals. In some years, however, a large ice field remains near the land in eastern Svalbard. When that occurs, there are usually large numbers of bears around the islands through the summer as well.

There is probably a similar pattern of movements of polar bears north and south with the ice around Franz Josef Land in the eastern Barents Sea, and other Russian island archipelagos, but this is not well documented. Periodically, a few polar bears continue to arrive on the north coast of Iceland with the pack ice during winter and late spring, although this is not common. Those that arrive have little chance of returning to the pack ice and end up being shot because of the potential threat to humans and their property, particularly sheep.

The most southerly dwelling polar bears live all year round in Canada's James Bay at latitudes as far south as Calgary, Alberta, or London, England. There, and in Hudson Bay to the north, the ice melts completely in summer so the bears spend the summer along the coastline, or on various of the islands, living on their stored fat reserves, waiting for winter to return. However, for the most part, few people live in the areas where they come ashore and hunting pressure is low, so unlike in southern Labrador, they have not either been driven away or hunted out of existence.

The northern limit

In 1969, the Transpolar Expedition travelled from Alaska over the pole and south to Svalbard in the spring. They reported seeing no bears between the pole and 82°N but found them in abundance further south, closer to the outer edge of the continental shelf.

Similarly, the Norwegian polar bear biologist Thor Larsen and his colleagues conducted a series of aerial surveys in the Greenland and Barents seas during the early spring, along with ship surveys in the summer. One of their objectives was to determine the northern limits of the distribution of polar bears in those areas. A very small proportion of the tracks they recorded from the air, and only three of 181 bears seen from the ship, were above 82°N, past the edge of the continental shelf.

Polar bears, or their tracks, have been reported, albeit infrequently, by various explorers almost as far north as the North Pole and at other locations deep in the polar basin. Similarly, a few bears carrying satellite collars have made brief forays into the polar basin. Although sightings at high latitudes have become more frequent with the advent of icebreakers taking tourists to the North Pole every summer, the overwhelming impression is still that there are very few bears, or even tracks, in the central Arctic Ocean. The reason is probably that (until recently at least) heavy multi-year ice floes characterize the area and the waters are very deep and stratified, a combination that results in very low levels of biological productivity and few seals, especially

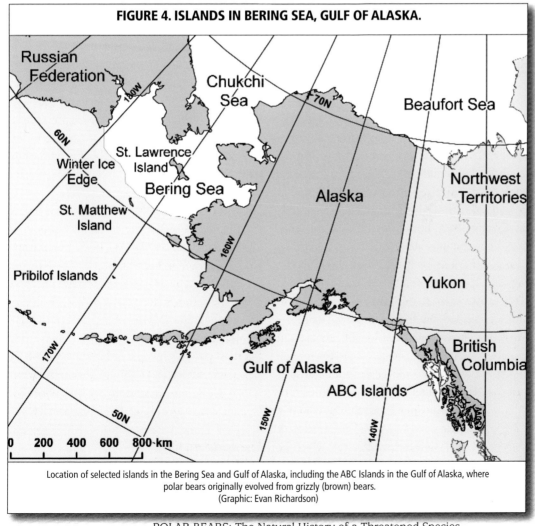

FIGURE 4. ISLANDS IN BERING SEA, GULF OF ALASKA.

Location of selected islands in the Bering Sea and Gulf of Alaska, including the ABC Islands in the Gulf of Alaska, where polar bears originally evolved from grizzly (brown) bears.
(Graphic: Evan Richardson)

when compared to the high levels of productivity over the continental shelf.

The edge of the continental shelf off the north slope of Alaska and along the western side of the Canadian Arctic Islands is fairly close to shore. In this area, most of the polar bears are found within a few hundred km of the coast at any time of year. North of Russia, between the Barents and Chukchi seas, the continental shelf extends offshore for several hundred kilometres in places, but how far from the coast polar bears are found on a regular basis in those areas is not well known.

Home ranges and subpopulations

From forty years of information on the movements and home ranges of tagged polar bears, and 20 years of tracking individual adult females with satellite radio collars in several different areas of the Arctic, it is clear these animals do not wander at random but remain within their individual home ranges. As noted earlier, the size of the home ranges of individual bears in the same area can vary considerably. However, each individual polar bear within a subpopulation, except for cubs with their mothers, determines its own home range and moves within it independently. Initially, bears probably learn the seasonal pattern of movements as cubs during the two years or more they remain with their mothers. As a bear gains in knowledge and experience, it builds on its mother's teachings to develop its own individual patterns of movement within its home range.

Since the movements and home ranges of individual bears are essentially independent of one another, subpopulations primarily result from concentrations of polar bears with independent but overlapping home ranges, in other words, significant clumping of home ranges within a continuum. However, home ranges are neither distributed at random nor spread evenly throughout the Arctic. Ecological conditions and the distribution of resources are too variable to permit that. Thus, in places where ice conditions may be too poor or variable for reliable seal hunting, there

will be fewer polar bear home ranges. Conversely, in areas where biological productivity is high and seals are abundant, there may be many overlapping polar bear home ranges. Similarly, the distribution of denning areas and land masses, the patterns of break-up and freeze-up of sea ice, and currents that change the distribution of pack ice

in a systematic or predictable fashion may also combine to influence the size and distribution of home ranges. The geographic clumping of home ranges, plus the fidelity that young animals have to the areas in which they were born, combine to form what we would call, for management purposes at least, individual populations. Even so, it is recognized that there can be a relatively small amount of exchange between subpopulations in the vicinity of their borders without negating the value of their value for conservation purposes.

From an initial analysis of tag returns, local knowledge, and the patterns of break-up and freeze-up in Canada, 8 subpopulations were

Typical area of extensive rough ice that provides poor hunting and difficult travel for polar bears.
(© Ian Stirling)

identified for management purposes, along with 3 extra subdivisions within areas where the boundaries were poorly understood, for a total of 11. With more data from all those sources but particularly when augmented by results from satellite tracking of bears throughout the Arctic, Canada was found to have 9 subpopulations within its borders while sharing 3 more with Greenland and one with the US (Alaska). The Polar Bear Specialist Group (PBSG) of the IUCN (International Union for the Conservation of Nature) now recognizes 19 subpopulations throughout the circumpolar Arctic although the proposed boundaries for some, particularly in Russia, might still be classified as "best guesses" based on limited information (Figure 5).

Although it has been suggested from time to time that there may be a bear population resident in the polar basin, it does not seem likely on the basis of what we know of polar bear distribution and movements at the moment. Although occasional bears with satellite radio collars have made long journeys north of the boundaries of the subpopulations in which they are resident, such movements appear, for the moment at least, to be more exploratory than indicative of residence in the polar basin.

Navigation

When you consider the extensive movements made by individual bears, and the seasonal fidelity they maintain to particular areas despite living within home ranges that can be up to several thousand square kilometres in size and devoid of obvious landmarks, you have to conclude they know where they are. From the high degree of seasonal fidelity they show, it is also clear they know where they want to be at particular times of the year, and how to get there, despite often having to travel long distances against the direction of ice drift, and occasionally needing to swim substantial distances. I have often recaptured polar bears out on the ice of the Beaufort Sea, far from sight of the nearest land, within a few km

of where they were first caught two, three, ten or, in one case, over twenty years earlier. In western Hudson Bay, when adult females leave their maternity dens south of Churchill in February and March, they take fairly straight routes to the sea on courses that are parallel to each other. It is intriguing, however, that the mean course taken by the bears is 39° true (close to northeast) even though the most direct route back to the sea ice would be to go straight east. Regardless, for whatever reason, the direction in which they want to travel is clearly predetermined. To me, the most remarkable evidence of a bear's sense of where it is, and its ability to navigate, comes from the females that den on the pack ice north of Alaska. There, a bear may enter a den in November and not exit with her cubs until late March, after drifting inside her den for up to 1,000 km (620 mi). Despite having received no visible cues, these females return against the direction of drift of the sea ice to the area they came from. At present, how polar bears accomplish such incredible feats of navigation is unknown.

How many polar bears were there in the 1960s and how many are there now?

This must be the most frequently asked question about polar bears and it reflects an enormously strong and enduring topic of public interest. In part, the question about the total population size recurs because there has been an ongoing perception in the public for many years that polar bears were threatened or endangered then, even though we now know they were not. Population size, and how much total numbers have gone up or down over the last 45 years or so is probably the issue about which the public at large has been most confused, in part because of the deliberate recycling of erroneous information by some with more of a political than scientific or conservation agenda.

One regularly sees statements suggesting that the polar bear population may have been as low as 5,000 back in the 1960s. This number appears

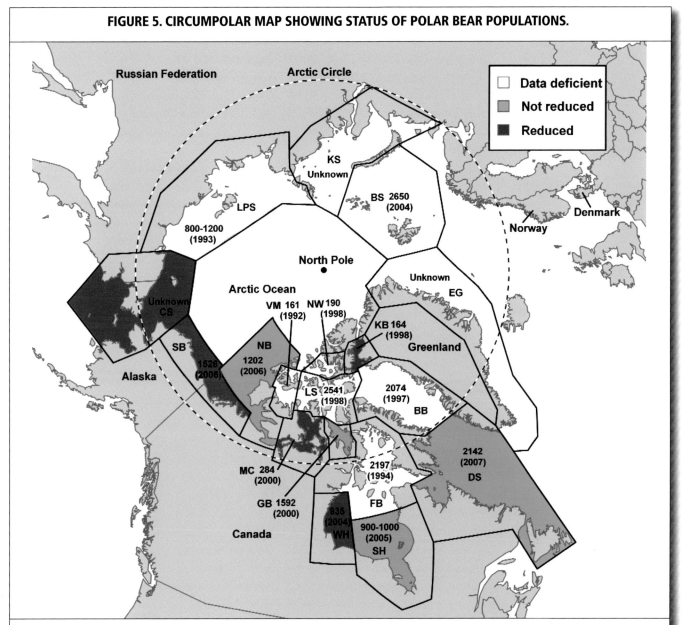

FIGURE 5. CIRCUMPOLAR MAP SHOWING STATUS OF POLAR BEAR POPULATIONS.

Map of the currently recognized populations of polar bears around the circumpolar Arctic. Where available, estimates of population size, the year of the last estimate, and the status of the population are also shown. (Based on summary from Polar Bear Specialist Group, 2009; pbsg.npolar.no) Southern Beaufort Sea (SB), Chukchi Sea (CS), Laptev Sea (LPS), Kara Sea (KS), Barents Sea (BS), East Greenland (EG), Northern Beaufort Sea (NB), Southern Hudson Bay (SH), western Hudson Bay (WH), Foxe Basin (FB), Davis Strait (DS), Baffin Bay (BB), Gulf of Boothia (GB), M'Clintock Channel (MC), Lancaster Sound (LS), Viscount-Melville Sound (VM), Norwegian Bay (NW), and Kane Basin (KB). (Graphic: Evan Richardson)

to originate with the report of the Russian Delegation to the First International Scientific Meeting on the Polar Bear, held in Fairbanks, Alaska, in 1965. The Canadian delegation cited Uspenski's 1961 estimate of 5-8,000 polar bears in the whole Arctic, while the Russian Delegation itself suggested there were "not more than 8,000 in the spring." But what that estimate was based on and whether the Russians or anyone else actually believed it is open to question.

It is informative to go back to the original reports by the late Savva Uspenski, as well as the actual estimates made by other scientists at the time. In 1956 and 1957, the Alaskan biologists Paul Tovey and Robert Scott carried out aerial surveys and concluded there were 2,000-2,500 bears in a 75 mi-wide strip off the Alaskan coast. By extending these densities around the polar regions, which involved making admittedly broad assumptions, they estimated a total population of 17-19,000 bears (not much different from the total estimated today). Uspenski also quoted a later estimate by Scott and others in 1959 of 19,000, along with their admission that the latter number could be an overestimate. In 1969, on the basis of aerial surveys made from fixed-wing aircraft in 1962, 1967, and 1968, Uspenski and Shilnikov reported a density of 1 bear per 711 km^2, from which they went on to estimate a population of 5.6-6.6 thousand in the USSR and a total of 10.7-13.6 thousand in the Arctic as a whole. Later, using only information from denning surveys, Uspenski went on to estimate a total population of 10,000 polar bears. In 1964, the Canadian polar bear biologist Richard Harrington combined information on denning, various aerial surveys, and the knowledge that there was considerable variation in densities of bears in different parts of the Arctic, to conclude "that the world polar bear population is well over 10,000."

Regardless, the paucity of information on the distribution, movements, and abundance of polar bears throughout the Arctic in the late 1960s, along with the rapidly rising levels of recorded harvest, provided a reasonable justification for concern that the worldwide population of polar bears might be in decline. There were concerns about possible overharvesting in areas such as Alaska, parts of Canada, and Svalbard. However, no bears had been legally harvested in Russia after 1956, and the recorded harvests in Greenland and some areas of the Canadian Arctic, though not known, were thought to not be excessive. Also, at that time, scientists did not know whether polar

bears were distributed in a single circumpolar population or, as we now know, occured in 19 different subpopulations. With the benefit of hindsight, it seems unlikely there were never fewer than 10-15,000 polar bears in the Arctic. That said, it is also clear that some populations, including a few that were shared internationally, were being severely overharvested and worldwide collaboration in research and management was needed to resolve the problems.

Throughout the 1980s and 1990s, the world polar bear population was considered to be reasonably secure, and in the range of 20-25,000 individuals, according to the IUCN Polar Bear Specialist Group. After all, they were still widely distributed throughout the ice-covered and biologically productive seas of the continental shelf throughout the circumpolar Arctic and occupied the majority of their original habitat. There was recognition that harvesting by aboriginal hunters was an important part of that culture and economy but needed to be done in a sustainable fashion. Population data were available for many populations although little was known about others, such as populations in East Greenland or Russia. Some of the results from widespread studies of various contaminants were worrisome but, overall, from a population perspective, it was felt that on an Arctic-wide basis, the situation was reasonably under control. Historically, the arctic marine system was assumed to be relatively stable and ecologically predictable over the long term. Thus, from a management perspective, the early view was that once you had a reasonable population estimate and calculated a sustainable harvest, one could just continue on that basis semi-indefinitely unless, for some reason, there was a need to do re-assessment. However, following recognition of the negative effects of global climate warming on sea ice, at its meeting in 1995, the PBSG declared polar bears "vulnerable" because of the threat of large-scale loss of habitat.

Even so, at the Fifteenth Working Meeting of the PBSG in Copenhagen, Denmark, in 2009, there was general agreement that the world polar bear population probably still numbered about 20,000, but also gave a possible range of 14-25,000. However, any of these numbers taken in isolation is misleading. For example, estimates of the size of some subpopulations are now dated and it is not possible to make direct comparisons of estimates made by such variable methods as mark-recapture, aerial counts, and shipboard surveys. In several areas, the estimates of population size are listed as "data deficient" because there is simply not enough information available to make a reasonable current estimate. Eight full populations are now listed as declining and the estimated risk of future decline was listed as very high for six. The probability of future decline could not be assessed for eight subpopulations, in part because of lack of sufficient data. Thus, Table 1 summarizes our present knowledge of the status of all 19 subpopulations, along with qualifications. In this context, it is important to remember that the estimated population, in 2009, of 20,000 is not as reassuring as it might seem at first glance.

TABLE 1. IUCN POPULATION STATUS TABLE

Population	Mark-Recapture Population Analysis/ aerial survey		Computer simulation		Status	Current Trend	Estimated risk of future decline
	Number (Year of estimate)	± 2 standard errors or 95% confidence interval	Number (Year of estimate)	± 2 standard errors or 95% confidence interval			
Arctic Basin	unknown				data deficient	data deficient	data deficient
Baffin Bay	2074 (1997)	1544-2604	1546 (2004)	690-2402	data deficient	declining	very high
Barents Sea	2650 (2004)	1900-3600			data deficient	data deficient	data deficient
Chukchi Sea	unknown				deduced	declining	data deficient
Davis Strait	2142 (2007)	1811-2534			not reduced	declining	very high
East Greenland	unknown				data deficient	data deficient	data deficient
Foxe Basin	2197 (2004)	1677-2717	2300 (2004)	1780-2820	data deficient	data deficient	data deficient
Gulf of Boothia	1592 (2000)	870-2314			not reduced	stable	very low
Kane Basin	64 (1998)	94-234			reduced	declining	very high
Kara Sea	unknown				data deficient	data deficient	data deficient
Lancaster Sound	2541 (1998)	1759-3323			data deficient	declining	higher
Laptev Sea	800-1200 (1993)				data deficient	data deficient	data deficient
M'Clintock Channel	284 (2000)	166-402			reduced	increasing	very low
Northern Beaufort Sea	1202 (2006)	686-1718			not reduced	stable	data deficient
Norwegian Bay	190 (1998)				data deficient	declining	very high
Southern Beaufort Sea	1526 (2006)	1210-1842			reduced	declining	moderate
Southern Hudson Bay	900-1000 (ON); 75-1000 James Bay (2005)				not reduced	stable	very high
Viscount Melville Sound	161 (1992)	121-201	215 (1996)	99-331	data deficient	data deficient	data deficient
Western Hudson Bay	935 (2004)	791-1079			reduced	declining	very high
Total							

Table 1. Summary of the status of polar bear populations throughout the circumpolar Arctic. Abbreviated from the assessments of each population as discussed and concluded by the Polar Bear Specialist Group of the IUCN in Copenhagen in 2009 (with some small updates in March 2010). (http://pbsg.npolar.no/en/status/status-table.html)

Chapter 2

THE ORIGIN OF

These adult male polar bears exhibit a relatively smooth, elongated profile from the top of the head to the nose
(© Stefan Lundgren)

THE POLAR BEAR

Until quite recently, it was uncertain when or where polar bears evolved because their fossil remains are so rare. Most of the handful of fossils (and sub-fossils) confirmed to be of polar bears come from northwestern Europe (mainly Scandinavia), likely because the western coastal regions of Norway, Sweden, and Denmark (northern Jutland) were colonized by

Female hybrid (left) standing beside her grizzly bear mother. Note overall light colour and presence of smaller shoulder hump than mother and less distinct rise of forehead. (© Alexandra Preuß)

polar bears in the late Weichselian to Early Holocene period, up to the end of the last ice age (10-15,000 years ago). A large jaw from an adult male found near Asdal in Jutland was dated at about 11,000 years BP (Before Present). Another eight partial specimens of similar age are known from Sweden, a nearly complete skeleton from Judaberg, Norway, and some bones from an 8,200-year-old specimen from Svalbard. Two other specimens carbon-dated as being 22,000 and 22-36,000 years old have also been reported from western and northern Norway. Undoubtedly, additional specimens are waiting to be found but, realistically, their apparently small numbers make the chance of discovery quite low. Regard-

less, it appears that the area of northern Scandinavia was important to polar bears during the last glacial period from roughly 110,000 to 10,000 years ago.

The paucity of polar bear fossils is not surprising, assuming that the behaviour and ecology of the ancestral polar bears were probably similar to their present-day descendents. These animals were likely distributed over vast areas of sea ice at low densities and their total numbers were probably never very large. When animals died, the remains of most would have sunk to the bottom of the ocean or have been left on the surface of the ground to rot near the coastline, as they still are today. As a result, it is unlikely that very many

POLAR BEARS: The Natural History of a Threatened Species

animals became fossilized in the first place, so the chance of finding remains scattered anywhere in the Arctic today is low. In addition, the polar bear developed fairly recently as a species. Consequently, compared to animals with a longer evolutionary history, polar bears have had much less time for fossils to be created and become available for eventual discovery. In fact, all things considered, it is rather surprising that any polar bear fossils have been discovered at all. Even arctic seals that lived in the same habitat for a much longer period of time and were far more abundant, are little known from fossil records.

Pleistocene ancestors

Until quite recently, much of what we know today about the origins of the polar bear was the result of years of painstaking morphological examination of the few existing specimens by the famous Finnish paleontologist Björn Kurtén (whose first name means bear). His studies traced the evolution of the bear family for about the last 2-2.5 million years or so, through a geological period known as the Pleistocene. The Pleistocene epoch fascinates modern zoologists because it was characterized by species that were much larger than their present-day descendents. It was the era of the woolly mammoths, saber-toothed tigers, Irish elk, giant beavers, and many other species of large mammals that have since disappeared, leaving behind their smaller relatives and descendants.

Some of the bears of the Pleistocene were also larger and must have been impressive to see. In Europe, the cave bear became one of the best known carnivores of that period because of its convenient habit of dying in large numbers in caves where the bones were well preserved. In one particularly famous cave in Austria, there are bones from an estimated 30,000 individual bears! (If Pleistocene polar bears had been considerate enough to die in caves as well, instead of out on the sea ice, we would know a great deal more about them.) North America also had a large Pleistocene cave bear that lived in Florida. However, the most impressive North American native was the giant short-faced bear, which had exceptionally long legs for a bear, indicating it must have been an extremely fast-moving animal capable of chasing and bringing down large ungulates. In fact, Kurtén describes it as the most powerful predator of the Pleistocene. Roughly a million years ago, the cave bears gave rise to a similar looking line, the brown (or grizzly) bears that have persevered to the present day in Europe, Asia, and North America. On the basis of morphological comparisons alone, Kurtén estimated that polar bears diverged from brown bears, possibly as recently as 70-100,000 years ago.

Exciting breakthroughs on the origin of the polar bear

By the 1990s however, exciting new techniques were developing in the field of molecular genetics that would yield spectacular new insights into the origin of the polar bear. By examining the mitochondrial DNA of brown and polar bears, Gerald Shields and colleagues from the University of Alaska not only re-confirmed that polar bears evolved from the brown bear but, for the first time, determined that their closest relatives were a group of geographically and genetically isolated brown bears that live exclusively in the Admiralty, Baranof, and Chichagof (ABC) islands of the Alexander Archipelago in southeast Alaska (Figure 4). They suggested polar bears may have split from these brown bears 250-300,000 years ago.

Then, in 2004, came one of the most important discoveries of the last 20 years with respect to the evolution of polar bears! Ólafur Ingólfsson, a Norwegian geologist working on a rocky outcrop at Poole Pynton on the west coast of Svalbard (the Norwegian Arctic), found the lower jaw of a male polar bear. Its age, determined in the laboratory using a process called infrared-stimulated luminescence, along with the age of the rock layer it came from, confirmed it was between 110,000 and 130,000 years of age—by far the oldest polar bear fossil ever found. The bone was about 10 cm

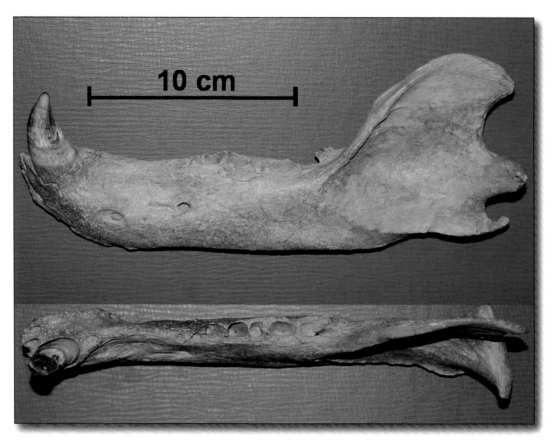

10 cm

(4 in) into the substrate which, in that location, was eroding away at a rate of about 20 cm (7.9 in) per year. Thus, if it had not been found when it was, it probably would have disappeared within a year or two and been lost forever. Even more exciting was that by applying the newest genetic sequencing technology to the ancient DNA extracted from the jaw, Charlotte Lindqvist and her colleagues at Buffalo University in the US were able to determine the complete mitochondrial genome of the fossil bear—an extraordinary achievement in itself. Furthermore, by comparing this with the genome of modern-day polar bears from Alaska, and brown bears from the ABC islands, they were able to confirm that the Svalbard bear had been alive soon after the time that polar bears separated from brown bears, which was likely about 150,000 years ago. The suprisingly recent time frame for the divergence of the polar bear from the brown bear, suggested by Lindqvist, was recently confirmed by John Davison and col-

leagues from Estonia. From their analysis of ancient DNA from a 115,000-year-old polar bear rib from a cave in northern Norway, Davison estimated an evolutionary age for the polar bear of about 160,000 years.

Analyses of the stratum in which the fossil was found also uncovered bivalve molluscs (clams) and other marine fauna, and indicated the bear was living in an open marine environment influenced by input of fresh water from glaciers and warm North Atlantic water, similar to that of the environment in the same area today. Furthermore, from the molecular dating, and stable isotope analysis (from which one can determine where in the food chain an animal feeds), it is also clear that by very early in their evolutionary history, polar bears had become inhabitants of the arctic sea ice and were carnivores feeding at the top of the food chain. Taken together, the stable isotope data, genetic analysis of the fossil bear and its relatives, and the geo-

logical environment where the fossil was found indicate that the ancient polar bears adapted very rapidly both morphologically and physiologically to their present form, probably within 10-30,000 years of diverging from the ABC brown bears, and that within 100,000 years, they had spread throughout the circumpolar basin.

Evolving into a polar bear from a brown bear

At the time the polar bear was evolving from the brown bears of the ABC islands, about 150,000 years ago, the world was in a glacial maximum known as the Wisconsin glaciation. Polar ice extended south through Bering Strait into the Bering Sea down on a roughly NE-SW angle, just to the south of the Pribilof Islands and St. Matthew Island to the north side of the Aleutian island chain (Figure 4). Glaciers extended out

from the shoreline in much of the northern and northeastern Gulf of Alaska and it is likely that annual ice formed in the northern portions of the Gulf of Alaska as well.

It is hard to know just what the ecological stimulation was that caused grizzly bears to begin venturing onto the ice to hunt seals. However, I suspect the ecological setting may have had some similarity to the present-day situation in the eastern Beaufort Sea, along the Tuktoyaktuk Peninsula and Smoking Hills in the Northwest Territories, Canada. There, some of the relatively small present-day brown bears, known locally as barren-ground grizzlies, den and feed terrestrially near the arctic coast. Males first come out of their dens in mid- to late April when there is still snow on the ground and not much to eat. Thus, a few venture offshore, possibly attracted by the smell of the seals themselves or the carcasses of seals

An almost all-white grizzly with dark legs, undersides, and muzzle in the Mackenzie Mountains, Northwest Territories, Canada, illustrates the range of natural coat colour still existent in wild grizzly bears.
(© John Nagy)

killed by polar bears. There have been a several sightings of grizzlies feeding on seal carcasses out on the sea ice although whether they kill the seals themselves, or are simply scavenging, or both, is unclear. One large male I saw was about 60 km (37 mi) out on the ice, far from sight of the nearest land. Inuit hunters from Tuktoyaktuk have told me that they occasionally see grizzly bears hunting for seals in their birth lairs near the mouth of Liverpool Bay. In the area of the ABC Islands, there must have been an abundance of harbour seals, sea lions, and, when there was ice nearby, ringed and bearded seals. In such circumstances, it does not seem too far-fetched for a

the arctic coast. They range from very light brown to almost black, while a few are still almost as white as a polar bear. Thus genetically, it was probably not a long step to take for the coat colour of the majority of animals hunting on the ice to evolve to white in order to blend in with the snow and ice of their new environment, thus providing a degree of camouflage to make them less visible when stalking seals hauled out on the ice.

In overall body build, polar bears became more elongated. Similarly, the skulls and necks grew longer and less bulky than the brain case of a brown bear, possibly as an adaptation to make it easier for a polar bear to thrust the head deep into seal breathing holes or birth lairs when trying to capture a rapidly disappearing seal. Instead of the characteristically dished nose and face of the brown bear, polar bear males, in particular, often developed more of a Roman nose. Polar bear cheek teeth grew smaller but more jagged, including the development of carnassial teeth (molar and premolar teeth modified for shearing flesh by having cusps with sharp cutting edges), essential for life as a carnivore. In comparison, the cheek teeth of the grizzly are larger, but flatter and smoother, for grinding the vegetation which makes up a large portion of their omnivorous diet. As a further adaptation to life as a carnivore, the canines of the polar bear became larger and sharper for tearing seals apart. Their claws were shorter and more solid than the long, curved claws that are the trademark of the grizzly bear. The stubby-but-strong and sharp-pointed claws of the polar bear were probably less likely to bend or break under strain when digging through hard wind-blown snow or ice, and gave a better grip when running on ice.

Considering that anthropogenic unidirectional climate warming now threatens the long-term existence of polar bears as a species, it is ironic that it is possible that climate warming may have played a significant role in this bear's evolution in the first place. A few tens of thousands of years after polar bears separated from grizzlies and

grizzly to evolve into a polar bear by filling the hugely rich but vacant niche as the supreme predator of the sea ice.

Once started, the polar bear apparently evolved quickly. There was probably already considerable variation in the coat colour of the ABC grizzlies as there is today in the barren ground grizzlies of

moved onto the sea ice of the Bering Sea, much of the ice from the Wisconsin glaciation melted in the polar basin during the Eemian warming, known geologically as Termination II, about 125,000 years ago (Figure 6). As the southern boundary of the ice in the Bering Sea moved northward through the Bering Strait and eventually into the polar basin, polar bears would have moved with it. As the Arctic cooled again after the Eemian warming to the last glacial maximum, about 20,000 years ago, whatever residual population of polar bears remained probably moved south to the coastline and archipelagos of the polar basin, into Scandinavia, and into the Bering Sea again. By about 11-12,000 years ago, the Arctic began to warm again, a period known geologically as Termination I. As the southern edge of the ice in the Bering Sea moved north, the bears moved with it as they had previously, a fact confirmed by identification of fossil polar bear bones on St Paul Island in the Pribilof Islands (Figure 4) that date back about 4,000 years. The southern edge of the sea ice in the Bering Sea no longer comes that far south and polar bears have not been resident there in recorded human memory.

Differences between populations of polar bears

There is insufficient systematic variation in the skulls to warrant recognition of any living subspecies of polar bears, although Kurtén recognized a subspecies on the basis of fossil material. He named it *Ursus maritimus tryannus* because, like many other earlier forms of present-day mammals, it was markedly larger.

However, the application of modern genetic methodology by David Paetkau and colleagues provided fascinating new insights into how polar bears evolved and spread throughout the Arctic. He identified subpopulations of bears that are more closely related to each other than they are to more distant or geographically separated pop-

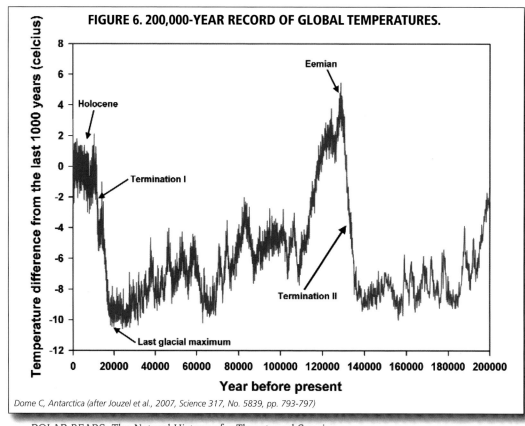

FIGURE 6. 200,000-YEAR RECORD OF GLOBAL TEMPERATURES.

Dome C, Antarctica (after Jouzel et al., 2007, Science 317, No. 5839, pp. 793-797)

POLAR BEARS: The Natural History of a Threatened Species

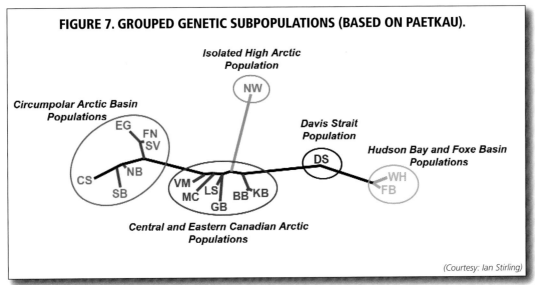

FIGURE 7. GROUPED GENETIC SUBPOPULATIONS (BASED ON PAETKAU).

Isolated High Arctic Population

Circumpolar Arctic Basin Populations

Davis Strait Population

Hudson Bay and Foxe Basin Populations

Central and Eastern Canadian Arctic Populations

(Courtesy: Ian Stirling)

ulations (Figure 7), but not sufficiently so to be called subspecies. From the Bering Sea, the bears would have had to first move into the Chukchi Sea, designated as CS on Figure 7. Although the next steps are not known, the bears likely spread out on the ice around the edge of the polar basin before retreating to a possible refugium at the northern end of the Canadian Arctic Islands and Greenland during the height of the Eemian warm period. As the polar basin cooled again, bears could have moved back to the coastlines and eventually further south along the southern border of the ice at the last glacial maximum, thus explaining the location of fossil polar bears in Scandinavia and near the seal populations of the Baltic Sea 8-11,000 years ago. As the ice retreated back to the north, the bears followed, though some ringed seals remained in the Baltic Sea and other southern water bodies, where they are still found today.

How, or when, the bears divided into groups centred on the geographic areas we know them from today, and then further subdivided into the groupings identified by Paetkau, is not known. However, the resulting pattern is fairly clear. One inter-related unit is spread around the coastline of the polar basin, probably dispersing along the system of shore leads and polynyas that characterize the area (Figure 2). These are the Chukchi

population (CS), the Beaufort Sea (SB & NB), East Greenland (EG), and Franz-Josef Land (FN). At some point, bears moved into the Canadian Arctic Islands, either from the Beaufort Sea (SB &NB) or the shore leads and polynyas along the northern coast of the Canadian Arctic Archipelago to East Greenland (EG). As bears spread though Baffin Bay, they likely moved on to Davis Strait and then into Hudson Bay, where they spread throughout the bay and adjacent Foxe Basin. Curiously, there is also a small anomalous but genetically separable group of bears resident in the Canadian High Arctic Islands, centred on Norwegian Bay (NW).

How different are polar bears from brown (grizzly) bears?

Polar bears and brown bears are both species of the same genus of carnivores, *Ursus*, which is Latin for bear. The polar bear is *Ursus maritimus*, which translates as the sea bear. The polar bear was first described by Phipps in 1774 from a specimen collected at Spitsbergen (now known as Svalbard). Between 1776 and 1908, there were subsequent suggestions for changing both the generic and specific names, but the right of priority of the original description held sway over time.

The brown bear is *Ursus arctos*, which is a little

repetitious since *arctos* also means bear, but this time in Greek. Taxonomists recognize the close relationship of the polar and brown bears by placing them in the same genus, despite the distinct appearance of both. So far, so good. However, this is where it starts to get interesting, since one of the original definitions of species is that they are reproductively isolated from each other and cannot produce fertile offspring. For example, although a horse and a donkey may mate, the resulting offspring, the mule, is sterile.

Interbreeding between polar bears and brown bears in captivity has occurred several times in zoos over the last 140 years or so, usually as a result of accidental mixing, but sometimes as a result of deliberate action. However, unlike the mule, the resulting offspring have been fertile, both when bred with each other in the case of siblings or with either parent in what animal breeders call a backcross. The apparent ease with which interbreeding takes place between these two species, and the high degree of fertility of the offspring, indicates that polar bears and brown (grizzly) bears have not become widely separated in the genetic sense, probably in part due to the short period, evolutionarily, that they have been separate.

Considerable variation has been reported in the colour of hybrid bears. Some were almost white at birth but changed to a bluish brown or yellowish-white as they aged. Others were darker with light patches, while yet others were half white and half gray-brown. For the most part, comments about the hybrids and comparisons to their parents have been more anecdotal than structured. For example, one hybrid in the Hellabrun Zoo in Munich, West Germany, was reported to be a much better swimmer than his brown bear mother, but not as good as his polar bear father, though not much other documentation is available on any of them.

In one of the few attempts to document some aspects of the biology of hybrid bears in more detail, Alexandra Preuß and Ute Mageira compared the morphology and behaviour of three-year-old male and female sibling hybrids in the Osnabrück Zoo in Germany. The mother was a brown bear and the father was a polar bear. In appearance, some of the characteristics of both parents were evident in each cub. In these cubs, the female was lighter in colour and looked more like a polar bear than did the generally darker male, though both had a dark stripe running from the top of the head to the upper back and were a light creamy brown overall. Compared to the fairly flat body contour of the polar bear, brown bears have a characteristic hump over the shoulders. Both cubs had a gentle, though distinct shoulder hump reminiscent of a brown bear (see the photo of the female hybrid standing beside her brown bear mother). The head was more evenly tapered and similar to the diametre of the top of the neck, like a polar bear, and with a less distinct rise of the forehead, characteristic of a brown bear. The ears were larger than a polar bear's but smaller than a brown bear's.

Variations in the internal structure of the hair of the parental species and hybrids were also interesting. The hairs on the paw of the brown bear mother were solid, while those on the body were a mixture of both solid and hollow hairs. In the hairs examined, the hollow core made up 18-40% of the cross section. The inner core itself was made up of large aerial regions separated in half by a partition. The cores of hairs from the hybrids had larger hollow areas than did those from the brown bear, but were smaller than those from the polar bear. There also seemed to be variation in the size of the core in light-coloured hairs compared to dark ones on the same animal. Although the dark coloured hairs had open spaces within them, they were smaller than were the light-coloured ones. Although this study was preliminary in nature, there is clearly much more of interest to be investigated on hair structure because there has been speculation in the past that the air spaces in a hollow hair core of a polar bear, if they existed, might add insulative value. From

the work of Preuß and Mageira, the fact that the hollow sections seem to be more developed in polar bears than in brown bears, and apparently more so in the light-coloured hairs of the hybrid cubs than the dark-coloured hairs, is intriguing.

For subpopulations of any species to develop significant genetic differences usually requires an extended period of geographic isolation and the turnover of many generations. Under these conditions, mutations or other naturally occurring inheritable variations become embedded in that population and help to make it unique. In a slow-breeding animal with a long generation time like a polar bear, this takes much longer than it would, for example, in mice. The low degree of genetic variability in the polar bear, along with the demonstrated ease of interbreeding with brown bears, supports Kurten's belief, subsequently demonstrated genetically to be true, that the polar bear is a very young species in an evolutionary sense.

Hybrids in the wild

Although hybrids between polar and brown bears have been well known from zoos for many years, it came as a considerable surprise when a wild hybrid was shot on the sea ice in the eastern Beaufort Sea in the spring of 2006. The bear was

Male hybrid born of a polar bear male and grizzly bear female. Note the darker colour than the female hybrid (P. 42), the more grizzly-like face, and short claws on front paws.
(© Alexandra Preuß)

mainly white, which, at a distance, was why the hunter thought it was a polar bear. However, when it was approached, there were some obvious differences. It had black around the eyes, a noticeable hump like a brown bear, and longer claws than a polar bear. It was a male and, from a tooth, it was determined to be five years old. Its mother was a polar bear and its father was a grizzly bear. Then, again, in 2010, another male hybrid bear was shot in Amundsen Gulf, again in the eastern Beaufort Sea. This time however, it was the offspring of a hybrid female and a male grizzly bear. It was largely a creamy brown on the body and a dark brown on the legs—quite a different-looking animal.

The presence of a hybrid in the wild was unexpected, largely because the two species occupy different habitats most of the time and the peak of the breeding season for the polar bear is a month or more earlier than that of the grizzly. Even so, it is likely that grizzly bear males, like most mammals, produce viable sperm well before and after the peak of the breeding season to ensure fertilization of females that may come into breeding condition earlier or later than the peak periods.

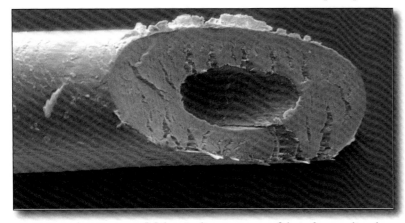

Cross section of a hair from a male hybrid bear showing a hollow centre more characteristic of a polar bear than a grizzly.
(© Alexandra Preuß)

Male grizzlies come out of their dens earlier than females, in late April and early May. Because the ground is often covered with snow then, leaving little to eat, they are more likely than females to go out on the ice, possibly in search of the remains of seals killed by polar bears to scavenge on. In this circumstance, encountering and mating with a female polar bear (probably a young and inexperienced one) could be possible, if highly unlikely in most instances. In fact, in one other circumstance where an adult grizzly met a subadult polar bear on the sea ice, the grizzly killed and ate it. In recent years, possibly partly because of a warming climate, or more likely just an expanding population, the number of grizzlies seen on Banks and Victoria Islands, and north to Melville Island on the north side of the Northwest Passage, has become more frequent. Certainly the two wild hybrids from the eastern Beaufort Sea caused quite a stir in the popular press. While interesting in their own right, these animals are probably not of a lot of additional biological significance. Personally, I doubt their occurrence will become frequent enough of be of any biological significance past being a curiosity.

Size of present-day polar bears

Although modern polar bears are smaller than their Pleistocene ancestors, they are still the largest non-aquatic carnivores presently alive anywhere in the world. Adult males may weigh from about 350-650 kg (770-1430+ lb). Females normally weigh 150-250 kg (330-550 lb), although super-fat pregnant individuals occasionally approach 500 kg (1,100 lb).

At one time, it was suggested that there was a gradient in the size of polar bears across the Arctic, with the smallest ones occurring in the area of Svalbard and becoming larger as one progresses west to the Bering and Chukchi seas. If this was true, one might expect that sizes would become smaller again as one proceeded from the Bering Sea across northern Russia back to Svalbard. However, with the benefit of more research and larger sample sizes, it is clear that the proposed cline was not real and probably resulted from small sample sizes or possibly the way the samples were collected from each area. For example, many of the skulls measured from Svalbard were collected at a time when the population was heavily overharvested, so the bears may not have reached

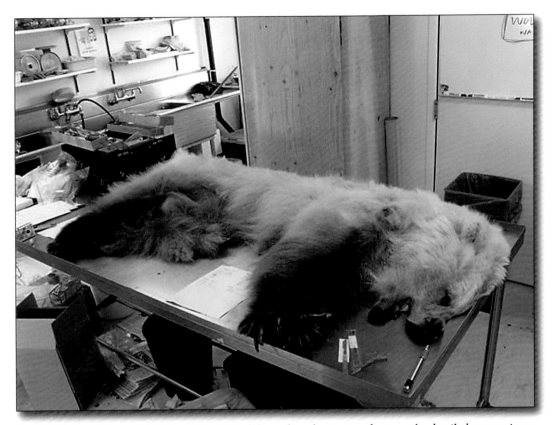

their full growth potential before being killed. In the Bering Sea, a large number of skulls were collected from bears that were being killed far offshore in a highly selective hunt that used small planes to find the biggest trophy bears. The tendency would be for these bears to be larger on average. The principal weakness of the earlier studies on geographic variation in size is that they were also done before accurate methods of age determination were developed. Thus, comparisons could only be made between pooled samples of adults representing a variety of ages. The skulls of adults continue to grow very slowly for several years after they reach maturity. Thus, a more rigorous comparison of the size and growth rates of bears from different areas had to wait until enough measurements were available from bears of known ages so age-specific growth curves could be compared.

By the late 1990s, Andy Derocher was able to use the ages and measurements taken from 6,208 individual polar bears from six areas of the Canadian Arctic in order to make detailed comparisons of growth rates and assess if there were clear trends that could be interpreted ecologically. The areas were: Western Hudson Bay, Foxe Basin, Davis Strait, the Central Arctic, the High Arctic, and the Beaufort Sea. Although a number of differences could be identified, the patterns were not always consistent and the possible significance of most of the differences was even less clear. For example, at 1.4 and 2.4 years of age, females in western Hudson Bay were longer than those in other populations. By the mean age of first breeding (4.1 years), females from western Hudson Bay had reached 97% of their adult length while those in other populations took 4.5 to 5.5 years to reach the same proportion. However, despite taking longer to reach the same length, females from the other populations still bred for the first time at the same age, except for those in the Beaufort Sea which did not breed for the first time until a full year later, at age five, even though they grew slightly more rapidly than bears in Davis Strait or

Hide from a cross between a hybrid polar/grizzly female and a grizzly male. This bear was much browner than a wild cross between a polar bear female and grizzly male that was almost all-white. Note the long claws on the front paws like a grizzly. (© Eugene Rees)

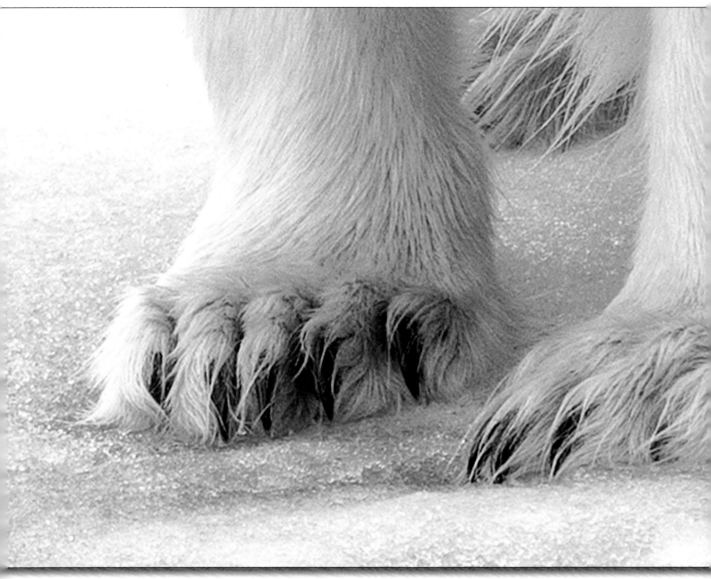

Front and side views of the short, sharp claws on a polar bear's front feet.
(© Mark Freedman)

the High Arctic. Adult males from western Hudson Bay and Foxe Basin were longer than those in the High Arctic and the Beaufort Sea, but males in the Beaufort Sea still grew more rapidly than those from Foxe Basin. In a later analysis of the growth of 361 female and 298 male polar bears from Svalbard, Derocher found both the males and female were shorter and lighter than in other studied populations, but again, possible explanations have not been confirmed.

In summary, while there appears to be some variation in the adult size and growth rate of polar bears from different areas, most differences ap-

pear small, and possible explanations for the variation are lacking. These variations seem to relate to a variety of possible ecological, and likely genetic, differences that we don't fully understand. Bears in populations at high densities or in areas of lower biological productivity probably grow at slower rates than those living at lower densities or in areas of high biological productivity. It also seems logical that bears which travel large distances in the course of a year (because they live on sea ice that is constantly moving) must use more energy for locomotion and have less left over for growth than those that have more local-

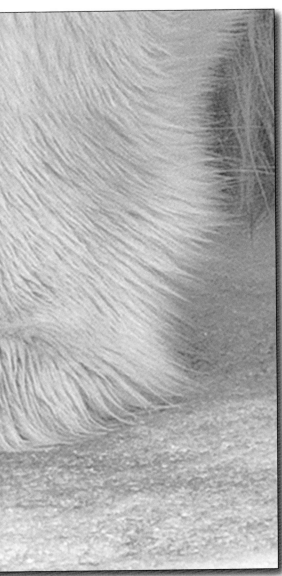

written as 3/3, 1/1, 4/4, and 2/3, a reference to the number of incisors, canines, premolars, and molars respectively. The first number of each pair indicates how many teeth of each type there are in the upper jaw, the second gives the same information for the lower jaw. Allen's Rule applies with respect to the size of a polar bear's tail and ears: it says that the farther north an animal is found, the smaller its extremities get because of the need to conserve energy. Smaller surface areas lose less heat than large ones. Desert foxes, for example, have huge ears while those of the arctic fox are tiny. Similarly, it always seems to me that the black bears of the southern United States have large ears like sails when compared to the small ears of polar bears. Polar bear legs are much larger and thicker in overall proportion to the rest of their body than those of their grizzly cousins to the south.

Polar bears have huge feet, much larger than those of grizzlies or black bears, in relation to their total body size, in what seems like a contradiction of Allen's Rule. This is probably an adaptation to two major selective pressures related to their existence in the pack ice of the Arctic Ocean. First, polar bears swim a lot, so large, oar-like feet help with propulsion. Second, while searching for seals just after freeze-up or when travelling from one area to another in early winter, they must often cross areas of thin, newly-formed ice that may not yet be thick enough to support a heavy animal with small feet. Their huge paws function like snowshoes to spread out their weight and keep them from breaking through in places where a human could not walk. Sometimes if the ice is really thin, a bear will get down on its elbows and knees, spread out its weight, and avoid breaking through.

Another interesting adaptation of polar bear feet to life on the arctic sea ice was discovered in an unusual way. Two English Doctors, Derek Manning and John Cooper, were involved in studying industrial accidents in Britain (over a million a year) caused by people slipping. They

ized movements. Similarly, rates of growth in the same area may change over time with changes in ecological conditions. In western Hudson Bay over the last 20+ years, the weights and body lengths of adult females have slowly been declining as conditions for feeding in the spring have deteriorated because of progressively earlier break-up of the sea ice. This confirms a logical link between the ability to feed and the potential rate of growth.

Morphology

Polar bears have 42 teeth. Their dental formula is

watched a polar bear on television as it ran on some ice, wondered why the bear didn't slip, and asked if I had any ideas. Apart from suggesting that their stubby, strong, and sharp claws would improve their grip, and the soles of a polar bear's paws are heavily furred, particularly in winter, I did not have a clue. I obtained some footpads from a bear killed by an Inuk hunter and sent them over for microscopic examination. The doctors also examined the footpads of two tranquilized bears in a local zoo. It turned out that the pads of a polar bear's foot are covered with small, soft papillae, which increase the friction between the foot and the ice. There are also small depressions in the sole, but their role is less clear. It is possible that these depressions function as little suction cups and briefly increase the grip of the bear's paw on the ice when it runs, but that is still only speculation at this stage. Regardless, it is fascinating to think that studies of the structure of the paw of the polar bear might one day influence the design of safer soles for shoes worn in the workplace.

Fat composition of the milk

To nurse their young, female polar bears have four functional nipples, a reduction of two from the six that their brown bear ancestors have. This may be an adaptation to having smaller average litter sizes. Mothers breast-feed their young for up to two-and-a-half years on milk that is higher in energy than that of any other species of bear. The average fat content in seven milk samples examined by the physiologist Robert Jenness and his colleagues was 33.1%, with variations ranging from 23.8% to 48.4%. More detailed analyses done by John Arnould showed, however, that the fat content varied with the age of the cubs, being about 31% in females with cubs-of-the-year but only 18% in the milk of females accompanied by yearlings. Some, but not all, females with two-year-old cubs cease nursing during the winter before the cubs are weaned. In comparison, the mean values for the fat levels of brown and black

bear milk were in the range of only 22-24%. Only one sample from the small (45 kg or 100 lb) tropical Malayan sun bear was analyzed but it had a fat content of just 11%.

The richness of their milk helps polar bear mothers to raise their young in a cold environment where energy is in high demand; hence the marked contrast to the milk from the sun bear.

The high fat content may also be important to polar bear cubs for another reason. Unlike brown bear cubs, after they leave the shelter of the dens they are born in, they do not escape the cold of the following winters by hibernating. They remain active and consequently have a higher energy demand in the two winters during which they follow their mothers before being weaned.

The rich milk of the female polar bear is comparable to that of other marine mammals. The young of whales and walruses, for example, have very high demands for energy because they grow rapidly and must quickly lay down a fat layer of their own for insulation when swimming in cold water. Milk samples from blue, fin, sperm, and white whales all have a fat content in the range

A polar bear spreads his legs out widely to help spread out his weight so he won't fall into the water as he crosses a patch of thin ice. (© Dan Guravich/ PolarBearsInternational.org)

of 30-40%, which is quite comparable to that of the polar bear. Only the milk of some of the seals that wean their pups in three to four weeks exceeds that of the polar bear. The fat content of elephant seal or Weddell seal milk is 45-55%, while the milk of the hooded seal, which weans its pup in only four days, has a fat content of 61%.

Why a marine bear at all?

Bears first became recognizable as bears about 20 million years ago in the geological period known as the Miocene. The first bears were tiny, about the size of a fox terrier. They were confined to land, where all bear species, except for the polar bear, continue to reside today. Bears evolved into much larger animals with the passage of time, but not until about 150,000 years ago did the first polar bears abandon land for sea ice. Consequently, the ecological problems other species of bears had to solve as they dispersed over all the continents (except Australia and Antarctica) were those of land animals. Although the evolutionary origin of the bears lies with the carnivores, they became more vegetarian in their food habits. Except for scavenging, they preferred plants as food. Kurtén has suggested that the large Pleistocene cave bears of Europe and southeastern North America were specialized vegetarians. Their large size and strength came about more for protection than for predation. An exception was probably the giant short-faced bear (*Arctodus*). With long legs, *Arctodus* seems to have become a superpredator. Today a few bears like the pandas of China, the sun bears of southeast Asia, and the spectacled bear of South America are almost entirely vegetarians. Other living species, including brown and black bears, are predominantly plant eaters, but some populations, and some individuals within populations, may feed on salmon, moose or caribou calves, or to some degree, even livestock at particular seasons.

Plants stop growing during the winter in the more northerly areas and high in the mountains, and those close to the ground become covered with snow. Some of the potential prey species, such as ground squirrels and marmots, hibernate in inaccessible burrows deep in the frozen ground. Although bears are admirably equipped for killing animals at close range and tearing them apart, their lumbering gait is not suited to chasing prey. In most areas, animals large enough to be worth killing, such as deer, moose, or caribou, are usually too wary and fleet-footed to allow a bear close enough for a successful attack in most circumstances. Consequently, the predominantly plant-eating bears of the northern and high mountain areas had to evolve an ability to hibernate through the winter.

Why then, if the bears were all so well adapted to being land animals, did a marine bear suddenly evolve? The expression "Nature abhors a vacuum" offers a clue. Brown bears of the ABC Islands may have first encountered seals along the coastline. Maybe they did not until they wandered out on the ice to explore. Possibly these bears scavenged on dead seals initially before they discovered they could catch live seals at cracks in the ice simply by sitting still and waiting for their victims to come up for breath. Bears learn quickly, so it is easy to imagine that when an individual somehow learned to catch a seal, the reward would be strong enough that the practice would soon be repeated. Other animals would come to scavenge and quickly learn by imitation. Cubs would be taught the trick by their mothers. Suddenly there was a new way to make a living, an opportunity ecologists call a niche. Most important, this was an unoccupied niche, with no other animal taking advantage of it.

As the polar bear evolved, it had to cope with different ecological factors from those confronting land bears. As long as the bear remained on the ice, it could catch seals throughout the year. Consequently, there was no longer a need to hibernate during winter in order to survive the food shortages that occurs at that time for brown bears. Pregnant females still went into dens during the winter because the tiny young required shelter until they grew large enough to withstand the cold and follow their mothers as they hunted on the open sea ice. The present-day polar bear is smaller than its Pleistocene ancestors, although it is still the largest of the modern non-aquatic carnivores. There is a good reason. They had and continue to have an abundant and rich food supply (seals) and a larger body is a more efficient conserver of energy than a smaller one.

The seal population, meanwhile, was not standing still. Under pressure of predation by polar bears, seals began to develop avoidance strategies. Over thousands of years of attack or escape, living or dying, bears and seals shaped each other's ecology and behaviour, habitat use, reproductive strategies, and population dynamics. In the process, the polar bear has become a true arctic marine mammal, in the sense that it now depends entirely on the sea for its existence and, without sea ice, will likely not survive. Throughout this book, the underlying biological theme will be how the polar bear has evolved to meet the ecological and energetic requirements of its unique life and how it is now coping with its most recent and potentially stressful environmental strain: modern man and a warming climate.

Chapter 3

POLAR BEARS AND HUMANS

A subadult polar bear looking at ecotourists in a
nearby small boat (out of photo)
(© David Merefield)

Early arctic people and polar bears

About 3,500 to 4,000 years ago, the Paleoeskimos crossed the Bering Straits from Siberia, probably on the frozen ice, and spread across the North American and Greenland Arctic. Archaeologists refer to the culture as the Arctic Small Tool tradition because their stone harpoon tips, arrowheads, and knives were so small.

Remains of Thule houses at Radstock Bay, Devon Island. Note the predominance of skulls and ribs from bowhead whales.
(© Ian Stirling)

A distinct cultural change, referred to as Dorset first appeared about 2,500 years ago in the areas of Hudson Strait and Foxe Basin in the eastern Canadian Arctic. The first artefacts from the culture were identified by Diamond Jenness, an ethnologist at the National Museum of Canada in 1924. The Dorset were elaborate and skilled carvers of miniatures of people and animals in ivory—ranging from detailed replicas to stylized and abstract portrayals. Apart from human and human-like faces, the most common image in Dorset art was that of the polar bear. The preva-

lence of bear carvings was probably partly because of the Dorset people's respect and fear of the sheer power of the creatures, but likely also because the polar bear was most like themselves. Only bears and the Dorset people were capable of hunting sea mammals. The bears occasionally killed humans as well. No doubt, an occasional Dorset hunter also killed a bear, probably with a spear when it was in a maternity den or swimming. The physical resemblance the bears bore to people probably also influenced their prevalence in Dorset carvings. For example, bears stand up

different postures such as swimming, standing, or sitting might simply represent the artist's appreciation of the natural beauty of the animal itself. More stylized images with the hind legs stretched out might represent the spirit of a magical or legendary bear swimming or flying. Flying bear images in particular have been recovered from several Dorset village locations in the eastern Canadian Arctic. Some appear to have abstract skeletal parts, such as ribs, vertebrae, and major joints delineated. A few of these locations, as well as sometimes the top of the head, are also marked with plus signs. Whole animal carvings, or sometimes just the bears head, have holes in them, suggesting they may have been sewn to clothing or worn on a thong around the neck as an amulet. Although it is impossible to reconstruct the exact significance of such carvings, their abundance and variety indicate they carried great significance, probably as protectors, providers of good luck, and for shamanistic activity. Unfortunately little more is known about the Dorset people. When the first Viking explorers arrived in southwestern Greenland a thousand years ago, only the ruins of the Dorset dwellings remained. What is clear, however, is how much the great white bear was valued and respected.

As the Dorset people disappeared from the eastern Canadian Arctic and Greenland, possibly influenced by changes in the climate, the Thule culture developed on the northern coast of Alaska. The Thule people were supreme maritime hunters of the Arctic and developed large, open skin-covered boats called *Umiaks* for hunting marine mammals in open water. So advanced were their skills that they even developed successful techniques for hunting bowhead whales (mostly young and subadult). The Thule people spread rapidly across the Arctic, reaching northwest Greenland by about A.D. 1200. They are represented in modern times by the present-day Inuit. Bowhead whale bones dominate the remains of pre-historic Thule houses, but bones of other arctic marine mammal species may be found there

on their hind legs, and sometimes walk a few steps, like a human. When dead and skinned, a bear's torso has an uncanny resemblance to that of a human. Taken together, these similarities likely helped the bear to become an influential spirit creature as well as a dominant feature of the natural environment of the Dorset people.

Because so little remains from the Dorset culture, it is difficult to interpret exactly what the different types of images of bears might mean. However, there is speculation that some of the tiny but elegantly accurate portrayals of bears in

as well, including the skulls of polar bears.

Much of the knowledge and tradition of the Thule people has been passed down to their Inuit descendents. Through the journals of explorers, traders, missionaries, and, thank goodness, scientists like Boas and Rasmussen, we have some detailed records of the relationship between the early Inuit and polar bears before extensive European contact changed things forever. The Inuit also have a strong tradition of oral history through which they have preserved a considerable record of past history and observations of the natural history of the wildlife species they hunted. Because contact with European civilization is still relatively recent in some areas, considerable and very important efforts are now being made to

A Greenland hunter wearing his polar bear pants cuts up seal meat for his dog team while out hunting.
(© Erik W. Born)

record and preserve as much oral history as possible before it is lost forever.

Use of polar bears by Inuit

The Inuit killed polar bears for clothing, sleeping skins, and food for themselves and their dogs. Historically there were also a number of specialized but local uses. For example, a hunter waiting for a seal to come up to its breathing hole in the bitter cold of winter might sit on a piece of polar bear skin on a snow block to make a warm, dry seat. He might rest his feet on another skin to help keep the cold from penetrating. Apparently hunters in the Ungava area of northern Quebec sometimes used a pad of polar bear skin to protect their elbows when crawling up on seals. In earlier times, when dog sleds were the predominant mode of transport, Inuit commonly used a piece of polar bear skin as a brush to spread water on sled runners in order to coat them with ice in the cold weather. The bear's canine teeth were often used for making ornaments or amulets, sometimes in the shape of a bear.

Most polar bears killed by hunters with primitive weapons were likely speared when swimming or when in a den. Dogs were used to sniff out female bears with cubs in their maternity dens. The hunters would then carefully cut a hole in the roof of the den and kill the bear by plunging a spear into the animal. Hides of cubs were particularly sought after because of their softness and warmth, while the meat was regarded as a special delicacy. Bears were also sometimes killed on the open ice while hunters were out looking for other animals such as seals. In such circumstances, hunters would sometimes follow a fresh track. When they neared the bear, hunters would unleash the dogs to let them rush at the bear and distract it by barking and snapping at its heels. This gave the hunter a chance to close in and shoot the bear with arrows, or impale it with a lance.

The so-called Polar Eskimos of northwestern Greenland hunted and used polar bears more than any other group. They also appear to have developed some of the most elaborate rituals involving bears. To this day, the wearing of polar bear pants by a hunter is a sign of status.

Some Inuit spiritual beliefs and practices concerning polar bears

As important as polar bears were for food and other materials, they were not the mainstay of life as were seals or caribou. Consequently, we must explore the cultural and spiritual aspects to gain a deeper sense of the polar bears' traditional significance to the first polar bear watchers.

The pre-historic Inuit had a dual relation with many animals. They knew how to kill and use their bodies, but when they did so, they believed they had to defer to their spirits. This required

that hunters act according to quite specific beliefs and rituals, or the animals would be offended and would withhold themselves from the hunters. An Igloolik Inuk hunter, Ivaluardjuk, explained the essence of these beliefs to the famous Danish ethnologist Knud Rasmussen as follows: "The greatest peril of life lies in the fact that human food consists entirely of souls. All the creatures that we have to kill and eat, all those that we have to strike down and destroy to make clothes for ourselves, have souls, like we have, souls that do not perish with the body, and which must therefore be propitiated lest they should revenge themselves on us for taking away their bodies."

Beliefs and practices varied between areas but there were some common themes. One was that the spirit of an animal might be chosen to be the *tornaq* (spiritual guardian) of a particular individual. With the exception of Sedna, the legendary goddess of the sea who was generally held to be the supreme being, the most powerful spirit of all was that of the polar bear. Consequently, the shaman usually had the polar bear as his *tornaq*. It is certainly no coincidence that when the mighty *angakoq* (shaman) of ancient Greenlandic legend made his daring and adventure-filled trip to the moon and back, he was accompanied by his polar-bear *tornaq*.

Another powerful concept was that the spirits of men and bears were interchangeable. Bears were the most powerful and dangerous of all the animals, so the killing of one was a major event. More significant, as pointed out by American anthropologist Irving Hallowell, is the fact that bears have so many "human-like" traits. Besides standing up, walking on their hind legs, and having musculature reminiscent of a human, they also eat many of the same foods, both plant and animal, that people do. Sometimes, they sit and lean against something as if resting and thinking. These similarities undoubtedly explain why, in so many Inuit legends, when the polar bears are inside their own houses they become people; they put on their hides when they go outside to be bears again. There are parallels in legends involving humans and other species of bears throughout the Northern Hemisphere.

A common theme in Inuit culture is the belief that a bear would give itself to a hunter only if it was to be treated properly after death. Thus, hunters were careful to observe various ceremonies after killing a bear. The most widespread practice was to observe a strict taboo against hunting polar bears after killing one to allow sufficient time for its soul to return to its family. Rasmussen recorded a legend from the Netsilik Inuit ("people of the seal") of the central Canadian Arctic that outlines this belief. In it, a woman had unwittingly entered an igloo inhabited by a family of polar bears. She became frightened and hid behind some sealskins that were hanging on the inside walls. As she listened to their conversation, she learned how the youngest bear had gained respect for the Inuit, who he had once thought were just figures of skin and bone. This bear had been out hunting humans and had been killed by a man who later gave him a death taboo and several wonderful presents. These actions set the bear's soul free and he was able to return to his family again after four days. Later, when the woman escaped, she returned to her village and told the people what she had learned. Because of this legend, in earlier times, the Netsilik, Copper, and Inland Inuit observed a strict taboo on hunting for several days after killing a bear. Curiously, this abstinence apparently lasted for five days after killing a female bear but only for four days after killing a male.

The non-hunting period during which the polar bear's spirit was thought to linger was three days in the Hudson Bay and southeastern Baffin Island areas. This was also identical to the length of time believed to be taken by a human spirit in those areas to leave its body and return to its ancestors.

The Copper Eskimos had another practice linking human beings to bears. If a male bear was killed, the hunter would give it a miniature bow and arrow, while a female bear was given a needle holder because, like humans, the man needs his hunting weapons, and the woman, her domestic tools.

In rituals, parts of a bear usually were used to represent the entire animal. The skull was most important to the Asiatic Eskimos, Greenlanders, Polar Eskimos, and those in the central Canadian Arctic. To the Polar Eskimos, as well as those of inland Alaska, the Mackenzie Delta, and the central Canadian Arctic, the skin was also of particular significance. Parts of the animals' intestines were apparently also important to the Inuit of Baffin Island, the Chukchi Sea, and the Igloolik areas.

In parts of Greenland, before contact with Europeans, some of the practices were apparently quite elaborate. The Scandinavian anthropologist Helge Larsen reported that the Polar Eskimos also regarded the soul of the polar bear as more dangerous than that of all other animals. Consequently, post-hunting rituals had to be carried out especially carefully. Particular attention also focused on the head of brown and black bears in boreal areas of Asia and North America. As an offering to the soul of a male polar bear, a harpoon was hung over its snout for five days, along with an offering of blubber and meat. A female bear would be given a piece of sealskin as well.

A hunter in southern Greenland placed the head of the bear on the lamp platform facing southeast, the direction bears came from in that district. He covered the eyes and blocked off the nostrils with moss or other materials so the bear's soul could not see or smell him. Fat was smeared on the jaws and articles such as boot soles, knives, or beads were placed on top of the skull. The fat on the mouth was to appease the bear because they were known to prefer eating it. Materials on the head were for the ancestors of the hunters who, they believed, had sent the bear to collect them. Like their kin to the south, Polar Eskimos also refrained from hunting polar bears for five days after a kill in order to allow sufficient time

for the bear's soul to return to its home.

American anthropologist Charles Hughes reported that in the days before the acquisition of firearms at St. Lawrence Island in Alaska, bears were killed with lances. The hunter who accomplished this particularly dangerous feat was honoured by five days of ceremonies similar to those judged appropriate for a whale. The head of the bear was put in a corner of the room with its

mouth open, and decorated with beads and so on, appropriate to its sex. All hunting ceased while stories were told and songs were sung. After five days, the skull was boiled and the pieces of flesh that became dislodged were either thrown into the air for the spirits or placed in the fire to appease their forefathers. Afterward, the hunter put the skull on the graves of the clan's ancestors, along with other bear skulls. St. Lawrence

This adult female and her tiny cub are very thin, but it will be three months before the ice freezes again and they can hunt seals. The cub will probably die and the starving mother may be dangerous if near human habitation.
(© David Merefield)

Islanders also believed that a hunter who wounded a bear must track it down and kill it so as to release its soul. If this was not done, the animal's soul would be deeply offended and cause sickness and harm to the hunter.

A polar bear legend

There are many Inuit legends and tales about polar bears. One of my favorites, *The Great Bear*, was recorded by Rasmussen (1921, p. 81) on the coast of West Greenland in the early 1900s. It goes as follows:

"A woman ran away from her home because her child had died. On her way she came to a house. In the passage way there lay the skins of bears. And she went in. And now it was revealed that the people who lived in there were bears in human form. Yet for all that she stayed with them. One big bear used to go out hunting to find food for them. It would put on its skin and go out, sometimes staying away for a long time, and always returning with some catch or other. But one day, the woman who had run away began to feel homesick, and greatly desired to see her kin. And then the bear spoke to her thus: "Do not speak of us when you return to men," it said. For it was afraid lest its two cubs might be killed by the men. Then the woman went home and there she felt a great desire to tell what she had seen. And one day, as she sat with her husband in the house, she said to him: "I have seen bears."

And now many sledges drove out, and when the bear saw them coming towards its house, it felt so sorry for its cubs that it bit them to death, that they might not fall in to the hands of men.

But then it dashed out to find the woman who had betrayed it and broke into her house and bit her to death. But when it came out, the dogs closed round it and fell upon it. The bear struck out at them, but suddenly all of them became wonderfully bright, and rose up to the sky in the form of stars. And it is these which we call Qilugtussat, the stars which look like barking dogs about a bear. Since then, men have learned to be-

ware of bears, for they hear what men say."

I particularly like that story because it seems to contain much of the essence of the mythological relationships between the Inuit and the polar bears before the arrival of Europeans. The bear as a particularly powerful spirit is shown by its ability to turn dogs into stars. It incorporates the recurrent theme from many legends that the spirits of men and bears are interchangeable. Finally, there is the clear expectation of how one should behaves toward bears and talk about them, along with the consequences of not doing so.

Talking respectfully about polar bears is still deeply ingrained in many Inuk hunters today, especially older and more traditional individuals. For example, a few years ago, an exceptionally good hunter who is a friend of many years confided to me that two young fellows who were out hunting polar bears would not succeed. "They been bragging too much about getting the bear. The bear won't let himself be killed by someone who talks like that." I made no comment because the two young hunters were headed for an area where I had seen several bears and a lot of tracks in the last few days, so I thought it quite likely they would each get one. Consequently, I was a little surprised when they came back empty-handed. My friend, on the other hand, saw nothing unusual and made no further comment on the matter. I have often thought about that conversation and the deep respect that hunter had for polar bears, and still has for that matter, for I feel the same way myself.

Polar bears and the Nenets of northwestern Siberia

The Nenets people, who live along the arctic coast of the Soviet Union, from the White Sea to northwestern Siberia, also gave polar bears a special place in their traditional beliefs. They erected altars of bones from several species in noticeable places. The skulls of polar bears were especially featured. The late Soviet polar bear biologist Savva Uspenski measured one such ceremonial mound of reindeer and polar bear skulls to be about five metres in diametre and three metres high. Another had fifty-five polar bear skulls in it. In northern Yamal, Uspenski was given permission by the Samoyeds to remove some skulls for scientific studies, but they asked him not to take any of the fresh ones because it might affect the success of next year's hunt.

The Nenet people also practiced other rituals in earlier times, such as the taking of an oath while holding the muzzle of a skull or a paw. In some regions, women were banned from eating polar bear flesh. Canine teeth were used as amulets against visits by deceased persons and attacks by brown bears.

Modern humans and polar bears

The history of human expansion into the wilderness has been one of continuous competition with large carnivores for space and resources. Humans have sometimes also represented potential prey for some large carnivores, including polar bears. In earlier times, human appropriation of habitat for agriculture and ranching over the entire Northern Hemisphere, or just plain fear of predators, drove species like the wolf and the brown bear into remnant populations and local extinctions throughout much of their original range.

Although polar bears are still distributed throughout most of their historic range, pressure from human habitation and industrial activities, along with the effects of climate warming, are resulting in an increasing number of negative interactions between humans and bears. Most conflicts of course take place along the coastlines of the polar seas and arctic archipelagos but, as humans travel and work more extensively in the sea ice further offshore, the chances of meeting polar bears greatly increase.

Besides simply scavenging at sites of human habitation such as coastal villages, Inuit hunting camps, weather stations, or settlements, hungry polar bears are more willing than other bears to prey upon humans. By way of comparison, few black bears ever attack humans. Although more humans are attacked by brown bears than by black bears, a high proportion are mauled but still left alive; not a pleasant prospect, but better than being killed. A polar bear attack on a human usually ends only when one of them is dead.

In the following sections, I will try to summarize some of the sorts of broad circumstances in which polar bears and humans come into conflict.

Being stalked by a bear on the sea ice

When a polar bear attacks a human, the victim is often unaware of the bear's presence until it appears at close range. The circumstances can vary greatly but the element of surprise is fundamental, as a couple of examples will illustrate.

On July 1, 1961, Tony Overton and three colleagues from the Canadian Department of Energy, Mines, and Resources were doing some seismic studies on the sea ice near the southwest coast of Ellef Ringnes Island. Normally, all four men slept in a large tent but one night, because one of the fellows had spilled liquid on the floor, the other three decided to sleep outside on the sea ice since the weather was mild. They had not seen any signs of bears, or even of seals, during the time they had been camped there. Even so, Tony put his loaded rifle on the ice by his right hand before crawling into his sleeping bag and going to sleep. To this day he doesn't know why, but for some reason he suddenly woke up at about four o'clock in the "morning" (24-hour daylight prevails in the High Arctic in summer) and saw a polar bear approaching about 65 m (215 ft) away. He reached for his rifle but before he could lift it, the bear charged. It seized him by the arm as he was raising it over his head in a last-minute act of self-defence. The bear dragged him out of his sleeping bag and about 15 m (50 ft) across the ice. Tony desperately shouted at his slumbering colleagues three times before finally managing to wake the now-deceased Bill Tyrlik. Bill quickly assessed the situation and swept up the rifle to shoot. By that time, the bear had

Six bears feeding in the Churchill Dump. Two can't even be bothered to stand up while they have their heads in garbage.
(© Ian Stirling)

dropped Tony and was charging him instead. Bill did not even have time to aim before the bear reached him, so he shot from the hip. He dropped it, with one lucky shot between the eyes, on the end of his sleeping bag. (One of Tony's other companions commented some time later that he had heard all three of his yells but thought he was just having a nightmare!) It seems likely the bear thought the men looked like seals on the ice from a distance, but when it seized Tony it knew it had something different. There was another instance where the bear dragged a scientist from his tent and was shot as it dragged the person away. On a third occasion, a bear clamped its jaws around the head of a young Inuk hunter inside a tent and was trying to drag him free while a second hunter scrambled outside and shot it. I have often wondered if the bear's hesitation from biting and crushing the men's heads immediately, as it would nor-

POLAR BEARS: The Natural History of a Threatened Species

"Don't move." Jimmy does not fool around, so Tom froze. In a single motion, Jimmy swung his rifle over Tom's back and pulled the trigger, killing a polar bear with a single shot just as it was breaking through the back wall of the tent.

In two other instances I am aware of, a large polar bear stalked a person to within a few feet in some pressure ridges. In both cases, when it was within a few feet of its prey, it let out a slight puff of air just before attacking. One was with the famous arctic explorer Vilhjalmur Stefansson, and the other was with Jimmy. Both men had been around polar bears enough that their reflexes took over and they were able to save their lives by instantly shooting the bear. However, had the bear not given a momentary warning before attacking, neither man would have lived to tell of the experience.

Having watched so many polar bears hunting over the years, I am particularly intrigued by this momentary pause when bears seem to blow out some air just before attacking a human. Clearly, such a noise can warn a person of an impending attack and possibly allow enough time to respond in defence. I doubt polar bears blow air out when they hunt seals because a seal could probably disappear in less time that it would take a human to react, although I have never been close enough to be able to confirm such small details of what might happen as a seal is caught. However, this breath when they are close enough to a human to attack, especially in a wilderness setting, suggests that because the bear is hunting something different, which might be a little dangerous, they may make a momentary last minute use of their sense of smell to give themselves a bit more information about their objective before attacking. It is interesting to speculate that even a polar bear might get a little nervous at times. The point of these stories is that one always has to be alert in polar bear country. Or, as Jimmy once said to me while we were working out on the sea ice, "If you don't keep looking, the bear is gonna get you."

mally do with a seal, might possibly be because of the unfamiliar scent. Whatever the reason, the bear's delay provided enough time for the humans to be saved.

On another occasion, Tom Smith and the inimitable Inuk hunter, the late Jimmy Memorana, had just set up their tent on the sea ice one cold evening in early April. They were unpacking inside and Tom was kneeling over his gear doing something when Jimmy matter-of-factly said,

Identification of a problem

For a number of years, wildlife agencies generally discouraged the killing of so-called "problem bears" of all species unless it was deemed absolutely necessary. Even so, few people actually worried much about those that did get shot. It was often difficult to obtain accurate figures on how many polar bears were being shot in "defence of life and property" (such cases are identified as DLPs). For many years, an unknown number of bears were killed when they came into settlements, but they were often not included in the quota, so their numbers were additive. In other cases, a dead problem bear was simply allocated a quota tag but the reason for its death was not recorded. In recent years, recording of the reason for a polar bear death, such as normal legal hunting, as a problem bear, or for other causes, is reasonably good in most jurisdictions, though there is still room for improvement.

Ray Schweinsburg, formerly the polar bear biologist for the Government of the Northwest Territories, worried about the number of problem bears being killed, and rightly so. He frequently pointed out that the annual quotas for Inuit hunters were already near the limit of the estimated sustainable harvest for each subpopulation. This meant the unregulated kill of "problem bears" was additive and might make some populations vulnerable to being overharvested. A few numbers make his point. In 1977, the recorded kill of problem polar bears in the Northwest Territories was ten. Five years later, it was over forty. At the time, the number of additional problem bear kills in the rest of Canada might have been another twenty or so per year but there was no way of knowing the total. The overall total is likely much higher today because many more hungry bears are now being shot in areas affected by climate warming such as Western Hudson Bay, Baffin Bay, Davis Strait and the northern coast of Russia. The lack of an accurate review of this problem and ongoing difficulties with ensuring accurate recording still likely results in an un-

derestimate of DLPs. Documentation of problem bears killed in Alaska was hampered for the first few years after the Marine Mammal Protection Act came into effect because it placed restrictions on the ability of government agencies to monitor the harvest taken by native people. However, much better records have been kept since 1988 with the signing of the Management Agreement for Polar Bears in the Southern Beaufort Sea (see

Conservation chapter) which required an accurate system of reporting harvest.

Nor was the problem solely a North American one. At the 1981 meeting of the IUCN PBSG in Oslo, Norway, a different but interesting perspective emerged. The Soviet Union had given the polar bear protected status in 1956 and Norway did the same thing in Svalbard in 1973. At the time, the populations were probably depleted in both areas and, as a result of being overharvested, the hunting pressure probably helped the bears to maintain a healthy respect for people. Initially, few bears were seen, but then things changed. At least partly because of the lack of hunting, the polar bear populations probably grew larger and their fear of humans declined. After only five or six years, the weather stations and settlements in Svalbard began reporting increasing numbers of

Ecotourists photographing a curious polar bear from the back of a Tundra Buggy.
(© Ian Stirling)

polar bears in the winter. Soon, half a dozen "problem" bears were being shot each year. At the 1981 meeting in Oslo, the late Savva Uspenski showed us some incredible photographs of polar bears wandering about in small villages on the northern Siberian coast. In one, a lady was standing on her doorstep calmly feeding an enormous male by hand. Uspenski said the bears were becoming "quite brave", which understandably raised concern among Soviet authorities at time.

These parallel experiences with polar bears in Svalbard, the Soviet Union (now the Russian Federation)and, to some degree Canada, also serve to underscore an especially important point when it comes to the conservation of large carnivores. Cessation of all killing of these animals is not a guaranteed means to save the species, as preservationists would like to think. Polar bears, like other large carnivores, are dangerous animals. Although most individuals are remarkably good natured and will avoid inhabited areas given half a chance, they do sometimes kill people and cause serious damage to property. Consequently, people responsible for polar bear management must have a variety of options open to them, including the authority to remove individuals when the occasion demands it. Today however, some of the reasons for the occurrence of problem bears in the first place are aggravated by a different influence: climate warming. The greater presence of hungry bears around areas of human habitation is often caused by longer and more geographically extensive periods of open water which have a negative affect on the bears' ability to hunt adequately for their natural prey. This aspect is discussed in more detail in the chapter on climate warming

What bears cause problems and why?

Before you can solve a problem, you have to define it. Which polar bears cause problems and why do they do so? At Churchill, Nick Lunn demonstrated that most of the bears that came to the dump were subadult males or females with cubs. In general, both groups were thinner and hungrier. In years when the bears came ashore lighter than usual, more showed up at the dump. Females with cubs tended to remain there. However, subadult males tended to wander more, and many of those that wandered into town were shot.

From 1973 to 1983, twenty-eight bears were reported killed as DLPs in the eastern Beaufort Sea. This is a minimum number because, for at least the first half of that period, problem kills in the villages and hunting camps were poorly documented and specimens were not always obtained. However, of the sixteen bears whose ages were determined, twelve were five years of age or less and two were cubs-of-the-year accompanying their mothers. The average age of the twelve subadults was 2.25 years. Similarly, in the eastern Beaufort Sea, the greatest number of problem bears were subadults. The bears that attacked Tony Overton and tried to enter Tom Smith's tent were also subadults. These are the bears that have the most difficult time hunting. They have just been turned out on their own by their mothers and they have not yet become proficient hunters. When they do kill a seal, they also have a higher risk of having it taken away from them by larger, more dominant bears. Scavenging is an important part of their strategy for survival. Consequently, subadults are more likely to be in poor physical condition during periods when food is less abundant. There may be little option for a small number of them but to try scavenging on garbage, and occasionally even preying on humans, in order to survive.

This was brought home rather forcibly and unfortunately in the eastern Beaufort Sea in the winter of 1974-75. The size of the seal populations had been greatly reduced by uncertain but natural causes in the previous spring. It seemed logical that if there was a dramatic reduction in the seal population, subadults might have an even more difficult time and, consequently, be in poorer condition. We predicted an increase in defence kills. Sure enough, there were seven problem bears killed that winter, compared to one or two in most winters. One of those bears killed a man at an oil company camp in January 1975. The seal populations remained low again the following summer and another seven problem bears were shot in the ensuing winter although no human was killed. After that, the seal populations recovered and the number of problem bears dropped back to one or two a year. Although females accompanied by cubs become problem bears less frequently than subadults, human deaths and property damage from them have been documented in the Beaufort Sea, the High Arctic, and Western Hudson Bay.

With polar bears, the common thread in problem incidents is that hungry, sometimes starving, animals have nothing to lose by trying something different. After all, investigating new possibilities is the hallmark of success for carnivores because it is the mechanism by which they discover new food sources or new ways of capturing their usual prey.

Although it is clear that nutritionally stressed bears enter human habitations, it is less certain whether any particular age or sex group is more dangerous than another out on the ice in prime polar bear habitat. Few adult male polar bears become problems at dumps for example, which is just the opposite of the case with black or grizzly bears. But, would they be more aggressive toward humans out on the sea ice? My impression is that adult males in most of the Canadian Arctic at least have learned to be wary of people, (probably because of centuries of being hunted), and are less likely to be a threat. At Cape Churchill in the fall, when we hung out a smelly bait specifically to attract bears so we could tag them, we consistently noticed it was the largest and fattest males that were the most cautious about approaching: many only came close at night. Similarly, Savva Uspenski maintained that along the Siberian coast, the large males were the most wary of all age and sex classes, and also usually only came into the villages in the middle of the night. Over the years,

our consistent impression has been that the bears in the best condition overall were the adult males. Since they experience the smallest amount of nutritional stress, they probably investigate human habitations least often. Also these bears, having learned to be cautious of humans and settled areas, are less likely to be shot, thus creating a positive feedback to being shy in terms of survival. Even in some areas where polar bears are not hunted, the largest males are still the most wary about approaching eco-tourists wanting nothing more than a nice viewing and a photo taken from either a Tundra Buggy (an all-terrain vehicle rather like a high-rise bus mounted on huge tires) near Churchill or an ecotourism ship in Svalbard.

The human factor

Another important aspect to remember when considering human-bear conflicts is that sometimes these are not the fault of the bear. Feeding polar bears and otherwise acclimating them to close human presence sets the scene for problems. Bears are individuals and they learn quickly. They are also adept at spotting opportunities for a meal while not giving any indication of their intentions. Two incidents illustrate this.

A a field research tent after a bear entered through the back wall. No one was hurt as the tent was empty at the time. (© Mark Mallory)

In one incident near Cape Churchill, an experienced polar bear photographer got a little careless while taking pictures from the Tundra Buggy. A large thin bear had been hanging around for a few days, sometimes disappearing from view beneath the vehicle. One day, a rare ivory gull landed nearby, causing great excitement among the photographers. The man hung his arm out the window to support his camera as he photographed the bird. Seeing his opportunity, the bear quickly emerged from under the vehicle, stood up on his hind legs, and seized the man's arm in his jaws. The tour guide pounded on the bear's head hard enough to make him let go but not before the photographer's arm was badly ripped open. A dramatic rescue operation across the tundra to the hospital in Churchill saved his arm and his life. Graciously, but appropriately, the man blamed himself, not the bear.

In 1983, the polar bears along the coast south of Churchill came ashore much lighter than usual which meant they had less stored fat to live on until they could return to the ice. That fall, the bear patrol recorded one of the highest numbers of problem bear calls ever. Everyone knew there were lots of bears around. Yet, a local man went to scavenge in the remains of a burned-out hotel late one night after leaving the bar. He stuffed his pockets full of meat and other food from the abandoned freezer and was apparently walking off in the dark when a bear attacked him from behind. The man was killed and the bear dragged his corpse down the main street, where the bear was finally shot. The townspeople were outraged and the press had a field day with headlines about a northern town under siege by polar bears.

As unfortunate as these incidents were, in each case, the human was more at fault than the bear. The bears were simply behaving naturally. Someone who places himself in a polar bear's mouth, so to speak, has only himself to blame if he is bitten. Similarly, when there are open garbage dumps near settlements and the remains from seals, whales, or other animals are not disposed of near hunting camps, polar bears will continue to be attracted. In polar bear country, it pays to observe the Manitoba motto: "A Safe Bear Is a Distant Bear."

Detection and deterrents

One of the main reasons a polar bear can be so dangerous is that its appearance is often so unexpected that people are caught unprepared. If there is a warning system of some kind, then people can be alerted and can take steps to try to scare the bear away or, if it is sufficiently threatening, shoot it. In earlier times, Inuit depended on their dogs to bark and warn them that something was approaching the camp. More recently, electric fences that deter a bear by giving it a shock have been fairly effective when deployed for small tent camps on land, but are less successful when applied on snow because they don't ground as well. Trip wire fences that set off an alarm provide a warning to a person inside a tent or building that something is around. At the same time, one of the most important single things to do consistently is simply to keep a camp as clean and devoid of attractive smells as possible.

Once one is aware of the presence of a bear, the real problem becomes *how* to scare it away without harming it, something that is often more easily said than done. Experience has shown that unexpected loud noises, such as gun shots or cracker shells and flares, can be quite effective on naïve bears in a wilderness setting. Similarly, being chased for a short distance with a snow machine or an all-terrain vehicle can also be quite effective when dealing with naïve, or relatively naïve animals. However, in situations where the bears are familiar with humans and return repeatedly to the same place, either in a single year or subsequent years, loud noises alone are less effective at frightening the animals away because they often get used to the sounds and ignored them.

Giving a bear what science calls a "negative stimulus" at the same time as making a loud noise can be quite effective, for short periods at least. This approach relies on the bear experiencing something unpleasant, maybe temporarily painful, but not harmful. The initial experiments with this approach were done with a 38 mm riot control gun at a distance of 40-60 m (130-195 ft). The sudden impact of a rubber bullet half the size of a pound of butter served that purpose admirably. There was no ignoring the smack of a fast-moving rubber baton on the backside, and the results were unequivocal. In an experimental situation, all of the 404 bears hit with rubber bullets from 1981 through 1983 fled immediately, except for one. He was a large but very thin adult male who still would not move, even after he had been hit five times. This degree of determination illustrates why a starving bear is so dangerous. The principal concern of such a bear is to find something to eat because he is starving. He will risk death to get it.

A few bears came back a second or even a third time but the "negative stimulus" of the riot gun still sent them scurrying once again. The indication was that they had learned quickly and were not about to stay for more. Although testing continued at night with the aid of spotlights, a few bears learned to wait until the biologists went to bed. Then they investigated the area under the cover of darkness. Again, the speed with which polar bears can assess and adjust to new situations should never be underestimated.

Although the 38 mm rubber bullet gun, originally developed for police use, is not legally available to the general public, it confirmed the value of a negative stimulus being delivered at the same time as the noise. More recently, a 12 gauge shell with a rubber bullet has been developed to "encourage" bears to leave an area by delivering a non-lethal but unpleasant experience without hide penetration or other injury. Field tests have proven this product to be quite effective on bears.

Polar bear safety video

A particularly valuable educational contribution to help people, especially newcomers to the Arctic, travel as safely as possible is the 2005 film, *Polar Bears: A Guide to Safety*, available on video or DVD. This program contains important information on how travellers can reduce their chance of encountering a polar bear and how to best respond if they do meet one.

The film was a collaborative effort of the Safety in Bear Country Society and many people knowledgeable about staying safe in polar bear country, including Inuit elders and polar bear hunters, other northern residents, scientists, wildlife managers, and operators of the bear-viewing vehicles. The program is 27 minutes long, and available in English only from: http://www.macecanada.com/unitedstates/Products/polar_video2us.htm.

Chapter 4

Things to consider before starting

Studying polar bears is challenging. Consider some of the problems. To begin with, polar bears are large, equipped with big teeth and claws, and are capable of doing a lot of damage to a person quickly. Working safely with them requires caution and patience. If immobilizing and handling bears is needed, one has to be equally careful about safety for both humans and bears, and always treat each individual bear with respect.

HOW DO YOU STUDY A POLAR BEAR?

A bear that has been darted in the shoulder
walks slowly as the helicopter lands and waits
until he goes to sleep.
(© Daniel J. Cox/NaturalExposures.com)

Even in places where there are lots of bears, they are usually distributed at low densities over vast and remote areas whenever they are on sea ice. When they are offshore in drifting pack ice, (which is much of the time), these animals are usually only accessible by helicopter. Sometimes you search all day and only catch three or four bears, though on other days one may catch a dozen or more. Occasionally, you don't even see one. Depending on the objectives, it is not unusual for a study to take several years to complete.

The weather can be cold, windy, or foggy. Sometimes several days may pass before the weather is good enough to fly again, or clear enough to be able to continue observations of undisturbed animals. In some areas, it is necessary to work at distances of 240 km (150 mi) or more from the nearest fuel cache. Mechanical failure of aircraft is always a possibility. In not that many years, people working on my project alone have been involved in two helicopter crashes, two fixed-wing crashes, two helicopter engine failures, and too many narrow escapes to even recall. Miraculously, no one has been hurt while working with me, though three polar bear biologists have been killed in aircraft accidents while undertaking their own field studies. Clearly, conducting research on polar bears is expensive, time-consuming, and potentially dangerous. On the other hand, there are few animals anywhere in the world as fascinating and rewarding to study.

These days, most scientific studies of polar bears can be divided into a number of broad categories. Some require immobilizing and handling animals and while others rely primarily on observing undisturbed wild animals, either for very brief periods such as when surveying from aircraft or for longer periods of observation from a semipermanent observation camp in order to quantify their undisturbed behaviour in natural habitat. A more specialized but very important category for a number of quite specific questions involves studies of captive animals in zoos. More recently, in addition to the scientific approach that most

western readers are familiar with, considerable contributions are coming from collations of interviews with experienced hunters and documentation of their observations, thoughts, and interpretations. Such information tends to be dependent on opportunistic observations, the

interpretations of which are sometimes difficult to test using western scientific methods. Regardless, considerable effort is being made these days to ensure inclusion of aboriginal hunters and their knowledge into the planning and execution of projects, as well as in the interpretation of results.

What methods one might apply to a project depends largely on what kind of information one wishes to gain from it, and with what degree of accuracy. In the following chapter, I will briefly outline and illustrate some of the techniques biologists have used over the last few decades to

It is important to keep a bear's head out of water while it is being tranquilized. (© Ian Stirling)

Measuring the straight line body length on an immobilized polar bear.
(© Ian Stirling)

discover all manner of new things about the life of wild polar bears.

Determining population size using tagging studies

Initially, the primary stimulus for conducting research on polar bears was international concern that population sizes might be declining because of kill levels that were not sustainable. Thus, a very large amount of the research conducted in the first 20 years or so, as well as much that followed, has been focussed on population ecology. To assess the size of a polar bear population, and whether it might be increasing, decreasing, or stable, there is pretty much universal agreement that,

overall, "tagging studies" provide the most reliable information.

Basically, this means immobilizing a large sample of bears with tranquilizer darts, usually fired from a helicopter. In practice, you capture as many animals as you can in the first year and mark them individually. In the following years, usually at least two, you go out and capture additional samples. In the second year, some of the animals will be marked and some will not, so you use the ratio of marked animals to unmarked animals in your second sample to estimate the size of the population. For example, suppose you tagged 100 polar bears the first year. In the second year, you caught 100 more, of which 10 had been tagged the previous

POLAR BEARS: The Natural History of a Threatened Species

year. This would suggest that 10% of the total population was tagged because 10% (10 of 100) of the animals you caught were marked. Therefore, since you caught 100 in the first year, and that was 10% of the population, the total would be 1,000 bears.

Unfortunately, like most things in life, the theory is simpler than the practice. For the mark-recapture method to be successful for estimating the size of animal populations, you must make a few basic assumptions. These are: (1) all tagged and untagged animals in the population have an equal chance of being captured each year; (2) animals do not enter or leave the study area; (3) tags on all recaptured animals can be identified. These conditions are not easy to meet when sampling a polar bear population because different age and sex classes of bears often segregate themselves into different areas or habitats. For example, one area may have more adult males while another may have more females with cubs. To compensate for this potential source of bias, you have to spread out the capturing effort over all kinds of habitat so that every bear has an equal chance of being captured or recaptured. For example, in the Beaufort Sea in the spring, we found that the preferred habitat for most bears was the area of active leads at the interface of the land-fast ice and the moving pack. Seals were more abundant there, and perhaps easier to catch, so lots of bears of all ages and sexes were there, but especially adult males. At the same time, in the stable, drifted pressure ridges, far from the floe edge, there were many more females with newborn cubs and some subadults. To accommodate this difference, we had to ensure an adequate amount of searching in all types of ice habitats.

Collection of the tagging samples in the field is usually repeated for three or four years in a row for the population in question. In simple terms,

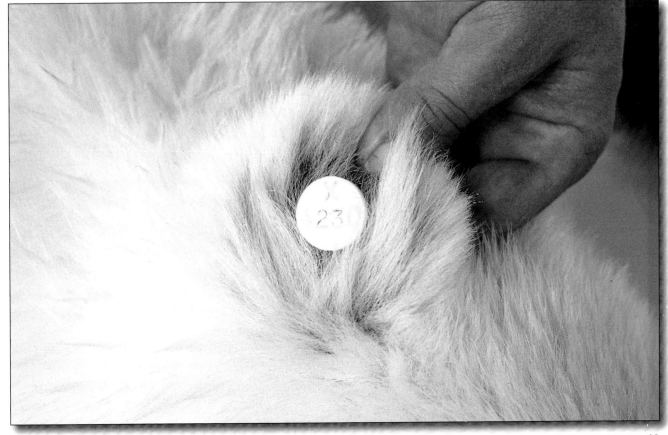

Polar bears don't notice a white ear tag and so don't bite them off.
(© Ian Stirling)

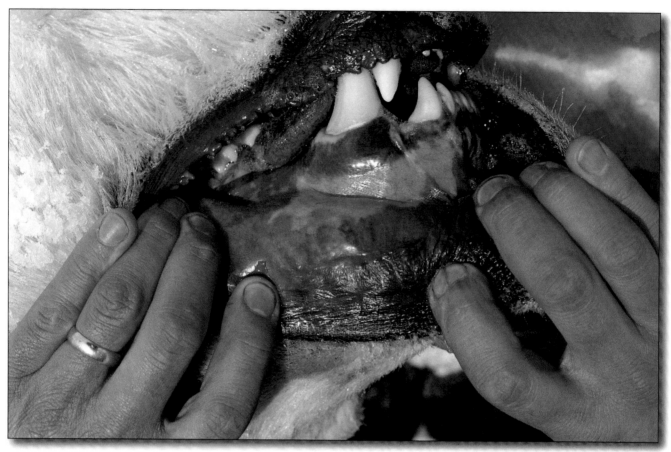

This lip tatoo, X687, was put on the bear 20 years before this photo was taken. The X means it was tagged in Canada.
(© Ian Stirling)

by calculating the ratios of previously marked animals to unmarked ones in the capture samples for all years, mathematical models can be applied to assess population size. Then, by simulating the populations in further models that include factors such as age structure, reproductive rates, litter sizes, survival rates, and population growth rates, an estimate of the sustainable harvest for Inuit hunters can be made within a range of confidence intervals. Because no such study is perfect, and there is always the possibility that estimates of population size or sustainable harvest levels may not be quite right, it is usually best to apply the "precautionary principle" and recommend a quota that is a little lower in order to provide a bit of added protection to the bear population.

What do you do with a drugged polar bear?

After an immobilized bear has been safely ap-

proached, it is first checked to ensure it is lying comfortably and able to breathe properly. Then a series of standardized procedures are undertaken. The length and axillary girth (around the body under the armpits) are measured. Sometimes, scales are used for weighing the bears, although the weight may also be estimated fairly accurately using a formula developed from the length and girth of a sample of bears that have been previously weighed. White delrin tags, each with the same identifying individual number, are put into both ears. In some of the early years of research, we also used coloured tags, but the bears appeared to notice them and sometimes groomed them off each other. This was particularly true of mothers and cubs. However, polar bears do not seem to notice the white tags and leave them alone. A tattoo with the same unique identification number as the original tag is put on both sides of the inner surface of the bear's upper lip. If an ear tag is missing on a subsequent capture, the bear is given a new set with different numbers, but they are still referenced to the bear's original tattoo number in the computerized database. The numbering system for the tags is coordinated between all the countries that have polar bears (Canada, Denmark, Norway, USA, and Russia) to ensure that the same number is not used twice. A small premolar tooth about half the size of a cribbage peg is removed from just behind the canine tooth so the age of the animal can be determined. In the laboratory, we soften the tooth in acid, slice it in very thin sections, stain it, and then count the annual growth lines. It is rather like counting the rings on a tree stump, though more difficult because the lines are not usually nearly as clearly laid down. Being able to assign different reproductive and survival rates to bears of different ages greatly improves the accuracy of the computer modelling

process for estimating population growth rate and possible levels of sustainable harvest.

Another huge side benefit of immobilizing and tagging animals is the ability to collect additional samples such as blood, fat, and hair, from which studies of diet, disease, pollution, and genetics can be undertaken.

Does handling have a negative effect on the bears?

Both scientists and Inuit hunters have been concerned about whether drugging and handling of polar bears causes any significant negative effects, particularly those that might influence their survival and reproduction. For example, hunters in the eastern Beaufort Sea asked if tagged bears could still hunt seals. Would bears chased by helicopters be too afraid to be able to hunt properly? Their concern was based on a local notion that if

Longitudinal section of the root of a small tooth, showing lines in the outer layer of cementum used for aging. The individual lines are clearest on the upper right hand side. (© Ian Stirling)

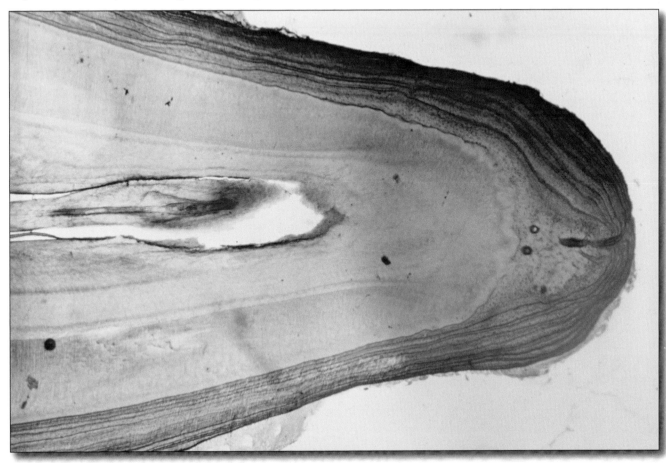

a bear was badly frightened by a hunter, it might be too nervous afterward to be able to sit still when waiting for a seal to surface at its breathing hole. An approaching seal might hear the bear moving and go elsewhere to breathe. If that happened enough times, a bear might starve to death. When hunters saw thin bears out on the ice, they sometimes wondered if they had escaped another hunter at some earlier time. Thus, they were concerned that the same thing might happen if a bear was frightened by a helicopter.

In other areas, hunters asked if bears would leave the area after being tagged and not come back. These were important questions and we addressed them in two ways. In our behaviour studies at Radstock Bay (Figure 8), we compared the behaviour of marked and unmarked bears of the same age and sex categories (i.e., adult males, adult females with cubs, and so on). We found no differences in the number of seals killed or the amount of time spent in various other activities such as sleeping or walking. Nor did marked animals leave the area. In fact, we were pleasantly surprised to find that overall the bears seemed remarkably unaffected. Most went about their business after waking up in much the same manner as they did before. From the longer-term studies of marked animals, it also soon became clear that they continued to come back to the same areas year after year despite, in some cases, having been caught there several times.

Several years ago, the late Malcolm Ramsay and I reviewed data on almost 3,000 records in the Polar Bear Project's computer files on bears that had been captured all over the Canadian Arctic, going back for about twenty years. We checked aspects we thought might be important, such as body weights, litter size, survival of cubs, and behaviour. We found no significant differences. Recaptured mothers appeared to be a little lighter, but not significantly so, but their cubs showed no difference. Now, with the benefit of hindsight, it seems more likely that the lighter weights of females captured a second time a few years later

Following the tracks of a female and her yearling cub as they hunt along pressure ridges.
(© Ian Stirling)

POLAR BEARS: The Natural History of a Threatened Species

The observation tower at Cape Churchill. A biologist is checking on an immobilised bear. (© Ian Stirling)

their den sites in fall with those that were not. We also found that adult females that were handled moved from the original den site they had chosen to a new one before settling down for the winter, but there were no detectable differences between the two groups in either their survival or their reproductive success.

Over the last 20 years, there have been several more studies to assess whether there have been any detectable negative effects on the bears as a result of handling. Francois Messier from the University of Saskatchewan reviewed information from 3,237 immobilizations, many of them recaptures of individuals in subsequent years following their initial capture. He conducted 25 independent analyses of the long-term effects of tagging, of which 24 showed no measurable effects. Similarly, he conducted 29 independent analyses to test for measurable effects of radio collaring, of which 27 showed no effects, one suggested a positive effect and one suggested a negative effect. He concluded that, overall, the long-term effects of tagging and radio-collaring polar bears were either not measurable or were negligible. Similarly, in analyses of data on female polar bears captured in the Beaufort Sea, some several times, Steve Amstrup found no evidence that being captured influenced litter sizes or the physical size of cubs. Separate analyses by Lily Peacock indicated there was no difference in the body condition of adult females captured once, twice, or three times and, similarly, the number of times a mother was caught did not affect the size of her litters in the following year.

Another concern raised by Inuit hunters was whether the meat of bears that had been immobilized was safe to eat. Based on the results of a detailed technical study, Health Canada initially recommended not eating meat for a year after handling but since revised the timeline for safe consumption down to 45 days.

Overall, it is pretty clear that if handling of polar bears for research purposes is done properly,

were simply the first indications of the long-term decline in condition, caused by climate warming and earlier break-up of the sea ice, and had nothing to do with handling. Several pregnant female polar bears caught in earth dens in October moved about 25 km (15 mi) to new den sites before settling down again for the winter. In a later study, Nick Lunn and I compared the movements of radio-collared bears that were handled around

there are no serious negative effects on survival, reproduction, behaviour, or movement patterns.

Aerial surveys for estimation of population size

In recent years, despite the lack of evidence that handling bears for population studies has a negative effect on the animals, there has been growing resistance to mark-recapture studies from some Inuit groups, particularly in Nunavut, simply because they object to the process. At the same time, there are also areas such as the vast areas of offshore pack ice in places such as the Chukchi or Barents seas, where it is probably not possible at almost any cost to conduct mark-re-

capture studies, so aerial survey, despite its shortcomings, is probably the only option.

Consequently, there is now a new focus on developing methods of using aircraft to search for bears and use data such as the distances away from the aircraft that bears are sighted, and how many are seen or not seen by two observers on the same side of the aircraft (determined by recording observations independently during the flight and comparing later). Jon Aars and colleagues from the Norwegian Polar Institute successfully applied this methodology to obtaining a first estimate of population size, with confidence limits (albeit wide) for polar bears in the Barents Sea. Currently, test surveys are being conducted in

The camp for observing polar bears in late winter and spring at Cape Liddon, Devon Island.
(© Ian Stirling)

parts of Nunavut, Canada, which are showing some encouraging results, at least for obtaining an estimate of total population size. Managers hope this approach may be adequate for management and quota setting purposes in areas where there is strong resistance to the handling of bears. Realistically, at least until some experience with the methodology increases confidence levels, it will be very important to ensure some application of the precautionary principle. It remains to be seen how accurate or repeatable this approach will be as development is still in the early stages and most of the surveys are not being done at the same time as a comparable study with a proven technique, such as mark and recapture, with which to compare results.

There are also a couple of serious negative aspects to using aerial surveys for assessing population size in polar bears. One is that with the exception of large adult males and females accompanied by dependent cubs, most experienced polar bear biologists do not think it is possible to reliably determine the sex of the majority of the single animals seen from the air. Also, of course, because no teeth or other specimens are collected, no other aspects of the biology of the bears in question can be considered, such as age structure or age-specific survival and reproductive rates. Thus, the main piece of scientific information obtained for management purposes is a single number, along with information on the distribution of bears at the time the study was done. Second, the

Caswall Tower has a commanding view of the ice and polar bears in Radstock Bay. (© Ian Stirling)

Observing polar bears through a telescope from Caswall Tower in early summer.
(© Ian Stirling)

cost of doing a quantitative aerial survey is very expensive, and in some cases likely exceeds that of a mark-recapture study, which weakens its value to me in a cost-benefit sense since so much less information is obtained. However, the history of science also tells us that when we start doing research on new topics, much of what we learn is unexpected, so it will be interesting to see what

the longer-term benefits of using aerial surveys to count polar bears might be.

What time of year is best for a population study?

To estimate populations accurately, you need a representative sample of all the bears in an area. Yet scientists are often limited in what they can

treme cold is hard on equipment and people alike, which makes the work difficult and potentially dangerous. In areas like the Beaufort and Chukchi seas, or the Canadian Arctic Islands, most population studies are done between late March and mid-May. During that time period, the most representative sample of the polar bear population is likely to be present on the coastal landfast ice and adjacent floes. There are several reasons for this. Females with cubs-of-the-year have come out of their dens, and thus, data on productivity and maternity denning can be collected. In most areas, adult females with yearling and two-year-old cubs, and subadults, seem to prefer the area where the fast ice and floes meet, as well. Some of the adult females will be looking for mates, and this pulls in the adult males that are often farther offshore. Coincidentally, long days and reasonably stable weather conditions tend to prevail in spring, making it possible to get more work done. Finally, tracking conditions are best at that time because there is still a covering of snow on the ice, so a larger number of bears can be captured than is possible by simply trying to spot them on the ice.

In places where the ice melts completely in summer, forcing the whole population ashore, such as in Hudson Bay, the situation is quite different. On shore when the snow is gone, white bears are highly visible, so they can be found easily. In late summer and early fall, the days are long and the temperatures reasonable. Taken together, these factors make it possible to do some of the most cost-effective work in the world on polar bears. Although the weather further north is colder in the late summer and early fall than in Hudson Bay, the best time for population assessment work in the seasonally ice-free areas of Foxe Basin, Davis Strait, and Baffin Bay is also in the fall rather than the spring when the bears are out on the sea ice.

What do undisturbed bears do?

What do polar bears do when they are not

do by the amount of money they have to work with. If money is short, then sometimes you must concentrate on the most productive time and places. Population sampling during winter is pretty well out of the question. Twenty-four-hour darkness makes it impossible to even fly and look for bears with helicopters and, of course, many of the females and cubs are in maternity dens. Ex-

running away from Inuit hunters on snow machines or biologists in helicopters? Over the years, we have caught many thousands of polar bears all over the Arctic in different seasons, habitats, and geographic areas. Many bears are found on the sea ice by following their tracks, often for 100 km or more (60 mi). When following tracks on the wind-drifted ice, it is easy to lose them, so your eyes are glued to the ice and snow in front of the helicopter. You note every turn the bear makes, every ridge it walks over or around, and the areas it walks through without stopping. He (or she) follows refrozen cracks in the ice because past ex-

perience tells the bear that where there are seal breathing holes, there are seals. Periodically, you lose the tracks in an area where the wind has covered them with drifting snow, or they get mixed up with the tracks of other bears. Occasionally, the tracks seem to just disappear for no apparent reason. Where did the bear go, and why? Usually you find the track again, though sometimes you don't. But, whether you realize it or not, in the process of deciding where to look to relocate them, you are applying your knowledge of their behaviour, accumulated from previous years of following them. You see where bears have tried to catch seals but failed. Blood stains and remains on the ice confirm where a meal was consumed. From such observations, you begin to understand what kinds of ice habitat are best for hunting seals. The intervals between rests, periods of nursing by cubs, or defecations are all recorded in the ephemeral format of snow on the sea ice. However, even after thousands of kilometres of tracking, you see tracks or signs of activity you are not sure how to interpret.

In order to try to gain a greater understanding of what it means to be an undisturbed polar bear in places like the sea ice of the High Arctic or the western coast of Hudson Bay during the open water season, we established a couple of small, rather spartan, camps from which we could observe undisturbed polar bears for extended periods with telescopes. Obviously, the total area we could see from such camps was a miniscule portion of the habitat of a free-ranging polar bear. However, for the periods they were in our continuous view, ranging from hours to several days, we saw things and gained insights we could not have accomplished in any other way. At Radstock Bay, on the southwestern coast of Devon Island we built two small cabins (Figure 8). One, on top of Cape Liddon at the mouth of the Bay, we used in spring when the bay and Lancaster Sound were both completely frozen. On Caswall Tower, we had a small cabin we used in early summer when the ice in Lancaster Sound had broken up, forcing bears to hunt on the ice that still remained within

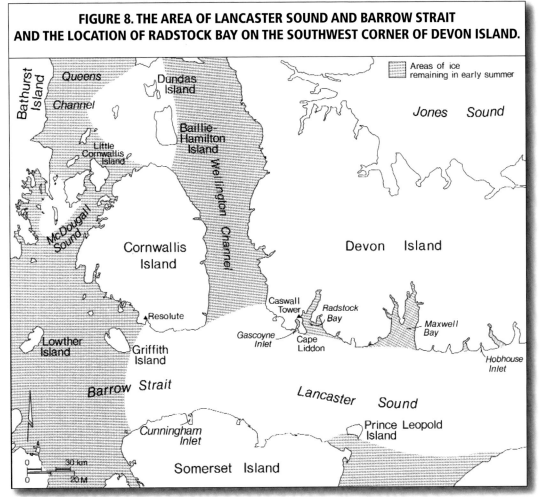

FIGURE 8. THE AREA OF LANCASTER SOUND AND BARROW STRAIT AND THE LOCATION OF RADSTOCK BAY ON THE SOUTHWEST CORNER OF DEVON ISLAND.

(Courtesy: Ian Stirling)

Radstock Bay. Because of 24-hour daylight, we were able to observe bears around the clock, provided the visibility was good and the bear didn't go somewhere it couldn't be seen. We used the cabin for working and an unheated polar pyramid tent away from the cabin for sleeping.

Western Hudson Bay is very flat. There are no cliffs that one can build a cabin on top of in order to observe undisturbed bears several km away. Thus, through colleagues at what is now called Manitoba Conservation, we scrounged the first 14 m (45 ft) of an obsolete fire lookout tower that had been dismantled near The Pas, in northern Manitoba. The steel was railed to Churchill, flown to Cape Churchill in a Twin Otter, and assembled with the help of a couple of professional steel riggers from Manitoba Hydro. On top, we assembled a 10-foot-square observation hut and the whole unit was guyed down with heavy cables as a precaution against the strong winds the area is so famous for.

Together, these camps provided the opportunity to let the bears tell us a little about what they did when undisturbed and what was important to them. In particular, we gained a whole new appreciation of how they gained the energy on which they survived and how they subsequently used it as parsimoniously and efficiently as possible.

Where do bears go throughout the year?

As we tagged more bears and recaptured them, or had tags returned by Inuit hunters, we quickly began to get a sense of the boundaries of the various subpopulations around the Arctic. The big breakthrough, however, was made with the development of collars that sent signals to a satellite and then back to earth. This technology made it possible to know where bears were throughout the year, including the 24-hour darkness of the arctic night. Although the radios and data were expensive, they were no more so than flying vast distances over the arctic sea ice in all kinds of weather conditions searching for signals from radio collars that had to be re-located using antenna attached to conventional aircraft—not to mention, considerably safer. The data simply kept coming in while the scientists could be doing other things. From a temperature sensor on the outside of the collar, one could tell if the bear was in a den or outside in the elements. From another temperature sensor, on the inside of the collar, one could know if it was still on a live bear. If the collar fell off, or the bear died, the temperature on the inside of the collar was the same as on the outside.

The current generation of these collars can send

An adult female with a satellite radio scavenges on the remains of a whale skeleton. The radios are waterproof.
(© Ian Stirling)

POLAR BEARS: The Natural History of a Threatened Species

a signal many times a day if desired, which, when analyzed in conjunction with satellite imagery of the ice the bear is on, is providing enormous amounts of new insight into the details of habitat selection and use by bears far out on the polar pack ice at all times of the year. The collars can also be programmed to simply drop off if they are not recovered, so a bear does not carry it any longer than necessary.

The main shortcoming of the radio collars to date is that they can't be used on adult males because their necks are bigger than their heads, so the collar won't stay on. Even with adult females, it is mainly the ears that keep a collar on, so if a female really doesn't want to wear it, she can take it off. Although the occasional bear does that, it is fairly uncommon. A current line of active, if frustratingly unproductive research to track adult males and subadult bears is the testing of various models of satellite radio attached to an ear tag. However, judging from the results obtained to date, there is still considerable innovation required to solve the problem.

Chapter 5

WHAT MAKES A POLAR BEAR TICK?

Adaptive needs for arctic survival

The Arctic, like the desert, has a highly variable and often severe climate. For much of the time, the life of a polar bear is one of uncertainty about where the next meal is coming from. In the late spring and early summer, the temperature is relatively mild and seals are abundant, but this when polar bears can least afford to take time to relax. They must maximize their hunting efficiency every day when hunting is good in order to deposit as

Polar bears may swim many kilometres in cold arctic water.
(© Stefan Lundgren)

Four kilometres an hour (2.5 mph) is a comfortable walking speed for a polar bear.
(© Jenny E. Ross)

much seal fat on their bodies as possible, in preparation for the times when stored energy reserves will be the key to survival. In a nutshell, the essence of a polar bear's survival primarily revolves around energy: in particular, accumulating it as rapidly as possible when it is available and then using it as frugally as possible when it is not. This chapter is about some of the remarkable ways in which the physiology of the polar bear has adapted to cope with its environment.

Take a moment to remind yourself of some of the environmental stresses in a polar bear's envi-ronment. During the winter, subzero temperatures prevail for months at a time, made more severe by incessant wind. Periodic blinding snowstorms hinder vision. The structure and distribution of sea ice can be highly variable, alternating between being frozen during cold calm weather or broken up with large areas of open water during polar gales. In some parts of the Arctic, the ice may drift several km a day. Annual patterns of freeze-up and break-up can vary, causing unpredictable changes in the distribution and abundance of seals. The result is a continuing

POLAR BEARS: The Natural History of a Threatened Species

search for prey in a changing environment.

To survive, the polar bear has two major physiological problems to solve: keeping its body at the right temperature and storing enough energy to last between meals, whether that turns out to be a few days or a few months apart.

Learning from captive polar bears

Much of what we know about the physiology of polar bears is the result of a series of brilliant studies by the late Norwegian scientist Nils Øritsland. Nils was a particularly resourceful scientist who seemed to think like a polar bear and had a sixth sense of what made them tick inside. He and several of his students built a unique physiology lab in a deserted military building near Churchill where they discovered most of what we know about how a polar bear regulates its body temperature.

One of their ingenious creations was an enclosed respiration chamber big enough to hold a large polar bear. The Chamber had instruments for measuring the oxygen and carbon dioxide in the air breathed by an undrugged resting or exercising bear. The chamber also had a treadmill so the bear could walk at different speeds while the scientists monitored the temperature, heart rate, and breathing.

Regulation of body temperature

The normal body temperature of a resting polar bear is about 37°C (98.6°F) which is much the same for most mammals. A bear's thick fur, tough hide, and blubber layer, which can be up to 11 cm (4.5 in) thick, provide such efficient insulation against the cold that the bear does not have to change its metabolic rate (in other words, burn any more energy) very often. Its body temperature and metabolic rate remain at normal level even when the thermometre drops to -37°C (-34°F). As long as the bear is relatively inactive, and is not exposed to wind, it does not need to burn excessive energy in cold weather.

The negative aspect of being so well insulated is that the bear overheats quickly. Just think of putting on all your warmest winter clothes and climbing a steep hill on a hot sunny day and you will appreciate its problem. Consequently, polar bears, especially large fat ones, cannot run very far without overheating, even on a cool day.

At temperatures ranging from about -15°C to -25°C (about -4 to -13°F), a polar bear's body temperature remains fairly constant at walking speeds of up to about 4 kph (about 2.5 mph). After that however, the temperature begins to climb rapidly until by about 7 kph (4 mph), it is

The late Ralph Nelson collecting a breathing air sample from an immobilized polar bear.
(© Ian Stirling)

almost 39°C (102°F), which is a fever temperature in a human. When moving at this relatively modest speed, a bear burns thirteen times as much energy as it would if it was lying down. From these results, it is easy to understand the slow, steady, plodding march that characterises a polar bear searching for seals on the sea ice. The bears have simply adjusted their walking speed to the point where their stored energy (fat) is burned most efficiently and overheating is avoided.

The comfort level with different walking speeds was clearly demonstrated to Øritsland by one of the bears he trained to walk on the treadmill. That bear frequently moved off the treadmill completely for short periods of time when the speed was increased, and he sometimes lay down

The late Jimmy Memorana, the legendary Inuk hunter from Holman, Northwest Territories, with whom I was fortunate enough to work on a number of occasions, once told me that in the old days, if he was hunting with his dog team and a large male polar bear heard them, it would immediately try to escape by going into the roughest ice possible because it was often too difficult for the dogs to pull a sled through. However, Jimmy maintained he could easily run a bear down on foot himself in a few hours, and did so successfully on at least two locally well-known occasions. At the time I was a bit puzzled, but now it seems understandable. Large male bears use so much energy to move, and they are so well insulated, that they quickly overheat when they try to run. Thus, they soon slow to a walk, even in very cold weather.

Polar bears regulate their temperature by both physiological and behavioural means. Measurements made with infrared sensors by Øritsland on an exercising polar bear revealed "hot spots" on the muzzle, nose, ears, footpads, and insides of the thighs. These are the points where the bear dissipates excess heat. Dissections of dead bears revealed that they also have thin layers of muscles, which are richly supplied with blood vessels, lying only a few millimetres under the skin in the shoulder region. This network brings warm blood from deep in the body to the surface where some of the heat may be given off.

The late Ralph Nelson, a medical physiologist from the University of Illinois, used infrared equipment to examine the shoulder areas of resting animals in air temperatures a little below freezing. He found that when the animal was resting, the shoulders did not give off enough heat to be detectable. That reminded me of a photograph I saw many years ago that was taken by an Alaskan scientist. He was trying to find out if infrared photography could be used to detect polar bears out on the ice. To test the idea, he found a bear and took some pictures. However, the bear was so well insulated that it gave off no detectable heat from its body at all, at least nothing that

and refused to walk at all! He also growled if the treadmill was run at too slow a speed for his liking. The bear's fairly specific comfort zone with walking speeds suggested that not only were faster speeds less efficient but maybe slower ones were as well. Whatever the reasons though, it was clear the bear knew what speed it wished to walk at, and what speeds it didn't.

could be detected by the equipment of the day. There was however, a spot on the infrared photo, just ahead of the bear's head—made by its breath! Not every creative idea achieves a breakthrough.

The conductivity of water is about twenty times that of air, so swimming is a good way to cool off quickly. On a hot day in summer, we often see bears swimming along the Hudson Bay coast or in lakes in the inland areas. We often observed that a bear running away from a helicopter would dive into a lead or a lake when chased, in part probably because of overheating. We soon learned to use that behaviour to our advantage during the ice-free period in Hudson Bay. By letting the bear go into a nearby lake first, and then darting it just as it went back onto land, its wet fur helped keep it cool on a warm day.

On the other hand, cooling from extended swimming is dangerous for small cubs that are only a few months old. After a cub had been swimming, Øritsland found that its deep body temperature did not begin to rise until it had been exercising for an hour. This probably explains why females with young cubs are reluctant to swim across leads with them in the cold weather that prevails after they leave their maternity dens. The cubs would likely become too cold and might die from hypothermia. Adult females have occasionally been observed carrying a newborn cub on their backs while swimming between ice floes. Females with cubs older than six months do not show the same hesitation about swimming for modest distances of up to a few kilometres, although they do not do so unless it is really necessary.

Bears adopt different postures when sleeping or lying, depending on whether they want to get rid of heat or conserve it. On warm days, they may sprawl out and sometimes lie on their backs with their feet in the air. On colder days or in snow storms they may simply curl up, sometimes covering the heat-radiant muzzle area with a paw, possibly to reduce heat loss. When sleeping on a warm day in the shelter of a pressure ridge, a bear

may sprawl over and around the irregular ice blocks, looking more like a jellyfish than the ultimate arctic carnivore.

On the western coast of Hudson Bay during the summer, bears spend most of their time lying around doing nothing. There is no point wasting energy when there are no seals to catch. If a bear gets hot, it costs energy to pant, increases the heartbeat, and requires metabolising

water to cool off again. Consequently, they remain largely inactive most of the time, especially on warmer days.

When obese, pregnant females first come ashore, they usually do not begin to move inland to the cool dens in the frozen peat banks of the maternity denning area until the sea breezes create a drop the air temperature, or until it begins to rain. Clearly, the objective is to avoid the high energy cost of moving a heavy, well-insulated body on a warm day.

The cost of walking

Another fascinating result from the treadmill studies done by Øritsland and one of his students, Ricki Hurst, relates to the energetic cost of locomotion for a polar bear. There is a general formula one can use to calculate how many

In a cold snow storm, a young bear finds a comfortable spot to sleep in a snow drift.
(© Sue Flood)

calories a mammal must expend in order to run at a particular speed. Most species fall close to the predicted value for their weight. However, there are some interesting exceptions to the rule. The polar bear is one of them. Weight for weight, a polar bear uses more than double the energy to move at a particular speed than do most other mammals. This relatively low efficiency of movement may result from the combination of its bulky build and massive limbs and paws which contribute to a slight but perceptible lumbering motion in the bear's forward movement, especially in larger or fatter individuals. Regardless, the high cost of walking likely

also helps to explain the polar bear's frequent preference for lying and still-hunting over stalking, even when there are seals lying about and visible on the ice. Quite simply, given a choice, still-hunting is the most energetically efficient way to hunt in an environment where calories can be hard to come by but easy to spend. The cost of running and associated overheating may also explain why bears rarely hunt musk-oxen or caribou, even though their ranges overlap in several areas. The energy cost of chasing speedier ungulates, even if some might be surprised at relatively short distances, is probably too great. It this context, it is interesting to note that

son Bay coast, and during the summer when they moult, the birds are flightless. Although polar bears have often been seen walking through some of these goose colonies, they almost never chase them. Using some of the results from the treadmill studies, Nick Lunn worked out the likely explanation. To gain the calories contained in an average snow goose, a 320 kg (700 lb) polar bear must catch it in only 12 seconds of running. Otherwise, it will cost him more energy than the bird would yield. A flightless goose can still run quickly and swim, although it seems possible it might be caught if a bear pursued it for a longer period. However, even most young bears seem to know better than to waste energy chasing flightless geese.

Heartbeat

Øritsland and another of his students, the late Robin Best, examined heart rate in several polar bears. They found that the heartbeat of resting bears was quite irregular, unlike humans. One female polar bear had a heart rate that varied between 53 and 64 beats per minute when she was sleeping undisturbed at an air temperature of minus 28°C (-18°F) on a cloudy day. Another sleeping female had a heart rate that average about 80 beats per minute on a sunny day when the temperature was just above freezing. Four 230 kg (500 lb) males at unspecified air temperatures had a sleeping heart rate of 33 beats per minute. When awake but lying down, the heart rate in these same bears averaged 46 beats per minute and increased to 58 beats per minute when the animals sat up. At walking speeds that varied between about 3-6 kph (1.5 to 3.5 mph), the heart beat increased more rapidly in relation to speed, rising to about 148 beats per minute.

Digestibility of ringed seals

It may be several days between meals for a polar bear, but when it does eat, it makes up for lost time. When a bear kills a seal, it may eat for an hour or more, depending on the size of the seal,

another mammal that requires about twice as much energy to move as predicted is the male lion. It too lies in wait or stalks slowly before making only a short charge, after which it quickly gives up if unsuccessful. Female lions do most of the running and killing following a stalk. These brief examples illustrate how much even a partial understanding of the physiology of these two predators helps us to interpret important aspects of their behaviour and ecology.

Knowing how much energy it costs a polar bear to run, and how quickly a bear can heat up, also helps to solve another puzzle. There are several large colonies of snow geese along the Hud-

with only short pauses to wash, look around, or clean itself by rolling in the snow. Captive bears in zoos can easily eat 10% of their body weight within 30 minutes. There are records of polar bears killed in the Soviet Union with 10-71 kg (22-156 lb) of food in their stomachs, although the size of the bears was not recorded. Robin Best estimated that a bear's stomach capacity could hold 15-20% of its body weight. Best also established that polar bears, like other carnivores, have high digestive efficiencies for the principal dietary components of protein and fat. The polar bear assimilates an impressive 84% of the protein it eats and 97% of the fat, for an overall energy intake of 92% of that which is available in the diet. According to Best, an average active adult polar bear would need about 2 kg (4.5 lb) of seal fat per day to survive. This means that any seal more than a month old could satisfy a polar bear's needs for a day and an adult seal could provide enough energy for about eleven days, while the bear continued to hunt.

This explains why the bears hunt fat, newly weaned, young seals so intensely in the late spring and early summer. It is the bear's annual opportunity to lay down the majority of the fat stores it will need to survive the open-water period of late summer. The extended duration of the fasting period for pregnant female polar bears in southwestern Hudson Bay is even more impressive. They must put on enough fat to not only survive through the open water period of late summer and autumn, but the duration of the maternity denning period as well, while nursing their tiny newborn cubs up to 10-15 kg (22-33 lb). To do all that means a total fast of about eight months, living on stored fat alone. A large pregnant female in prime condition may come ashore carrying well over 200 kg (440 lb) of fat to survive upon though the fall and winter. Although bears of all age and sex classes, except for denning females, continue to hunt though the winter, it seems likely that their overall hunting success is not high. Consequently, most bears on

the sea ice through the winter are likely to be in an overall energy-deficit situation until they begin hunting fat young-of-the-year seals again the following spring.

The polar bear's unique solutions to hibernation and energy conservation

Hibernation is an adaptation that allows some species of mammals to store fat when the feeding is good, and then burn it off slowly at a lower metabolic rate while in a deep resting state when

food is unavailable, usually, but not always, during winter. True hibernators such as some of the rodents, bats, or insectivores have a marked drop in heart rate, their body temperature may approach 0°C (32°F), and it may take some time to wake up because they have to burn stored energy to warm the body back to its normal temperature before it can function properly again. The largest mammals that are true hibernators are marmots. Bears are too large to drop their body temperature to very low levels because they would simply not

have enough energy to be able to warm such a large mass back to its normal operating temperature. Bears also need to maintain a much higher body temperature than true hibernators because they also still need to be able to maintain the physiological demands of pregnancy, birth, and nursing the young. Although bears sleep soundly, they are easily aroused and can, if necessary, defend themselves.

Although most species of bears go into dens during the winter, they have some important dif-

A young male cools himself by sprawling on the ice on a sunny day.
(© Jenny E. Ross)

ferences from the so-called true or deep hibernators. From research done on captive bears, we know that the heart rates of hibernating black and grizzly bears are capable of slowing to 10 to 12 beats per minute, or even lower sometimes, but their body temperature only declines to about 31-35°C (88-93°F). The heart rate of a polar bear held in an artificial den decreased to 27 beats per minute after about a month. The deep body temperature of two female polar bears hibernating in natural dens during the winter ranged between 35 and 37°C (95-98.6°F).

The pattern of hibernation and seasonal food shortages for polar bears is quite different from that of black and brown bears. In the first place, only pregnant female polar bears enter dens during the winter, while the rest of the population remains active. Second, for many polar bear populations, the season of greatest food shortage is the open water period of late summer and early fall, just when black and grizzly bears are eating most intensively in order to deposit fat reserves with which to survive the coming winter.

One of the most interesting chapters in our understanding of the "hibernation-like" state in polar bears, and hence how they have adapted their physiological needs to the vagaries of the arctic environment, originated with the late Ralph Nelson. He wondered how black bears could hibernate through the winter at near-normal body temperatures without eating, drinking, or producing any urine or faeces. When hibernating, the black bear produces all the water it needs by chemical pathways from its stored fat; then it recycles the by-products without producing waste materials. Nelson thought if he could figure out how this was done, there might be enormous benefits to humans with kidney problems.

Watching a large bulky male walk illustrates the effort required to move large limbs attached to a heavy frame.
(© Jenny E. Ross)

Nelson found that he could define a bear's physiological state by the ratio of the concentrations of two chemicals in the blood, urea and creatine. Creatine is produced by normal muscle activity and its level in the blood remains pretty much the same all the time. However, the amount of urea in the blood goes up when an animal is eating and becomes very low when it stops eating and lives only on its fat.

After some experimentation, Nelson defined the urea-to-creatine (U/C) ratio (that is, the number of units of urea in a sample of blood divided by the number of units of creatine) of a hibernating black bear as anything less than 10. He then examined blood samples taken from non-feeding polar bears on the western coast of Hudson Bay during the ice-free period in the late summer and fall. He found that the U/C ratio was at a similarly very low level in them as well. Thus, even though the bears were not in dens and were still active, they were (in the physiological sense) hibernating. This gave rise to the rather intriguing term "walking hibernation".

A curious aside to this finding is the observa-

A thin adult male conserving energy in "walking hibernation" while waiting for freeze-up on the Hudson Bay coast in late autumn. Thin adult males like this one are dangerous. (© Jenny E. Ross)

The bear that killed this adult seal ate the fat from the whole body but left everything else for foxes and small bears to scavenge when it melts in warmer weather. (© Ian Stirling)

tion an old Inuk hunter on the Labrador coast, passed on to a visiting anthropologist, sometime prior to 1916. He said that old male polar bears hibernate in caves along the coast in the summer when there was no ice. As in Hudson Bay, open water prevails along the coast of Labrador for many months in the summer, so we now know that similar hibernation-like responses must occur in the bears there. It has always intrigued me that an observant Inuk hunter noted the parallel between the summer behaviour of polar bears in caves and the winter behaviour of bears in dens.

Nelson and some of his colleagues then came to Churchill to work with our group so he could learn more about how polar bears evolved to live in the arctic environment. We selected polar bears of various sizes for non-harmful experiments, sometimes while other bears wandered by and gazed curiously at the goings on. By looking at

the U/C ratios over the next couple of years, we found that female polar bears coming out of the denning area in the spring were in a similar physiological state to that of hibernating black bears. More interesting though, were the results from polar bears spending the late summer and fall along the Hudson Bay coast. At the same time that non-feeding bears were in "walking hibernation", polar bears feeding in the dump had the same U/C values as non-hibernating (feeding) black bears. The astonishing conclusion was that members of the same polar bear population could be in completely opposite physiological conditions at the same time and place, depending on whether they were feeding or not feeding. That is something a black bear cannot do.

Andy Derocher, Nelson, and I then conducted some preliminary feeding experiments on several polar bears being held in captivity. They had not been fed for some time and had the low U/C ratios characteristic of the hibernation-like physiological state. When they were fed for a few days, the ratios went up, as we expected. However, once food was no longer available, the U/C ratios dropped again after about a week. Remarkably, these results indicated that polar bears could move from the physiological state of a fasting bear, to one of a feeding bear, and back to that of a fasting bear, all within a period of a couple of weeks. The contrast with terrestrial bears is dramatic. If you stop feeding a black bear or a grizzly in summer, it will starve to death. Thus, it appears that one of the most remarkable physiological adaptations of the polar bear to life in the arctic environment, where the availability of food is both variable and unpredictable for much of the year, is its ability to change its metabolic state as needed. This allows the bear to maximize the efficiency of its use of stored energy, and not be limited to changes controlled by photoperiod or other seasonal signals.

No subsequent research on this topic has yet been done, though it could be very informative to repeat and extend those experiments one day. Recently, however, another study on wild polar bears gave some results similar to those obtained from the captive bears. From direct observation, we know that when searching for a breeding female, or when courting one, male polar bears may not actively hunt for extended periods of time, although if one of them catches a seal, or they encounter a carcass, both the male and female may feed on it. In an analysis of the U/C ratios of polar bears from the Beaufort Sea in spring, Seth Cherry found, again, that bears in the same area at the same time could be in either a hibernation-like or non-hibernation physiological state. In particular, a larger proportion of adult males were not feeding, apparently maximizing their time for searching for breeding females and then courting them. They could afford to do this because the major feeding period of the year overlaps, but largely follows, the most active part of the breeding season. Thus, a temporary shortfall in energy intake can be compensated for fairly soon afterward. Most important though, since active hunting may absorb up to a third of a bear's time under normal conditions, it allows the male to slow its metabolic rate slightly and make maximum use of its stored energy to increase its searching and courting time which in turn will improve it chances of finding a mate and passing on its genes.

Polar bears and human physiology

It remains to be seen if discoveries about how a polar bear's biochemical pathways enable it to change it physiological state, and recycle its wastes without using its kidneys, or about its other adaptations might one day be applied to human medicine. However, Nelson believed that if these biochemical mechanisms could be isolated and applied to humans, it could be as important to kidney disease or obesity as the discovery of insulin was to diabetes. These seemingly esoteric studies on the physiology of wild polar bears are a prime example of how discoveries in one area of scientific research can be related to another if someone is imaginative enough to bring them together. It also underscores the importance of maintaining basic research in areas where economic benefits are not always immediately obvious.

Chapter 6

REPRODUCTION

Basic characteristics affecting reproductive behaviour of bears

The reproductive biology and social behaviour of all bear species are broadly similar, despite the fact that some bears in different parts of the world have evolved characteristics that are fascinatingly diverse . Black and brown bears are omnivorous while polar bears are carnivores; sloth bears are myrmecophages (eaters of ants and termites), and pandas specialize

An adult female and her two newborn cubs descends from her maternity den on an inland slope on their way to the sea ice. (© Doug Allan)

A large and battle-scarred old male.
(© Dan Guravich/ PolarBearsInternational.org)

on the leaves of a small number of species of bamboo. All of these species are medium to large-sized mammals that live to 20 to 25 years of age, and sometimes more. With the exception of family groups or breeding pairs, bears live largely solitary lives as adults although they may aggregate (while still feeding independently) at locations such as a salmon spawning stream, a dead whale, or a human garbage dump where food of some sort is super-abundant. Males and females do not breed for the first time until they are several years old (usually males are older than females). They come together only to mate, and produce small numbers of altricial offspring that require extended periods (one or more years) of maternal care before they are capable of living independently. Males do not aid in raising the young.

Territoriality, competition between males for breeding, and sexual dimorphism

The location of reproductive female polar bears for mating by adult males is more difficult than for their terrestrial counterparts, primarily because of marked differences in the stability or predictability of their respective habitats. Land bears defend territories which may vary in size, depending on the abundance and quality of food present, but location remains constant because food sources occur in the same place each year. As a result, once a terrestrial bear establishes a territory, it may live its entire life within a fairly small area, since there is little need to roam elsewhere in search of food or mates. The territories of adult males are usually larger than those of females and tend to overlap part or all of several adjacent adult female territories. Because of this, a territorial male usually has the opportunity to mate with more than one female. Through aggressive interactions, a territorial male can reduce or eliminate access to females by competitors, which results in intense competition between males for mating privileges. Bigger individuals win more fights and consequently do more mating, and thus there is a strong evolutionary selection pressure for larger body size. This leads to "sexual dimorphism," which means a pronounced size difference between males and females. Sexual dimorphism in body size is present in all modern bears but the difference in size is greater in the larger species. Similarly, as far as we have been able to determine, sexual dimorphism characterized most of the extinct Pleistocene bears as well. Some of the most extreme examples of sexual dimorphism in other mammal species (as a result of competition for reproductive advantage) include terrestrial-breeding seals such as the elephant seal or the northern fur seal.

POLAR BEARS: The Natural History of a Threatened Species

Sexual dimorphism is related to success in reproductive competition and is not limited to body size. The Japanese scientist M. Kadosaki and his colleagues compared the skull morphology of brown bears and Asiatic black bears in Japan. In both species, they found that although sexual dimorphism was detectable in all measured parts, the difference was significant only in the canine teeth. Since the diet of males and females within each species is similar, the significant enlargement of the male canine teeth (beyond that which would be expected because of their larger size) probably functions as male threat display and as a weapon. Canine teeth of male polar bears are also much larger than those of females, which is probably important for threats and fighting, as males battle for mating privileges with females. Old adult males often have badly broken canines. If this was simply a result of old age and wear from a lifetime of hunting seals, one would expect to see similar breakage in older females, but it does not occur. The most likely explanation is that the males break their canine teeth during intense fights with each other as they compete for females during the breeding season. A broken canine tooth can develop into a severe root canal infection. It is unknown whether this causes mortality of adult males or not, but sometimes a large scar on the side of an adult male's nose indicates where the infection was sufficient to break through the skin before subsequently healing. Males also show battle scars on their heads, necks, and shoulders once they become old and large enough to begin to compete for mates. Similar, though even more exaggerated development of canine teeth characterized other Pleistocene predators such as the saber-toothed cats and the giant short-faced bear, and the difference likely also functioned more for social display rather than for feeding.

Sexual dimorphism between males and females is also often apparent in the length of the guard hairs on the back of the front legs, with those on males usually being longer. In some individuals, this greater length is readily visible and may play

Broken canine teeth of a mature male from fighting with other males over females. (© Ian Stirling)

a signaling role of some sort to other males and females alike.

The influence of sea ice habitat on reproductive behaviour in polar bears

The sea ice habitat of the polar bear differs from that of the rest of the terrestrial bears in one major way: it is far more variable in almost every important aspect. Even something as simple as the location of the best feeding habitat can be far more variable between seasons and years than it is on land. A difference in the annual pattern

Exceptionally long guard hairs on the front leg of an adult male function as a secondary male sexual display organ.
(© Ian Stirling)

of freeze-up or break-up might eliminate suitable ice for hunting seals in an area where they were abundant just the year before. The distribution of the seals themselves may differ markedly from one year to the next for some unpredictable reason. Usually, there is some overall consistency, atlthough it is not uncommon for the location of the best seal habitat to shift within the same general area, from a few to over a hundred kilometres between years. This lack of predictability eliminates the potential benefit of defending a territory. Thus, polar bears are not territorial. Many bears of both sexes have large overlapping home ranges, resulting in a general fidelity to the same overall area during the spring breeding season. Within those much larger shared zones, males search for potential mates over vast areas of sea ice, usually finding

them in habitats where the seal hunting is best because females are trying to maximize their energy stores ahead of potentially producing cubs.

Although the overall ratio of adult male polar bears to adult females in a normal healthy population is approximately even, females keep their cubs for at least two and a half years before weaning them. Unless she loses her cubs prematurely, a female will only be available to breed once in every three years. Thus, only about one-third of polar bear females are available for reproduction in a particular year, so in total numbers, there are at least three potentially available adult males for each breeding female. This substantial and continuing imbalance in the sex ratio of prime adult males to available and reproductively receptive females has resulted in such intense competition for mating rights that male polar bears are now at least double the size of females, and thus one of the most sexually dimorphic of all mammals.

Breeding behaviour

Polar bears mate on the sea ice in the spring. Female polar bears do not usually mate when they are still accompanied by cubs-of-the-year or yearlings. It seems likely that the hormones associated with lactation (the secretion of milk) also inhibit ovulation. In fact, females with cubs less than two years of age actively avoid adult males throughout the year whenever possible, probably because of the risk of predation on their cubs. With the exception of family groups, polar bears normally live a solitary existence and are widely dispersed at low densities over vast areas.

By the spring when the cubs are about two and a half years old, very few are still being nursed by their mothers. Although some females may initiate separation from their cubs at that time, most are probably frightened away by threats from an adult male when he begins to follow the female closely with the intention of initiating mating behaviour. Mating takes place in April and May but finding lone receptive females on the open and variable sea ice is hard work.

The habitat most preferred by lone adult females and those accompanied by two-and-a-half-year-old cubs, both of which need mates, tends to be near the floe edge, leads in the fast ice, or areas of moving pack where subadult ringed seals and some bearded seals occur. Beyond focusing on productive hunting habitats to build up their fat stores in preparation for a possible mating and subsequent pregnancy, female polar bears leave it to the males to seek them out. When capturing polar bears for population studies in the Beaufort Sea in spring, we also found adult males more frequently near the floe edge, probably because they are more likely to encounter females there. Inuvialuit hunters living and hunting in the Beaufort Sea area have traditionaly found that adult males are normally further offshore in the moving pack most of the year, where they are less vulnerable to shore-based hunters. However, in spring, males become more abundant closer to the coast and the outer edges of the landfast ice as they search for adult females to mate with.

Even so, finding a mate is still not a simple matter and males may travel long distances while trying to encounter a potentially receptive female. Meanwhile, the females themselves may walk at 4 kph for long periods, moving more than 50 km in a single day. I have tracked individual adult males as they plodded relentlessly in a more-or-less straight line across the frozen pack ice, or along the edges of leads, for 100 km or more (60 mi) non-stop, in search of a possibly receptive female. Because the priority of the males in spring is to find females, they often go several days at a time without hunting at all.

I don't know how a male identifies the track of a potential adult female from the dozens of other sets of footprints he might cross in a day, but recognition is instant. He can not only identify the track of a potential mate but, amazing to me at least, he is able to detect her direction of travel and immediately sets out to find her. It is possible that a chemical signature of some sort is given off in her urine, or maybe via specialized cells in some part of her feet, but at present this aspect is not understood. Regardless of how the female sends her signal, the male polar bear is not in doubt. He follows her tracks wherever they go until he catches up with her. If she is alone, he then begins to follow and try to interact with her. If she is already accompanied by one or more males, considerable fighting may follow until the most dominant male defeats his rivals. We have occasionally seen as many as five or six additional males in the general vicinity of a single male-female pair, which further underlines the intensity of the competition that produces the broken teeth and scars referred to earlier. Once a male has secured a female, whether after finding her alone or after displacing other males, the pair may stay together for two weeks or sometimes even longer before the preliminary encounters and eventual

copulations are completed.

One summary based on polar bears tagged in the spring over several years throughout much of the Canadian Arctic provides considerable insight into the continuous competition between adult males for access to receptive adult females. Only about 13% of captured adult males were associated with females, whereas almost three times as many of the adult females without cubs (32%) were associated with adult males. Furthermore,

14 of the 80 adult males captured with adult females in spring were accompanied by one to four additional males. Clearly, not all these individual males will eventually mate, resulting in intense competition and fighting to determine the suc-

cessful breeders. In another study, based on 261 adult males and 220 adult and available females in Lancaster Sound, the proportion of males and females in breeding pairs reached a peak around mid-April and was followed by a slow decline until the end of May. While 33.8% of sampled males and 40.7% of sampled females were paired in April, only 15.3% of males and 17.9% of females were paired in May. Occasional mating pairs of bears are also seen in late March and early June, but this is uncommon.

Further evidence of the intensity of the competition is that the median age of males accompanying females during the breeding season was 10.5 while that of adult males that were alone when caught was 8.0, a statistically significant difference. This probably reflects the fact that males continue to grow through their adult years and reach their maximum weight at about 15-16 years of age. Thus, the average 10- or 11-year-old male would be heavier than a male two years younger. It is particularly informative to compare the occurrence of broken canine teeth and scarring between adult males and females. Males were significantly more likely than females to have broken canines, open wounds during the breeding season, and old scars. The amount of simple wear on teeth was similar for both sexes, indicating that the damage did not result from the use of teeth for hunting and consuming prey. As males reached the age of eight years or more, they often had one, two, or even more canines partially broken so that the pulp cavity was exposed. Some teeth were broken off within a few millimetres of the gum line. No comparable breakage was recorded in females. Similarly, while older males were often extensively scarred or wounded on the head and shoulders, the same was not the case for females.

Much of our initial understanding of the substantial length of time required for mating to occur came from records of polar bear behaviour in zoos. Some observations from the Moscow Zoo in the 1950s are particularly in-

In a pack ice environment, a polar bear can never know where the ice and seals may be from year to year, so there is no point in trying to defend a territory.
(© Stefan Lundgren)

Adult males detect potential breeding females by the scent left on their tracks in the snow.
(© Jenny E. Ross)

teresting because they are so consistent with what we have since documented in the field many years later. A single male bear held with a small group of adult females suddenly began following one of the females for several days in late February and early March, although she continued to ignore him. Then, on the March 3, they began to mate and did so periodically for nine days before she again rebuffed him. He continued to follow her for another two days without mating before losing interest. On March 15, he began to follow another female and mated with her for four days beginning on March 30. The following year, he remained with and mated a third female for twelve days, from March 14-26, although it was less clear how long he had followed her for before mating.

The length of time the male stayed with the females in the zoo is similar to a number of less complete observations from wild polar bears, plus what we can interpret from their tracks.

A unique observation of behaviour through an entire mating event

During one remarkable period a few years ago, an adult male polar bear located an adult female with a single 2.5-year-old cub near our cliff-top observation hut at Cape Liddon on Devon Island. The male herded the female part way into the bay, away from the regularly travelled route used by other bears along the coast. Because of 24-hour daylight in spring, we were able to observe and record the behaviour of the bears in detail through the entire period, from the initial discovery of the female by the male, through their preliminary interactions and mating, to their eventual separation.

We first spotted the adult male on May 2, at

POLAR BEARS: The Natural History of a Threatened Species

2.56 AM, on the open sea ice of Lancaster Sound, about 5 km (3 mi) SE of Cape Liddon. He was following approximately 0.5 km (0.3 mi) behind an adult female accompanied by a single 2.5-year-old-cub. The male was very large and easily twice the size of the female. When first sighted, the female and cub were walking steadily NW away from the male, lying down periodically, or sometimes hunting. Although the female periodically changed directions throughout the day, the male continued to circle around her in order to direct her in a northwesterly direction until he eventually directed her into Radstock Bay. Throughout this period, the female continued to look behind her in order to keep track of where the male was, while her very nervous 2.5-year-old cub remained so close to her that at times they appeared almost as a single animal. Both adults occasionally stood upright on their hind legs to get a better look at the other.

The adult male spent most of the day following the female at variable distances of up to approximately 500 m (1650 ft). In the late afternoon, when they were within the bay, he closed slowly to about 200 m (650 ft). After they entered an area of pressure ridges and rough ice, the male still followed the female but continued to run ahead or around to her side in order to prevent her from leaving an area roughly 1 km (0.6 mi) in diametre immediately to the north of Cape Liddon, where they remained for the next 12 days. Shortly after 9 PM, the male approached to within 20 m (65 ft) and the female responded by running and lunging at him but without making contact. Then all three bears ran north a short distance, stopped, after which the male ran between the

Male and female polar bears mating on the sea ice in Svalbard.
(© Mats Forsberg)

An adult male pins his opponent and holds him down by the throat. (© Jenny E. Ross)

female and the cub. They all stood looking at each other for about a minute; then the cub ran about 20 m (65 ft) further away from the male and stood still watching again. After this point, the female made no further effort to reunite with her cub, or defend it from the male. The female then began to walk away, followed about 20-30 m (65-98 ft)behind by the male, and by the cub at a greater distance (200+ m). For almost two more days, the cub continued to follow the male-female pair, stopping and lying when they did, and walking when they moved. It was last seen in the mid-afternoon on May 4, walking NW away from the other bears. The cub was no longer a priority for the female and had been forcibly weaned by the male.

For the next seven days, the male and female interacted intensely, interspersed with periods of

sometimes standing on her hind legs, and occasionally making jaw contact and vocalizing. The male in turn kept approaching her but backed off when rebuffed. On the May 9 and May 10, they copulated for 10 and 41 minutes respectively, not at all on the 11th, and then again for 86, 66, and 150 minutes for the next three days respectively. On the morning of May 15, the female simply walked away. The male did not follow. The mating sequence was over.

During the time they were together, the male kept the female in the same area away from the most regular thoroughfare used by other bears along the outer coast only a few kilometres away. Regardless, at different times, two other large adult males arrived to challenge the dominant male. His complete dominance was dramatically illustrated by how quickly and completely he routed each male in turn. He would approach the challenger to within a few metres and then suddenly charge, throwing him down on his back while almost simultaneously seizing his throat. The now totally subordinate male lay passive and motionless on his back for possibly a minute, until the dominant male backed off and allowed the loser to slink away unharmed. I have seen males of apparently similar size and social rank spar before and fights can be both vicious and protracted. However, in the presence of a truly top-level dominant male, there was simply no contest. His sheer superiority dramatically underlined the potential benefit to the fitness of the female to receive the genes of such a successful male.

More about the biology of reproductive behaviour

From our past observations, other less complete accounts in the scientific literature, and observations from Inuit hunters, individual aspects of the full sequence described above have become apparent. In particular, the penchant of the male for herding the female deep into fiords, into secluded bays, high up on mountainsides or islands, or into areas of rough pack ice away from the prime feed-

lying or sleeping near each other on the snow, and sometimes hunting (unsuccessfully) for short periods. Most of the hunting was done by the female while the male stood nearby. The female's behaviour included running away from the male while he galloped ahead in order to herd her back to the area where he wished her to remain. Periodically, she ran at the male with her head held low but stopped just before she reached him,

ing areas has been well noted over the years. It is easy to recognize the tracks of a male-female pair because they go back and forth all over the same local area as the male continues to herd the female and keep her from leaving, eventually coming together in several different places where they stood and mated. Most likely, the purpose of herding the female to a secluded spot if possible is to reduce the chance of encountering competitors that might be successful at taking the female away or the risk that, even when victorious, the dominant male might still sustain some serious wounds from a challenger.

The fact that the male and female remain and interact together for so long is another clue to their reproductive biology. The majority of mammals, such as humans or seals, are "spontaneous ovulators," meaning that the females automatically release an egg for fertilization at the appropriate biological time because there is a high degree of certainty that there will be a male available to fertilize it.

The situation is quite different for a female polar bear. Because the adults are usually widely distributed as solitary animals at low densities, if a female ovulated spontaneously, there would be no guarantee a suitable male would be nearby to fertilize the egg. So, although it has not been demonstrated experimentally, what almost certainly does happen is that the female comes into a state of general physiological readiness for mating but does not actually release the egg for fertilization until she has been sufficiently stimulated. Only after several days of intense behavioural interaction have provided her with enough physiological reassurance does she proceed to ovulate and then copulate over the next few days (as was described above). This process is called "induced ovulation" and it probably occurs in terrestrial bears as well as polar bears.

There is another potential benefit to this reproductive strategy besides simply ensuring that the egg is not wasted. Because the pair remains together, interacting and mating, for several days before the female ovulates, this allows for the possibility that other adult males will locate them. If that happens, intense competition takes place between them before her eventual consort is determined. This increases the probability that her cubs will be sired by a large, dominant, successful individual. In this way, her cubs will receive the best possible genetic inheritance, which in turn will improve their own chances of survival. It also means the most dominant males may succeed in mating with several females in each breeding season, which further emphasizes the advantages of being bigger, stronger, and more aggressive than one's competitors. It has now been confirmed from genetic analyses that in a very small number of cases, different cubs in the same litter may have different fathers. From these results, it is clear that if a one male is displaced by another around the time of ovulation, both may be successful in passing on their genes.

Getting ready for denning

After the female mates in the spring, she has only a few short months in which to accumulate the large deposits of fat she will need to survive herself and to support her new cubs after she enters her maternity den in the coming fall. This is no mean feat since most adult females weigh only about 150-175 kg (330 to 385 lb) in the spring when they wean their cubs. They need to gain at least 100 kg (220 lb) of fat, and preferably twice that amount, to carry off a successful pregnancy. One of the most dramatic examples of how fast an adult female can change weight was provided by an individual we caught with two yearling cubs in the Churchill dump in early December. She was a bag of bones and weighed only 97 kg (213 lb). By the following spring, she either weaned or lost her cubs, and mated. When we recaptured her the following August, eight months later, she weighed over 450 kg (992 lb). Her fourfold increase in weight was mainly due to fat deposition. The following summer, she was recaptured with triplets. Her

weight change and production of triplets was exceptional but it clearly illustrates the high reproductive value of depositing a lot of fat prior to entering a maternity den.

The timing for weaning of cubs has probably evolved to occur in the spring because that is when the availability of prey (seals) is greatest and they are most vulnerable to predation. In late March and early April, millions of female ringed seals throughout the Arctic dig birth lairs in snowdrifts over their breathing holes in the ice, where they give birth to their pups. The newborn pups weigh 4-5 kg (10 lb). Six weeks later, when they are weaned, they weigh 22 kg (48 lb), at a weight gain of 0.43 kg/day (0.94 lb/day). At weaning, up to 50% of their total body weight is fat. At this young age, seals still have much to learn about avoiding predators, so polar bears feed on them intensively through the spring and early summer. It is this super-abundance of fat, naive seal pups that enables the pregnant female polar bears to accumulate fat so quickly. Later in the summer, after break-up, the young seals disperse in the open water

This pregnant female was so fat that walking could cause overheating. Her neck was too big for a radio collar, so she has a small radio glued to the top of her head.
(© Ian Stirling)

POLAR BEARS: The Natural History of a Threatened Species

where predators are unable to catch them. By that time, polar bears in most areas weigh more than at any other time of year.

Female polar bears sometimes eat a bit of vegetation after coming onto land in the summer or fall. Similarly, a few bears occasionally dig up lichen or other vegetation in spring, just after breaking out of the maternity den. Despite such anecdotal observations, it is clear that vegetation contributes little to their overall energy requirements while on land. They live on their stored fat reserves.

How long a pregnant female is able to remain on the ice to hunt seals and deposit fat on her body before going ashore and into a den, and how long she must then sustain herself on her stored reserves without feeding, can vary considerably between areas. In the Beaufort Sea for example, a female may remain with offshore sea ice somewhere in her home range throughout most of the year. So long as the southern extent of the pack ice lies over the continental shelf in summer and early fall, she can probably continue to catch some seals, though likely less frequently than in the spring and early summer before break-up. By mid- to late October, most pregnant females have gone ashore to dig a maternity den in snow banks formed by wind-drifted snow. In parts of the eastern Canadian Arctic, East Greenland, Svalbard, and possibly the New Siberian Islands, most bears must spend at least some time on land during the open water period in the summer. However, because freeze-up in these areas starts by late September to early October, pregnant females probably have time to catch a few additional seals before going into their maternity dens. At Svalbard or Wrangel Island in Russia (not to be confused with Wrangell Island in Alaska), most pregnant females continue to hunt in the drifting pack ice and do not come ashore until late October or November, when the floes drift south toward the islands from further offshore in the

Top left: An adult female peers out of her maternity den.
(© Norbert Rosing)

Bottom left: Looking toward the entrance tunnel of a maternity den from inside the den.
(© Ian Stirling)

Below: The maternity den chamber at the top of an upward sloping entrance tunnel traps any heat.
(© Ian Stirling)

Two four-month-old cubs still inside a maternity den.
(© Jenny E. Ross)

Arctic Ocean. Females in these areas spend about six months on land, including the time spent in maternity dens. In Hudson Bay, however, the sea ice melts in July, forcing all the bears ashore. Since freeze-up does not occur until late November, there is no opportunity for pregnant females to feed on seals again before they enter their mater-nity dens. Thus, pregnant females must survive for eight months or more, solely on their fat re-serves, give birth to cubs (usually two), and nurse them from a birth weight of about 0.6 kg (about 1.3 lb) up to a weight of 10-15 kg (22-33 lb) be-fore leaving their maternity dens to hunt seals on the sea ice again.

clear. Soviet scientist O.B. Lutziuk recorded observations of the behaviour of possibly pregnant females in the early fall at Wrangel Island, in eastern Siberia. Substantial numbers of polar bears den there every year. Pregnant females are relatively easy to observe on the treeless landscape when they first come onto land from the sea ice and walk about, seeking suitable den sites. In most years, polar bears move off the pack ice onto the land in late August or September, though some may continue to do so until early November. The females prefer the dense hard snow of the older drifts to the softer snow of freshly formed snow banks. Lutziuk also suggested that pregnant females will sometimes excavate and re-use old maternity dens, if they are present, and then remain in them through the winter. Although his observations only continued until about mid-September, some females that entered old dens in late August remained there through at least the first few snowstorms of early fall.

The females Lutziuk thought were settling into maternity dens were not displaced from them despite repeated visits by biologists, at least up to mid-September. Neither did the bears exhibit any signs of aggressive behaviour, even when their dens were probed with wooden poles to ensure they were still occupied. In contrast, bears in what he thought were temporary pits were easily frightened when approached.

Some of Lutziuk's observations are reminiscent of things we have seen pregnant females do in southwestern Hudson Bay in August and September. Of course there is no snow on the ground there when the pregnant females come ashore by the end of July in most years, but there is permafrost along some of the streambeds and edges of lakes under copses of black spruce trees. There are several old dens dug in the earth against the permafrost, and pregnant females re-use many of them for maternity denning (Figure 4). We have also noted that once into these dens, even in the early fall, the females do not want to come out and are fairly unaggressive when ap-

Finding suitable sites for maternity dens

No one has ever completely described the behaviour of individual pregnant females from the time they first come ashore through the period of selecting a den and remaining there through the winter. However, from a variety of anecdotal observations, the overall pattern seems reasonably

proached on foot at close range. Recalling that many of the pregnant females at Wrangel Island, like those of western and southern Hudson Bay, must fast for longer periods of time than polar bears in other areas, it seems likely that early fall denning behaviour, and the inactivity that goes with it, functions to conserve energy. We have confirmed that most pregnant females in Hudson Bay remain in their earth dens until snowdrifts form over them. Thus, it is plausible that the females observed by Lutziuk remained where he saw them throughout the winter. However, that detail remains unconfirmed.

Pregnant female polar bears that spend the summer on the pack ice hunting through the late summer and fall before coming ashore to den behave a bit differently. They have no need to look for an interim resting place. When they come ashore, in late October, they do so to find a maternity denning site. Their tracks are unmistakable as they walk from snow bank to snow bank, testing them for consistency or depth or whatever else is critical to pregnant female polar bears. From the number of test pits and holes they dig, it is obvious that they know exactly what they are looking for, and they may travel many km as they search. Provided there are suitable drifts around, a pregnant female probably selects a site within a few days.

Structure of maternity dens

In his classic work on the denning habits of polar bears in the Canadian Arctic, Richard Harington, the original polar bear biologist for the Canadian Wildlife Service, gathered data on over 100 maternity dens to find out what influenced the selection of sites by pregnant females. In the Canadian Arctic Islands, 61% of 113 dens were within 8 km (5 mi) of the coast and 81% lay within 16 km (10 mi). Similar distances from the coast have been reported from Svalbard, the Alaskan north coast, and Wrangel Island. In contrast, along the southwestern coast of Hudson Bay (in Manitoba and Ontario) many of the ma-

ternity dens are 50-60 km (30-35 mi) inland from the coast. Some are as far as 100 km (60 mi) or more. Differences in terrain and the pattern of snow accumulation in the fall may explain the variation. Much of the coastal and adjacent inland areas of southwestern Hudson Bay are flat and boggy. There are few banks along lake edges and

streams that are high enough to contain beds of frozen peat deep enough to facilitate the digging of maternity dens until one is well inland. This is critical because in most years, there is insufficient snow on the ground to form suitable drifts in which pregnant females could dig maternity dens before the cubs are born by late November or December. Consequently, pregnant females probably have to go farther inland to find suitable denning habitat in the frozen ground.

Harington found a tendency for maternity dens in the Canadian Arctic to face in a southerly direction where the northerly prevailing winds deposit the best drifts. There, too, the

An adult female rests near her den with her cubs as they acclimate to the cold before returning to the sea ice.
(© Daniel J. Cox/ NaturalExposures.com)

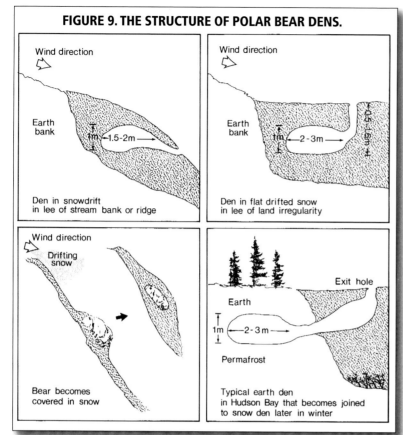

FIGURE 9. THE STRUCTURE OF POLAR BEAR DENS.

Wind direction

Earth
bank

1m ←1.5-2m→

Den in snowdrift
in lee of stream bank or ridge

Wind direction

Earth
bank

1m ←2-3m→ ↕0.5-1.5m↕

Den in flat drifted snow
in lee of land irregularity

Wind direction

Drifting
snow

Bear becomes
covered in snow

Exit hole

Earth

1m ←2-3m→

Permafrost

Typical earth den
in Hudson Bay that becomes joined
to snow den later in winter

(Courtesy: Ian Stirling)

Breakout hole from a maternity den showing tracks of bears walking, digging, and sliding down the hill.
(© Ian Stirling)

benefits of solar radiation are the greatest. In general, this is also true in southwestern Hudson Bay and on Svalbard.

On Wrangel Island, the distribution of snowdrifts seems to be quite variable, depending on which direction the winds come from in the autumn each year. Consequently, the orientation of the den entrances varied considerably between years. A tendency for some dens to face north was thought to be influenced by the regular use of old snowdrifts from the previous winter, which, of course, last longest on the north- and east-facing slopes.

Observations concerning den sites in different areas may seem contradictory, but the annual regime of snowfall could account for much of the apparent variability. In places like Southampton Island or the east coast of Baffin Island, there is usually quite a bit of snow. So, although there may be some variability in when it falls, there will be

lots of it and drifts will form that face in all directions. Consequently, a pregnant bear can choose a drift that faces whatever direction she prefers. The information available suggests that, given a choice, more females dig dens on southerly-facing slopes.

The High Arctic is a polar desert, which means that the total precipitation received in a year does not exceed what might be expected in a normal desert in more southerly climes. Because there is so much less snow, the distribution of the drifts is more strongly influenced by the direction of the prevailing winds. As a result, there can be considerable variation between years in the number of drifts present, and in their orientation. On Banks Island in the western Canadian Arctic, I have found dens facing all directions. On one particular hillside, I found dens in perfect-looking drifts two years in a row, while in spring of six other years there was so little snow you could see bare ground. In places where the distribution of suitable habitat is that variable, pregnant female polar bears probably do not have much opportunity to be selective.

Female bears everywhere construct dens that are quite similar. Most common is a single chamber, slightly elevated from the entrance tunnel so that the warmer air remains with the female and her cubs (Figure 9). Fourteen single-room dens measured by Richard Harington averaged about 2 m x 1.5 m (6.6 x 5 ft) and a metre (3 ft) high. The entrance tunnels are usually about 2 m (6.6 ft) long but very narrow, about 0.65 m (2 ft) in diameter. I have squeezed through some of these entrance tunnels myself and I am amazed that there is room for the pregnant females to squeeze in. Some females become more architecturally creative and dig two- and even three-room complexes, but I suspect most of these are done in the late spring when the cubs are becoming more active and are getting ready to leave. The cubs sometimes also dig small alcoves off to the side. In areas where the snow continues to accumulate, it may be necessary to scrape snow from the roof of the den to keep it thin enough for oxygen to

continue to pass through. A few authors report the maintenance of a small air hole for ventilation, but this has not been reported from the majority of studies.

Temperature in maternity dens

During his original research on denning areas back in the 1960s, Richard Harington poked a hole through the roofs of two occupied snow dens and lowered a thermometre in on a string. In one, the temperature was -9.9°C (14.6°F), about 21°C (37°F.) warmer than the outside air. In the other den, the inside temperature was -17.8°C (0°F), which was 7.8°C (18°F) warmer than it was outside. The dens were kept warmer by the body heat given off by the bears, by the insulating properties of the snow, and by their being out of the wind. Sometimes the roof of a den may have a layer of ice crystals indicating that on occasion, the inside temperature may have risen above freezing, so the moisture in the bears' breath solidified when it came into contact with the cold snow on the ceiling of the den chamber.

The relationship between the air temperatures outside compared to those inside the dens dug in the frozen peat in the denning area south of Churchill is particularly interesting. We knew that a den used in a previous winter had a higher chance of being re-used in the following winter, so we placed thermisters that would record temperature several times a day for a year into the ceiling of several dens. At each den, we also placed a thermister on a nearby tree so we could compare the temperature inside with that outside. That way, if a pregnant female bear occupied one of the dens, we could directly assess the influence her presence might have on the temperature in the den chamber when compared to exactly what was happening outside. We installed thermisters in ten dens well ahead of when we thought they might be occupied, partly because it was safer for us, but also because we didn't want to risk disturbing the females and possibly causing them to move.

Fortunately, one of the dens we instrumented

was occupied and provided us with internal temperatures from August through late January. Through the late summer and autumn, before the den entrance became covered with wind-blown snow that provided an insulating lair over the den, the inside temperatures generally tracked the outside temperatures, but were sometimes 2-3°C warmer. However, on the day in late November

when a big snow storm apparently plugged the entrance to the den, the inside temperature suddenly rose and remained at 1-2°C while the outside temperature plunged to -25 to -30°C (-13-22°F). For the next two months, despite temperatures that remained in the -20s and -30s most of the time, the internal den temperatures ranged between 1-2°C to as high as 5-6°C (35-41°F). The coating of peat that dried over the permafrost on the inside of the den, which has a very low degree of thermal conductivity, probably also acted as additional insulation to retain the small amount of heat that escaped from the bear and its breathing inside the den chamber. Then for some unknown reason, on January 23, when the outside temperature was -31°C (-24°F), the in-

Once onto the sea ice, the newborn cubs must follow their mother for hours each day as she searches for seals.
(© Norbert Rosing)

ternal temperature of the inside of the den plunged to -19°C (-2°F) and then -34°C (-29°F) the following day. Clearly, the female had suddenly and prematurely abandoned her den and her cubs, which most likely were no longer still alive. Even so, at that time of year, they would still be too small to survive, had they been able and tried to follow her. Whether she exhausted her fat supplies prematurely, the cub or cubs died, or whether she might have been disturbed in her den by some other animal, remains unknown. However, it was clear from the temperature record that she abandoned her den four to six weeks prematurely.

We hadn't expected the results from the unoccupied dens to be equally fascinating, but they were. Unlike the occupied den, until snow covered the den entrance, the inside temperatures generally tracked the outside temperatures but tended to be a bit lower on the hot days (>20°C; 70°F) days in late August. However, after the den entrances were plugged with snow, and the outside temperatures plummeted through the winter, the temperatures inside the unoccupied dens fluctuated but did not drop further than about -2 to -5°C (28-23°F). In other words, once the entrance to the den was sealed, the inside temperature remained no colder than the permafrost and did not appear as vulnerable to the same degree of cooling recorded by Harington in the snow dens. This probably resulted from the den being encased in permafrost, so its temperature reflected the temperature of the permafrost, not the outside temperature.

Thus, it appears that because the temperatures of dens in the frozen peat remained just above freezing, a female polar bear would have to use less energy to keep herself and her cubs warm than she would in a snow den. That in turn suggests she would be able to put more of her stored energy into her cubs in a frozen peat den than she could if she was in a snow den where she would be more influenced by the bitterly cold temperatures that prevail in mid-winter. That may be part of the explanation for the greater number of triplet litters in 1970s and 1980s, because polar bear females were in better condition and heavier because of carrying more stored fat; i.e., they simply had more resources to invest in their cubs than they do today when they are generally in much poorer condition prior to denning.

Delayed implantation and birth

Female polar bears mate in late April or May but, instead of embryonic growth continuing soon after the egg is fertilized, as it does in humans or dogs, further development is suspended until about mid-September to mid-October (in Hudson Bay) when the blastocyst implants in the wall of the uterus and the embryo begins to grow. (Implantation probably occurs up to a month later further north but this is not documented.) This phenomenon is called *delayed implantation* and it has been documented in many different species of mammals, for a variety of possible evolutionary reasons. In polar bears, delayed implantation allows for mating to take place at the optimal time for males to be able to search for and locate available females (on the sea ice in spring), but for the initiation of embryonic growth to be delayed so the eventual birth of the cubs can occur at the time when they will have the greatest chance of survival because they depart from the maternity den just as prey availability and accessibility is about to reach its maximum for the year.

Whether a pregnant female has entered what will become her maternity den as early as August, or not until late October, she will be there by the time her altricial (very undeveloped) young are born. Several newly born polar bear cubs in zoos have been reported to weigh 600-700 g (1-1.5 lb) which is tiny in relation to the large body size of their mothers. The cubs' eyes are closed at birth and they have such fine fur that its very existence has sometimes been overlooked, resulting in inaccurate reports of their being hairless. The same tiny size of cubs relative to much larger mothers is characteristic of all

bears, including the panda.

The late Malcolm Ramsay provided a possible explanation for why bears have such tiny cubs at birth. He noted that, when in a maternity den, the pregnant female does not eat, drink, urinate, or defecate. Instead she relies solely on her stores of body fat for energy while fasting and uses physiological pathways to recycle her metabolic waste products and those of her fetus. Although the fasting female is capable of breaking down the fatty acids she has stored on her body to provide energy, the fetus (like those of other mammals) cannot do so unless it has a supply of glucose (sugar) to act as the oxidizing agent. However, the female can only supply that glucose by breaking down her own body protein, a process she can only support until the physiological demands of the fetus increase to the point where they might jeopardize her own survival. By giving birth to her cub while it is still

*An adult female stops to nurse her cubs en route from her den south of Churchill to the sea ice of Hudson Bay.
(© Daniel J. Cox/Natural Exposures.com)*

tiny, and then nourishing it outside her own body, the female no longer has to support the fetus via the placenta, with the added physiological expense of removing the cub's waste products from her own blood. Once born, the cub can receive the fatty acids so critical to its growth directly from the mother's milk, which it is capable of digesting for itself when it receives it by drinking. Also, once the cub can defecate and urinate outside the female's body, the female no longer needs to use energetically expensive physiological pathways to remove the cub's waste products from the closed blood system of her own body. In this way, the female allows the cub to grow internally to the point where it can survive externally, albeit within a maternity den, by huddling close to her body and being fed externally. As such, the maternity den effectively functions as an external womb, allowing the weak, underdeveloped cub to be protected and to grow until it is large enough to leave the den and travel to the sea ice with its mother in the bitter cold of an arctic spring. This also explains why it is critical that females in maternity dens not be disturbed, so that they don't leave prematurely, as the cubs are not likely to survive.

Triplet litters of polar bear cubs are not common.
(© Jenny E. Ross)

Growth of the cubs

There are records of the birth weights of polar bear cubs from several zoos. A male and female cub born in the Topeka Zoo in 1971 weighed 706 g and 570 g (1.5 lb and 1.2 lb) respectively. For ten hand-reared cubs in zoos, the birth weights ranged between 570 g and 750 g (1.2-1.6 lb). Uspenski reported that there were three one-day-old male and female cubs in the Leningrad Zoo, two of which weighed 840 g and 725 g (1.8 lb and 1.6 lb) and 730 g and 650 grams (1.6 lb and 1.4 lb) respectively. The mean lengths of the male and female cubs were 30.2 cm and 28.9 cm (about 1 ft). From these few observations it appears that the male cubs may be slightly larger than the female cubs right from birth. By the time the cubs leave their dens, the males already weigh about 10% more than the females. Again, based on data from zoos, cubs may weigh about 3.5 kg (7.7 lb) at one month of age, 5.5 kg (12.1 lb) at two months, and 11 kg (24.2 lb) by three months. At the time of leaving the maternity den in spring, wild cubs weigh 10-15 kg (22-33 lb), 90-160 kg (198-352 lb) at one year of age, and 170-200 kg (374-440 lb) at two years of age, at which time they become independent. By two years of age, the males are often taller than their mothers.

The cubs in the Topeka zoo opened their eyes at 26 days of age (compared to 30 to 31 days in Leningrad), and their canine teeth first became apparent at about 50 days. Uspenski also reported that the ability of the cubs to smell first became apparent to him at about 50 days of age. Unsteady walking began at about 2 months of age in both zoos.

Getting ready to leave the den

Detailed observations of the distribution of maternity dens, and the behaviour of female polar bears with their three-month-old cubs, have been made in areas as widely separated as Køngsøya in Svalbard (Rasmus Hansson and Jorn Thomassen), the north slope of Alaska (Tom S. Smith), and Herald and Wrangell Islands in eastern Russia (Nikita Ovsyanikov). Taken together, their extended observations, made under impressively cold and windy conditions, provide us with a fairly thorough picture of what these bears do from the time they first break out of their dens until they depart for the sea ice.

At Køngsøya, as at Herald and Wrangel islands, there may be several dens in a small area, so at least some females are in sight of each other. For example, one spring on Wrangel Island, there were 12 maternity dens in a bank of snow only 2.5 km (1.5 mi) long, while in another spring on Køngsøya there were 20 dens within two square kilometres. This contrasts with almost everywhere else in the Arctic, where single polar bear dens are widely distributed at low densities, but it did provide situations where observations could be made on several families each year.

The adult females remain in their maternity dens, nursing their rapidly growing cubs on their rich milk (about 36% fat in spring) until late February to early April, depending somewhat on latitude. Most females did not break out unless the weather was generally favourable (not too windy), although there were exceptions. Even so, the air temperatures in all the areas studied were usually in the range of -25 to -40°C (-10 to -40°F). Mother bears break out of their dens later in the far north than they do in more southerly parts of their range where it gets warmer earlier.

In Svalbard, after the den entrance was first opened, it was still an average of two days before the cubs began to venture outside, but that did not seem to happen in either Alaska or Russia. During the time the families remained at the den site, they spent up to 85% of their time in the den in Alaska and 92% in Svalbard.

By the time the female breaks out of her den, the cubs are large and strong enough to be able to follow her outside. Most families remain at the den site for up to about two weeks before leaving, although some leave earlier and others leave later. It has been suggested that the cubs may need some time to acclimatize to the cold; although physiological studies indicate they already have a lower critical temperature of -30°C (-22°F) so the external temperature on its own may not be the only factor. It is also possible that because the cubs have had little opportunity to be active while still in the den, they may need to exercise a bit simply to develop some muscle tone before starting to walk behind their mothers for sustained distances. At this stage however, such suggestions are simply speculation, as no one knows for certain.

Once outside, most families tend to remain in the general vicinity of the den. In Alaska, the females were inactive and simply watched around the area about half the time. In contrast, cubs were active about 87% of their time outside the den, including 54% playing, 17% walking, and 10% just being generally active. Play in young cubs, and even those up to a year old, includes a great deal of chasing, rolling over each other, wrestling, and climbing up small hills so they can slide down again. Although the female did not participate in this behaviour, she always remained close by where she could keep an eye on things. The attentive mothers groomed and touched their cubs with their muzzles often. Nursing took place periodically with the female either sitting up or lying on her side, often in a temporary pit dug in the snow.

On both Herald Island and Køngsøya, females occasionally went on short exploratory walks during which they sometimes did some digging and grazing on grass. I have sometimes seen tracks and signs of digging adjacent to den sites in places as far apart as Banks Island and Hudson Bay, indicating that such activity is probably fairly common. When eating dried lichens and grasses in late winter, the females leave large stools of undigested vegetation, suggesting it is unlikely they receive any nutritive value from their intake. It may simply be that by this time the females have used most of their stored fat reserves, so having something in their stomachs reduces hunger pangs a bit.

At Køngsøya, Hansson and Thomassen noted that defecation and urination took place throughout the area but there was no indication of a scent-marking or territorial function. This behaviour has not been reported elsewhere. On Herald Island, Ovsyanikov noted that females that appeared to be older dominated those that looked younger. In some cases, older females were observed using an average of more than three different dens after the original occupants had departed, a behaviour that was also described on Køngsøya. In contrast, females that appeared to be younger used only their own dens. Three times on Køngsøya, females were observed using their paws to scrape snow over their own feces like a dog, while on a number of other occasions, they ate the feces of their cubs. Uspenski and Kistchinski also reported females eating the feces of their cubs on Wrangel Island. The insides of maternity dens I have entered have been devoid of cub feces which also suggests they are likely eaten by the mothers, possibly for their nutritive value. Cubs have not been reported eating feces.

When the female finally decides it is time to leave, the family begins its trek to the sea ice. The periods of travel are punctuated with rests and bouts of nursing in resting pits scraped out of the snow.

Age of reproductive maturity

Sexual maturity is the age at which a mammal is capable of mating and having young for the first time. In most areas of the Arctic, female polar bears breed for the first time at four years of age and give birth to their first cubs at the age of five. Some of these young females are smaller and inexperienced, lose their first litters, and mate again the following year. Depending on their physical condition, some females may not mate until they are five or six years old.

There are also some interesting differences between populations in the age of first breeding of females. For example, in the Beaufort Sea, females do not breed for the first time until they are five years old, so they have their first cubs at six, a year older than their counterparts in most other parts of the Arctic. A similar delay of one year in the age of first reproduction occurred with females in Viscount Melville Sound which, at the time the research was done in the early 1990s, was mostly covered with multiyear ice and had one of the lowest known densities of ringed seals in the Canadian Arctic.

A full year's difference in the age of first breeding between the polar bears of the Beaufort Sea and those of other areas is quite substantial. The reason is not known, but it is probably influenced by the overall biological productivity of the different areas. For example, it is often stated that the waters of the eastern Arctic, such as Baffin Bay and Lancaster Sound, are much more biologically productive than is the Beaufort Sea. Much of the water in the Beaufort Sea comes from the depths of the cold, stratified polar basin, which is supposed to be one of the least productive marine water bodies in the world. If the overall level of biological productivity is lower in the Beaufort Sea, the density of seals may be lower there than in other areas. If the seal populations are smaller or distributed at lower densities, polar bears might catch them less frequently, and it might take a little longer for female bears to grow to physical maturity. However, all that is speculation as there is little solid comparative information on the causes for differences in the age of first reproduction in the different populations.

The majority of male bears reach sexual maturity by the age of six years, but that does not mean they will succeed in mating at that time. Several more years must pass before most males grow big, strong, aggressive, and skilful enough to compete successfully for females. Most mating is probably done by males eight to ten years of age and older.

How often do females have cubs?

The rate at which a female can have cubs depends on how long it takes her to wean one litter, mate, and produce another litter. In most areas, females keep their cubs with them for two and a half years, which means they are capable of mating once every three years. Even though females in the Beaufort Sea mature a year later than do females in other areas, they keep their cubs for the same length of time.

In a small number of instances, females have been recorded keeping their cubs for three and a half years before weaning. This anomaly was reported most often from Viscount Melville Sound during a population study in the early 1990s, and one female there even had her cubs with her when they were four and a half years of age. Why this occurred more frequently there is not clear but one likely explanation, as noted above, is that the area was less biologically productive because of largely being covered by unproductive multiyear ice. This lower level of productivity is also reflected by Viscount Melville Sound, at that time, having one of the lowest densities of ringed seals anywhere in the Arctic. Thus, a reduced and possibly less accessible food base might have slowed the growth rate of the cubs, resulting in a delay in the age at weaning. It was also possible that, because the population had been heavily overharvested, the number of adult males was sufficiently reduced, that there were simply not enough males present to drive the cubs away and ensure mating of all available females. Because of climate warming in the Arctic, multiyear ice is now mostly gone in Viscount Melville Sound, so it is possible the area is more productive now because of being covered with annual ice. How such changes may be affecting the polar bears there is unknown.

In contrast, back in the 1980s, up to about 40% of the females on the western coast of Hudson Bay successfully weaned their cubs at only one and a half years of age. Consequently, at that time, many of the females in western Hudson Bay were capable of breeding every two years, which may have enabled some to have up to 30% more litters during their lifetimes. When we compared the survival rate of the yearlings that were weaned versus those that remained with their mothers for

An adult female with two yearling cubs. Two is the most common litter size for bears of all ages.
(© Stefan Lundgren)

an additional year, there was no significant differ-ence. Similarly, the survival rate of the cubs that were weaned as yearlings in western Hudson Bay was similar to those weaned as two year olds else-where in the Arctic.

We do not know why some of the Western Hudson Bay females were able to successfully wean their cubs as yearlings back in the 1980s, but there are a few possibilities. One idea con-cerns the minimum size that polar bears must reach to be able to hunt successfully. In our studies of the hunting behaviour of polar bears in the Canadian High Arctic in the spring, we noted that polar bears must crash through hard snow-

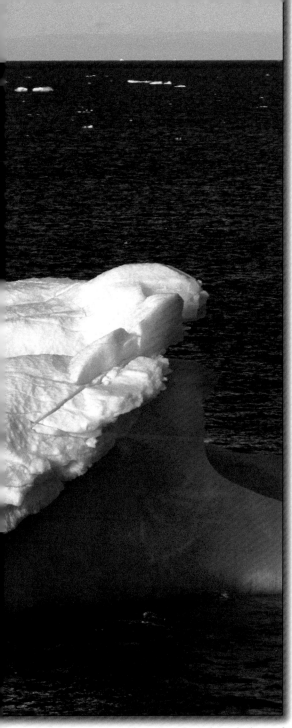

and easier to break into. If so, it might allow a smaller bear to hunt successfully. Another possibility is that Hudson Bay may be more biologically productive, thanks to the many rivers that discharge nutrients into it. This might result in larger seal populations and a greater number of seals could mean that bears of all ages might have less difficulty catching food. A third possible explanation relates to the relative abundance of the different species of seals available to be hunted. Hudson Bay has a large population of bearded seals, which are four to five times larger than the ringed seals. A bearded seal kill means a much larger supply of carrion left on the ice. Since young bears get much of their food by scavenging the kills of older bears, this resource might be enough to help yearlings survive until they are large enough to kill seals on their own.

Regardless, we will likely never know what enabled some female bears to successfully wean their cubs as yearlings because that behaviour has all but disappeared now, as is discussed in the chapter on the effects of climate warming.

Litter size

The third major reproductive variable is litter size. Throughout polar bear range, twins are most common and account for about two-thirds of the litters. Single cubs are the next most common, accounting for 20-30%. Triplets occur much less often and their frequency of occurrence varies by both geographic area and time frame. For example, of 119 litters caught in Western Hudson Bay in spring in the 1980s, 24 (20%) were cubs-of-the-year, 79 (67%) were twins, 14 (12%) were triplets, and one rare litter had four cubs. In comparison, only 1-3% of the litters caught in spring on the southeastern coast of Baffin Island, Svalbard, the Canadian High Arctic, or the Beaufort Sea during the same period were triplets. In the last decade or so in Western Hudson Bay, triplet litters are much less frequent than they were in the 1980s, though they are occasionally still recorded.

drifts to capture seals at their breathing holes and haul-out lairs (see also "Hunting Behaviour"). Yearlings may be too small to hunt this way on their own because they are not heavy enough to break through the snowdrifts in winter. At the lower latitudes of western Hudson Bay where it gets warm earlier, the snowdrifts may be softer

Litter sizes also vary because some of the cubs die. Simply because some cubs die of natural causes before they are weaned and become independent, one would expect the highest litter size to be recorded at the den before the family departs for the sea ice. The average litter sizes of cubs in spring from several studies in different areas range from about 1.5 to 1.9 in different areas. Andy Derocher looked at litter size in relation to latitude and found there was no relationship. Similarly, the litter sizes in the same area may be different in different time periods. Thus, it seems more likely that the major factors influencing litter size in any particular areas are more related to environmental conditions and prey availability than to something like latitude. Because of natural cub mortality, the average litter size tends to decline with age of the cubs. However, this decline is sometimes difficult to estimate without tagging and resighting known individual females over time because if you see an unknown female, alone or with a single cub, there is no way of knowing if she had more cubs with her at an earlier time.

Data on litter sizes of cubs in their dens are extremely difficult to obtain but it does confirm that some mortality occurs there as well. Most of what little information is available was collected by scientists (such as Harington) or other observers accompanying Inuk hunters several years ago, when the traditional hunting of polar bear in their dens was still legal. One of the most remarkable data sets was collected by Father Van de Velde, a Catholic priest who lived and travelled extensively at all seasons with the Inuit from Pelly Bay, in the central Canadian Arctic (Figure 10). Although the sample sizes of litters from within dens may not look impressive, we should remember that these data sets took several years to collect and usually involved weeks of travel at a time, by dog team, in bitterly cold temperatures in the early spring. During the winter, from 1937 through 1965, Van de Velde documented the size of 25 litters of polar bears while still in their dens. The average for 8 pregnant females was 2, while the average of 24 litters after their birth but still in their dens (December through February) was 1.88. The mean litter size of cubs-of-the-year caught on the sea ice in April during population studies in the same general area during the 1970s was 1.56. Even though that sample was collected several years after the records from within the dens, the smaller litter size is consistent with the idea that litter size declines as the cubs age, because of natural mortality.

Harington collected similar data from Inuk hunters during the early 1960s. On the basis of 16 litters of cubs still in their dens on Southampton Island, he calculated a mean litter size of 1.94. On southeastern Baffin Island, about 800 km (500 mi) to the east, the mean litter size of cubs as they first reached the ice in April in the late 1970s was 1.82, a difference of only 6%.

In his pioneering study of polar bears at Svalbard, the Norwegian biologist, Ødd Lønø, collected data from resident polar bear trappers from 1946 and 1967. He examined the ovaries collected from 14 adult female polar bears for evidence of ovulation. He found that 13 had released 2 eggs and one released 3 for an average of 2.07. During the same period, he obtained data from 24 litters of cubs after leaving the maternity dens and found an average litter size of 1.67. Even though the sample sizes from all these sources were not large, it is clear that a certain amount of egg loss, prebirth mortality, or postbirth mortality takes place in the den.

Of course, there is no way of knowing if a female with no cubs might have lost her whole litter unless she is tagged and you know her individual history at different stages of her life. In a study in western Hudson Bay in the 1980s, using tagged adult females with known histories, families experienced a cub loss of 38% between the time they left their dens in the spring and when they returned to shore again in late summer.

The largest average litter sizes of polar bears anywhere in the world were recorded along the western and southwestern coastlines of Hudson

Bay during the 1970s. Each spring from 1970 through 1976, Dale Cross, Dick Robertson, and others from the Manitoba Department of Natural Resources counted the tracks of polar bear families as they plodded through the black spruce forests inland to the coast. Their tracks are easy to see from the air, so by doing a series of flights to count new sets of fresh tracks after snowstorms, a total count could be made. Tracks can be followed backward to find the actual den sites. The number of cubs born can be estimated by summing the number of tracks and the number of cubs seen. Between 1974 and 1978, George Kolenosky and Paul Prevett did a similar survey for the Ontario Ministry of Natural Resources along the northern Ontario coast. In both studies, the average litter size was 2.0. A greater frequency of triplets in these areas yielded the high average litter size.

More about cubs

A genetic examination of the sex ratio of multi-cub litters indicates that most are fraternal, although a small number of identical twins have also been confirmed. Several factors can influence both the weights of individual cubs or the total weight of the litter in spring, but the most important is the weight of the pregnant female in the fall prior to denning. In a detailed examination of this relationship in polar bears in Western Hudson Bay, Andy Derocher found that litter size, total litter weight, and the weight of the females all increased with age until 14-16 years, after which it began to decline. Some females continued to have cubs well into their late 20s but most had single cub litters. Most importantly in the longer term, heavier females produced heavier cubs that, in turn, survived better. Also, single cubs in the spring weighed about 30% more when they were leaving their dens than did cubs from litters of two. In turn, cubs from litters of two weighed about 30% more than did those from litters of three.

In a small, but even stranger study involving ge-

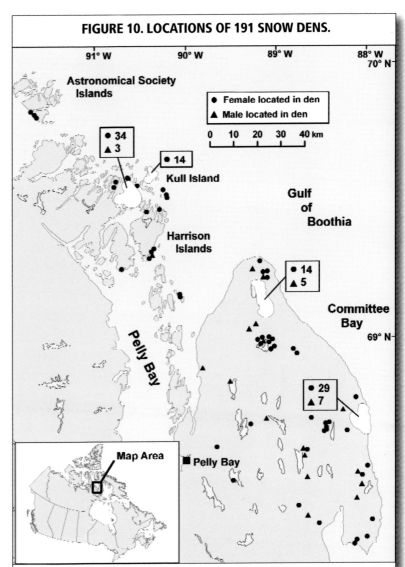

Locations of 191 snow dens occupied by polar bears in winter on the Simpson Peninsula and adjacent islands, provided from living memory by Inuit hunters in Pelly Bay to Father Van de Velde, OMI, between 1952 and 1955 and in 1968–69. (The density of dens in grey shaded areas was too high to plot individual locations clearly at this scale, so the total number in each is given in the attached box.). (From Van de Velde et al. Arctic 56:191-197.)
(Graphic: Evan Richardson)

netic analyses of family groups, three females were found to have naturally adopted cubs that were not their own. It was also shown that there was no relatedness between the adoptive mothers so kinship could not be involved. How such an event might occur in the wild is completely unknown, though disturbance of family groups in an area, resulting in separation of a mother from her cubs is likely a starting point.

Chapter 7

BEHAVIOUR

Sources of behavioural information

Our understanding of the behaviour of any animal comes from many sources of information. Sometimes you can watch an animal directly and, if you can do that for extended periods while the animal is unaware of being observed, that is obviously the best option. However, much of the time, impressions are drawn from more indirect sources such as tracks, the remains of kills, analysis of scats, or from speculating about anecdotal observations. In the case of a solitary carnivore like the polar bear which

A female with two cubs walks on ice to detour around a melt pool in summer to avoid getting wet. (© Stefan Lundgren).

lives at low densities over a habitat as vast and relatively inaccessible as the sea ice of the Arctic, much of our information comes, of necessity, from the indirect method.

years of experiences comes together. No longer are the bears just interesting specimens, scientifically identified by ear tags, or dots on a computer-generated map. They become what they are in real life: the ultimate arctic animal, entirely adapted to live comfortably on the sea ice, and an integral part of the ecosystem. In this chapter, I will discuss aspects of polar bear behaviour with the exception of hunting. Their hunting prowess is so evolved, proficient, and fascinating that I have devoted a separate chapter to "Hunters of the Northern Ice."

Occasionally, you see bears before they see you, and you have a brief opportunity to watch one doing something. These brief impressions are often difficult to interpret. Worse, they may lead to misleading ideas. Yet, sometimes, a glimpse at the right moment reveals a great deal. However, the frustrating part of gathering information in this manner is that often there are simply not enough facts to permit meaningful conclusions. Regardless, it is this backdrop of lore, accumulated from individual observations by Inuit hunters, explorers, and biologists, that forms much of the basis of our understanding of the behaviour of wild polar bears.

Given the ease of drawing incorrect conclusions from anecdotal information, it is no surprise that much of our best information on the behaviour of wild polar bears has come from the many long hours and months we have spent watching them from the observation points described in the chapter "How Do You Study a Polar Bear" Nothing quite equals the sense of total fascination and respect that overcomes me when I spend several hours or weeks at a time watching undisturbed bears. Everything from the kaleidoscope of many

Some bears will make extraordinary leaps over water to avoid swimming between floes. This probably saves them energy in the long run. (© David Shaw Wildlife)

Swimming

Polar bears are, rightly, renowned as strong swimmers. As they travel, they swim across bays or wide leads without hesitation. In the summer, they may swim for hours at a time along a floe edge or among the floes, likely looking for a seal, though at times they simply swim in open water for no apparent reason. Bears of all ages and sex classes swim in summer, but subadults do so the most. Even though polar bears are powerful swimmers, when walking across ice floes, they often take detours of a few or a hundred or more metres, apparently to avoid having to swim. Similarly, they may undertake some quite impressive jumps, sometimes covering a wide area in a rapid series of jumps from floe to flow. I have sometimes wondered if they might do this because of a possible energetic benefit from staying dry and avoiding immersion in cold water but, so far, the ecological reasons for this behaviour have not been clearly established.

I remember one July day, watching a large adult male who was identifiable by a big number on his back. He had been hunting in Radstock Bay, and otherwise behaving quite normally for several days when he suddenly he changed his direction of travel for no obvious reason. He walked over to the floe edge, jumped into the water, and swam south from the coast of Devon Island until he disappeared from sight. Later the next day, we got a radio message from a biologist colleague that he had seen the bear (with the number 10 on his back) walking along a beach on the north coast of Somerset Island, a straight line distance of about 100 km (60 mi) across the open water of Lancaster Sound.

Polar bears are sometimes seen swimming in open water several hundred km offshore in the Labrador, Greenland, and Barents seas. From

bears carrying satellite radio collars, it is clear that bears regularly cross distances of upto several kilometres on occasion (likely with the aid of in-termittent ice floes). However, for the most, their presence that far from land is likely accidental. In general, ice floes in the open ocean areas of the Arctic tend to drift south in the spring and summer and a few bears are probably inadvertently carried along with them. When the ice melts, the accidental

tourists are left to their own devices. Most prob-ably drown but such occurrences probably explain the origin of polar bears that end up along the northern coastlines of places like Iceland. In much earlier times, some of the bears found swimming in the open ocean were captured by sailors and taken back as gifts to the royalty of Europe.

Healthy polar bears are fairly buoyant because of their body fat. They swim dog-paddle style with their large oar-like forepaws. Meanwhile, their hind legs simply float out behind, occasion-ally serving as rudders. The fat of adults, or even subadults, appears to be adequate to keep them warm enough, even while swimming extended distances. However, probably because of the risk of hypothermia, females with cubs, especially those less than a year of age, avoid swimming long distances. Sometimes, if swimming is necessary but the cub is small, the female will carry it on her back where it is mainly out of the water and can keep warmer.

In the Beaufort Sea, the southern edge of the sea ice of the Arctic Ocean is now retreating pro-gressively further north away from the bears' prime feeding areas near the coast. Consequently bears that used to have to swim tens of kilometres to reach the ice now may have to swim 100 km or more. In one spectacular case George Durner

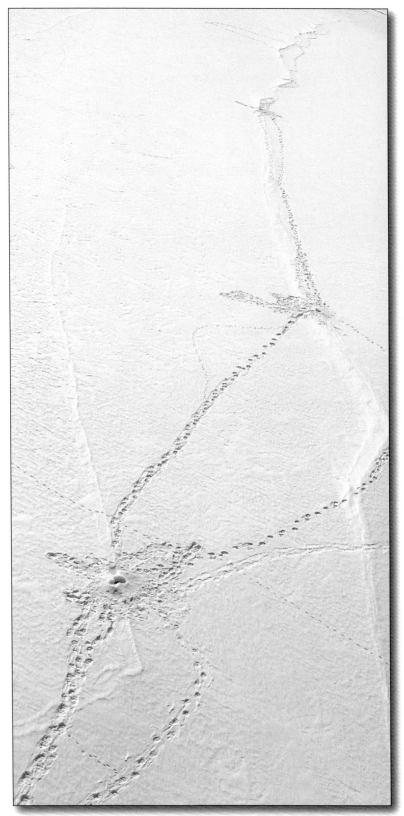

and colleagues documented a nine-day, non-stop swim of 687 km (427 mi) by an adult female. In the process she lost 22% of her body weight and her yearling cub.

When swimming, polar bears dive in two ways. The most common is to go down headfirst, leaving the rear end out of the water until the thrust of paddling by the forepaws pulls it under. I have only observed the second form of submerging during "aquatic stalks," which means sneaking up on a seal on the ice by approaching it in the water. During an aquatic stalk, the bear swims beneath the surface of the water and only its nose comes out of the water to breathe between dives. After breathing, it slips backward until it is below the surface and then continues to swim underwater. Most dives last about 30-40 seconds, though I timed one that lasted 62 seconds.

Bears will also dive for food underwater if it is not too deep. A common form of this behaviour, often observed by ecotourists in Svalbard, involves diving down to the remains of a submerged whale carcass, tearing a piece off, and bringing it back to the surface to chew on. Bears feeding in this way sometimes do so for an hour or more at a time, occasionally dragging larger pieces back onto the beach where they may eventually be scavenged by smaller bears. One of the most curious acts of swimming I have personally observed was a polar bear at Radstock Bay diving for kelp on a small reef just offshore from our camp on Caswall Tower. After bringing a piece of kelp to the surface, he lay on his back like a sea otter, picking out pieces to eat. However, even with the telescope at its maximum magnification, I could not discern whether the bear was feeding on bits of the kelp itself or on invertebrates that might have been attached onto it.

Sometimes when swimming, bears try to capture sea birds and ducks by diving underneath them and biting them from below. Successful

Tracks of hunting bears visiting ringed seal breathing holes on a refrozen lead.
(© Ian Stirling)

captures have been observed by a number of people and this practice seems to be successful mainly when the water is rough, probably because the wave action helps to keep the birds from noticing the approaching bear when it surfaces to breathe. It is doubtful that there is an energetic benefit to hunting this way, so it is most likely done mainly by subadults.

Sometimes a bear wants to cross a body of water covered with newly frozen ice too thin to hold its weight but too thick to swim through. In that case, the bear breaks through into the water and then dives and swims underwater until it needs to breathe and then breaks through again with its head. After breathing, it dives and swims again until reaching its destination and then breaks through, climbs out, and carries on.

Walking speed

When watching polar bears for extended periods or more briefly, one thing that constantly impresses me is that they rarely do anything quickly. Nowhere is this more apparent than when watching a bear walk. Their great heads swing gently from side to side, making them appear misleadingly ponderous and inattentive to their surroundings. Periodically, they stop to look around or raise the nose to test the wind before plodding

When a cub is small, the mother may carry it on her back to keep it from becoming chilled in the water.
© Angela Plumb

An adult female dives down to feed on the remains of a partially submerged whale carcass and brings up food to share with her cub. (© David Merefield)

on. However, when walking steadily, they move more quickly than it might appear. Their steady lumbering gait averages about 5.5 kph (3.5 mph) and can continue for hours at a time, sometimes covering tens of kilometres in a day. Some problem bears being chased away from town by a truck have been recorded running at speeds of 35-40 kph (22-25 mph) for short distances.

Sleeping

During the summer, polar bears spend a quarter to a third of their time sleeping. It is difficult to measure this precisely because sometimes bears fall asleep when they are lying still-hunting and it is difficult to tell with a telescope from a distance when the change occurred. When it is time for a nap out on the sea ice, a bear will usually just dig a pit in the snow on the lee side of a pressure ridge and lie down. If it is windy, the bear can be completely covered by blowing snow and may remain at the same spot for several hours or even days. On flat or open ice, a bear may simply lie on its stomach or side with its hindquarters or back to the wind. During the ice-free period in places

POLAR BEARS: The Natural History of a Threatened Species

like Hudson Bay, bears often sleep in pits dug into sand or gravel ridges along the beach.

Most bears like to sleep within an hour or two after a meal. In areas near the coast or in places such as Radstock Bay or Svalbard, there are usually hillsides with patches of snow on them. Subadults and females with cubs in particular often climb a hundred metres or more up one of these snow slopes and dig a big sleeping pit. Subadults do this as well. From the hillside, they have a good view of the area and are less likely to be surprised by another bear. Adult females with cubs in particular probably do this to reduce the risk of predation of the cub by an adult male .

In one sample of 17 sleep sessions longer than an hour, the average length was 7 hours and 45 minutes, not much different from what a lot of humans need. In the summer at least, there is also a tendency for bears to sleep more during the day than at night, although during 24-hour daylight

the difference is only relative. The apparent preference for being active at "night" may relate to the behaviour of the seals. Ringed seals feed at night when their prey species come up closer to the surface of the water. This may result in the seals surfacing more often, or more regularly, possibly increasing a bear's chance of catching one at its breathing hole as compared to during the day.

Sheltering

During winter, polar bears of all age and sex classes, except adult females in maternity dens, continue to hunt on the sea ice. Through the dark, cold, stormy winter, the windblown snow over breathing holes thickens and becomes very hard. The number of cracks available for seals to breathe at where they are accessible to bears is greatly reduced, especially during periods of intense cold. Most bears on the sea ice are at their lightest weight in late winter and it seems likely

Polar bears often feed on kelp, sometimes by diving for it in open water, eating it when washed up on shore, or sometimes pulling it up through seal holes. (© Ian Stirling)

Holes in young ice that is too thin to walk on. The bear swam under the ice and broke holes as he needed them to breathe until he reached the other side and could climb out.
(© Ian Stirling)

that for much of that time, it costs them more energy to continue walking and hunting than they take in as a result of catching seals. One might predict it could be more energy-efficient for a bear to dig a den for protection during the coldest or stormiest periods and fast on stored fat, much as the bears in Hudson Bay do during the open water period when there is no food available. Over the years, several Inuit hunters have told me they have occasionally seen females with cubs older than newborns, subadults, and adult males in snow dens during the winter. However, it is difficult to determine how often this might occur, or by what conditions it might be stimulated, when

POLAR BEARS: The Natural History of a Threatened Species

one only has anecdotal information and the conditions under which this might occur make gathering data so difficult.

Surprisingly, there are two very different but equally fascinating sets of observations that confirm both the use and importance of temporary dens, probably for energy conservation in the coldest times of winter by non-pregnant polar bears. In the early 1990s, François Messier and colleagues used satellite radio collars to track 17 adult female polar bears in Viscount Melville Sound over a three-year period. At that time, the area had one of the lowest densities of ringed seals anywhere in the Canadian Arctic and multiyear ice prevailed over much of the region, both of

which probably contributed to making hunting seals both more difficult and less productive. From the radios, the scientists obtained both movement data and activity levels. They found that in the coldest months of December through March, ten females not suspected to be in dens with newborn cubs showed a marked reduction in their activity and mobility during some of the coldest periods in winter. They speculated the bears were using temporary dens facultatively in order to conserve energy during cold periods when seal hunting might be less productive. This facultative energy-conserving behaviour was termed "sheltering." Similar behaviour has not been documented from radio-collared polar bears

A bear breathing at a hole he has made with his head while crossing a lead by swimming under the ice. (© Mike Lockhart)

A male bear lies sleeping on the beach, below a well developed coastal sleeping pit, in the gravel on a beach ridge.
(© Ian Stirling)

hunting in winter on more biologically productive and active areas of annual ice in areas such as the Beaufort Sea, Baffin Bay, Hudson Bay, or the Barents Sea.

From 1937 to 1965, when hunting polar bears in dens by Inuit hunters was both traditional and legal in Canada, Father Franz Van de Velde, a priest at Pelly Bay in the central Canadian Arctic, maintained a careful written record of the ages and sex classes of bears killed in snow dens on the Simpson Peninsula by local Inuit hunters. Five non-pregnant adult females were found alone in dens in January when temperatures ranged from -28 to -41°C (-18 to -42°F). Five females accompanied by yearlings were found: one in November, two in January, and two in February. The temper-

atures at Pelly Bay on the days the two females with yearlings were reported in January were -32°C (-26°F) and -52°C (-62°F). It was -57°C (-71°F) when the two dens were found in February. Two females accompanied by two two-year-old cubs were found: one in November and one in February. One adult male was found in a den in November and two in January, on days when the temperatures in Pelly Bay were -25°C (-13°F) and -41°C (-42°F) respectively. Overall, of 191 snow dens occupied during winter, 148 had females (alone or with an unspecified number of cubs), and 32 had lone males. The sex was not reported for the lone occupants of 11 dens. However, from these data, it seems highly likely that polar bears of all ages and sex classes without newborn cubs in maternity dens throughout the Arctic may seek "shelter" in temporary snow dens in order to use their stored energy reserves as efficiently as possible during periods of particularly cold weather in winter.

Tool-using behaviour

The ability of animals to use a "tool" of some sort to solve a problem, usually related to feeding, has often been regarded as indicative of a higher level of intelligence.

Historically at least, there have been stories and speculations about polar bears using blocks of ice or stones to kill other animals, particularly walruses. Perhaps the most famous example is the engraving in C. F. Hall's book *Life Among the Esquimaux* which depicts a polar bear on top of a cliff hurling a large stone down at an unsuspecting walrus. According to Hall's Inuk companion, this did not kill the walrus but only stunned it long enough to give the bear time to run down and finish the job.

In a variation on this theme, the bear carries a block of ice on its shoulder and, when the mo-

Illustration titled "Bear killing walrus" from My Life With the Esquimaux, *by C.F. Hall (1865)*

Large adult males aggregate non-aggressively while not feeding and waiting for the ice to freeze in late fall in western Hudson Bay. (© Dan Guravich/ PolarBearsInternational.org)

ment is right, stops to hurl it at another animal. Although the stories are widespread, witnesses are hard to come by. Various people, including the polar explorer Frederick Cook, tell of seeing bears stand up holding objects. Indeed, anyone who watches polar bears performing in a circus will see the same thing. An observation recorded by the arctic physiologist Kare Rodahl offers a possible clue to the mystery, in at least some cases. Rodahl saw a polar bear that narrowly missed a bearded seal and then "leaped up onto the floes and in his fury began to toss

POLAR BEARS: The Natural History of a Threatened Species

lumps of ice about." I have also seen bears show frustration after not getting a seal. Sometimes they will swat the snow, or a female will swat a cub that disturbed her hunt. One bear I watched stalked a ten-gallon oil drum on the ice for half an hour. When it made its final charge and then realized it was not a seal, it gave the drum a frustrated cuff and sent it spinning several metres across the ice. Polar bears are intelligent animals though, so I would be reluctant to categorically say one could not learn to use a "tool" in this manner. However, if they do, I

think it is a rare occurrence. My guess is that blocks of ice found around unsuccessful hunting sites were probably broken off in a moment of frustration.

There are a few fascinating illustrations which confirm that polar bears really do have a rather remarkable ability to envision the solution to a problem via clever use of an otherwise unrelated object, or "tool." In one case, I allowed a photographer friend and his colleague to stay in my research tower at Cape Churchill for a couple of weeks in order to photograph the bears. The tower has reinforcing steel struts between its main legs at about 4 m (12 ft) intervals above the ground. They put some boards across one corner on the first tier so they could stand lower down to get better photographs. There were also a couple of fuel drums off to one side, but still beneath the tower. A large gaunt adult male bear walked about below them for a few days, apparently not paying attention to anything in particular, and after a while, the men no longer paid any attention to him. One day, completely without warning, the bear suddenly ran under the tower, leapt onto the two fuel drums, and used them to vault upwards at one of the men. He managed to get a claw into the man's lower pant leg and tore it open before falling back to the ground, leaving the careless person shaken but hopefully a little wiser. The bear could not have jumped the full 4 m unassisted, but he figured out that he could reach the man if he got to the top of the drums first.

At the Tennoji Zoo in Osaka, a five-year-old

A young male bear in the Tennoji Zoo, Osaka, Japan, has learned to use "tools". Above, he throws a piece of plastic to dislodge the meat on a hook Below, he uses a pole to hit it.
(© Tennoji Zoo, Osaka)

male polar bear named GoGo demonstrated an astonishing, and previously unreported, degree of conceptual creativity to get access to food. The zoo staff had been devising forms of enrichment to keep the bear from becoming bored, so they hung a piece of meat about 3 m (10 ft) above his pool, but too high for him to

grasp. Initially GoGo tried to get it by jumping but he was unsuccessful. After about four months however, the ingenious bear invented two tools which he used successfully. In one technique, he began to throw a short, hard piece of plastic pipe at the meat (like throwing a basketball upward toward the net), until he

knocked it down. In the second method, he picked up the remains of a tree branch, about 2 m (6 ft) long, and used it to slap the meat off the hook. Initially it took him a couple of hours to get the meat by either technique but after a while he needed only five minutes.

In general, polar bears are considered to be very

Four large adult males aggregate unagressively at close quarters to feed on a floating whale carcass. (© Daniel J. Cox/ NaturalExposures.com)

In a rare and bizarre episode, a young male polar bear plays unaggressively with a dog who is similarly unperturbed.
(© Norbert Rosing)

intelligent predators, but from these few examples, it is clear that some are capable of thinking at a more conceptual level than most of us ever suspected.

When polar bears are not solitary

Although polar bears are usually described as being relatively unsociable and living solitary lives, except for family groups and breeding pairs, there are two circumstances in which several bears may tolerate each other at close quarters without interacting, either because there is nothing to compete for or, alternately, there is a sufficient abundance of food and simply no need to compete. Because polar bears are well

armed and can inflict serious damage on each other, it can be ecologically important to recognize when aggressive behaviour is not needed.

During the open water season, along the coast of western Hudson Bay, there is normally no food to compete for and it is the most distant time from the breeding season. Testosterone production is at its lowest point for the year and there is no need to compete for access to reproductive females. In this circumstance, groups of large adult males may aggregate, often within metres of each other and, for the most part simply ignore one another. The lack of testosterone and the absence of food probably also creates circumstances that make it possible for young adult males to "play fight," sometimes for extended periods, while on land, without either animal harming his jousting partner. More details of this behaviour are given in the chapter "Polar Bear Capital of the World".

The other circumstance where bears may aggregate without aggression is in places where there is an abundance of food, especially when satiation is reached before the food supply is exhausted. In some cases where a single dead seal is present, two animals of similar size may simply pull it apart and each feed on a piece without necessitating a fight for possession of the carcass.

Some unexplained behaviour

Normally, dogs and polar bears don't get along. Inuit have used their dogs to hunt bears and guard their hunting camps for centuries because most dogs bark immediately at the sight of a bear. Bears, for their part, sometimes kill and eat dogs that are chained up. Some Inuit hunters have told me that if you want to have a dog guard your camp, it is best for it to be loose because sometimes it knows it can't get away when chained up and may remain silent so as not to attract a bear's attention. Regardless, everyone around Churchill was surprised when a subadult male bear began to just visit and play with a couple of sled dogs chained to a dog line, unable to escape. It is clear from the two photos here that the dog is not at all afraid and the bear is not being the slightest bit aggressive. Quite amazing! Apparently, the bear wasn't hungry, probably because of having gorged himself from the unprotected supply of meat nearby. He continued to *(© Norbert Rosing)*

visit, eat from the dog food supply, and then play with the dogs for several more days, before eventually being moved away from that site by local conservation officers.

New innovations for studying polar bear behaviour

Two examples of imaginative applications of technology may help us study the behaviour of undisturbed polar bears in the future. One is the installation of remote cameras that can use a digital network to provide continuous viewing, and recording of observations. Polar Bears Interna-

tional did a highly successful trial of this technology at Cape Churchill. Each fall, from 2005 through 2008, they installed a continuously broadcasting video camera on our old observation tower so that designated school classrooms could log in with their computers and watch what the bears were doing in real time. It was enormously popular, but also very expensive. However, as the cost of technology continues to come down, similar applications may have significant scientific and educational potential in the future.

In a second, more recent development, John Downer Productions for the BBC used three

A polar bears surveys his surroundings, unaware that "Icebergcam," on the floe in front of it, is documenting every detail of his behaviour.
(© Philip Dalton/ John Downer Productions)

bird colonies, diving for kelp, indulging in courtship rituals, and of other aspects of their natural behaviour. From a very close distance, "Icebergcam" even documented how a group of bears could be non-aggressive in the presence of a surplus of food when seven bears shared a washed-up whale carcass. However, bears are also very curious, so their investigation of the units they eventually noticed resulted in some comical, but highly destructive encounters. The remarkable video gathered in this venture can be seen in the video *"Polar Bear: Spy on the Ice."*

In future, these and other ingenious applications of technology will continue to broaden our understanding of wild, undisturbed, polar bears.

Polar bears investigate everything. Here, an adult has noticed "Blizzardcam", demolishing it in the process of investigating it. (© Philip Dalton/John Downer Productions)

remotely controlled miniature devices equipped with high definition cameras to document the behaviour of undisturbed polar bears in Svalbard. They were: "Icebergcam," which was waterborne; "Blizzardcam," which travelled over the land like a small robot in all weather; and "Snowballcam," which was about the size of a football and could roll like one. The housing was white to help them blend in with their surroundings. By controlling the movements of the cameras from a distance, they were able to obtain extraordinary video of bears journeying across the drifting ice in search of seals, raiding

Chapter 8

An adult male stalks entrapped belugas breathing at a hole in the sea ice..
(© Sue Flood)

HUNTERS OF THE NORTHERN ICE

The role of the polar bear as the supreme predator of the sea ice most defines its overall significance in the ecology of the arctic marine ecosystem, its influence on the daily lives and evolution of other marine mammals, and its absolute dependence on ice for survival. The primary prey of the polar bears is the ringed seal. Although it is the most abundant and widely distributed seal in the Arctic, the ringed seal is

also the smallest, with adults weighing only 40-70 kg (90-150 lb). The small size of ringed seals is especially important to polar bears because it means that even small bears can successfully hunt and kill them. Most ringed seals live as single animals or in very small groups over the vast areas of Arctic sea ice.

Polar bears hunt seals in all seasons if they are able to be on ice but the most important times are spring and summer, prior to break-up. During winter and spring, adult ringed seals defend territories beneath the stable frozen landfast ice along the coast, in bays and interisland channels, and sometimes in large areas of stable pack ice. This means they are distributed over huge areas

during winter and spring but at fairly low densities. The seals need stable ice because they self-maintain breathing holes through the winter by constantly abrading the refreezing ice with the heavy claws on their foreflippers. In fact, if one uses a hydrophone (an underwater microphone) to listen for vocalizations of seals beneath the ice, one of the most common sounds heard is the periodic scratching of a nearby seal as it keeps a breathing hole open. Stable ice is important because access to breathing holes could be compromised in ice that is constantly shifting or piling up in pressure ridges during storms. When seals surface to breathe, they are vulnerable to capture by the bears. As a result ringed seals maintain access to several breathing holes or various openings along leads or in pools of water, so a bear cannot easily anticipate where his prey will surface next. During winter, rock-hard, windblown snowdrifts form over seal breathing holes, providing some protection from bears. Ringed seals come up through their breathing holes and scoop out small haul-out lairs in the overlying drifts, in which they can rest. Later, in spring, pregnant females give birth to their single pups in such lairs.

Ringed seal pups are born around the first of April and weigh about 5.5 kg (12 lb) at birth. They are weaned by six weeks of age, by which time they weigh about 22 kg (48 lb), having gained about 0.43 kg (0.9 lb) per day since birth, and are 50% fat by wet weight. The annual flush of seal pups in spring provides the most fat; the pups are not yet very experienced with predators. Their vulnerability to the bears is greatest from the time they are weaned up until the ice breaks up and melts in summer. To hunt seals, polar bears depend on the ice as the platform from which to capture their prey. Although the occasional bear has been known to kill seals in the water near the shoreline, successful hunting in open water is very uncommon. Seals are far more agile swimmers than bears, which makes expending energy by swimming both inefficient and ineffective compared to walking on ice.

By April, after the newborn ringed seal pups have begun to grow and deposit fat, many bears, (adult females with newborn cubs and subadults in particular), move into the stable landfast areas closer to the coast or in deep bays to hunt. It may be a bit more difficult for these smaller, lighter bears to break through the hard drifted snow over the seal lairs or breathing holes than it is for the large adult males. However, because adult males are known to sometimes kill and eat both cubs

An adult female polar bear stands still-hunting until she detects something in the lair beneath the snow in front of her. She then pounces down hard with all her body weight to break through into the lair below.
(© Per Michelsen)

An adult bearded seal with large whiskers and a head brown with iron oxide from the mud at the bottom of the ocean, where it searches for prey.
(© Ian Stirling)

and young independent bears, the use of habitat well away from the floe edge by more vulnerable bears may be partly to reduce their risk of being preyed upon.

While tracking polar bears for capture and tagging, we keep track of all attempts to predate seals, and how many of these attempts are successful. Success rates can vary greatly, even between adjacent localized areas. However, the overall impression is that polar bears sometimes travel long distances when hunting seals at birth and haulout lairs but experience relatively low success rates overall. Here are some numbers to illustrate the point. During a three-year period of high seal productivity in the Beaufort Sea, we tracked bears for a few thousand kilometres and recorded 556 attempts to break into seal lairs, of which only 48 (8.6%) were successful. A period of low seal productivity followed, during which we traveled similar distances but recorded only 120 attempts in

majority of the kills were pups though some subadults and adults were captured as well. For a polar bear, capturing a fat female seal before she has begun to nurse a pup is a huge bonus because she still has so much fat on her body.

In a series of studies, Tom Smith used trained dogs to locate ringed seal subnivean (beneath snow) lairs to assess the quality and importance of different sea ice areas as ringed seal breeding habitat. His records of how many lairs had been predated by bears give additional insight into the important role subnivean lairs play in protecting seals from predation. Over an eight year period in Amundsen Gulf (SE Beaufort Sea), the High Arctic, and southeastern Baffin Island, Smith and his dogs located 310, 363, and 239 lairs, of which bears had located and dug into 5 (1.6%), 110 (30.3%), and 47 (19.6%) respectively. Of the 162 lairs dug into, they made kills at 37 (23%).

Predation of other seals and marine mammals

The other main prey species for the polar bear, the bearded seal, is much larger, though far less abundant than the ringed seal. The "bearded" name comes from its large whiskers, which it uses to find food on the bottom of the ocean. Apparently, they sometimes put their heads right into the bottom sediments in search of prey, judging from the rust-stained faces of some individuals. Adults may weigh 225 to 360 kg (500-800 lb). Because of their large size, most bearded seals are killed by large male bears, although smaller bears often benefit by scavenging on the remains of kills, and may sometimes capture younger seals. Bearded seals are widely distributed throughout the Arctic in areas where pack ice lies over relatively shallow water. Like ringed seals, they are capable of self-maintaining breathing holes but usually prefer not to, normally remaining in drifting pack ice over relatively shallow water.

the same general area, confirming our conclusions from other sources that productivity of seals was exceptionally low. Of those attempts, 8 (6.7%) were successful, indicating that even when the productivity of the seals was low, the bears' success rate at the birth lairs that were located was similar. During several hundred kilometres of tracking bears by helicopter in a productive area for ringed seals in the High Arctic, 172 attempts to capture pups at lairs resulted in 11 (6.4%) kills. The great

In some areas such as Davis Strait or the Labrador Sea, harp and hooded seals haul out near the outer edge of the pack ice in March to

Subadult walrus killed
by a polar bear.
(© Rod Vallee)

give birth to their pups. Although many hundreds of thousands of seals are present at the same time, they remain at most for only a few weeks. Although there is an element of risk to a bear to hunt so far from land on ice floes that can break up at short notice, the caloric reward of access to so many pups just lying on the surface of the ice, is huge. Consequently, some polar bears walk several hundred kilometres from southern Baffin Island, feed heavily for a few weeks, and then walk north all the way back over the pack ice as it is steadily being carried further south by the Labrador Current. In some areas where harbour seals are locally accessible around leads in the pack ice or hauled out along the coast during the open water season, polar bears hunt them as well.

they haul out on land during the open water season. Usually only younger and smaller walruses are successfully preyed upon, because the adults are too large, protected by very thick skin, and well armed with lethal tusks. Again, it is mainly adult male polar bears that are capable of killing walruses. In some areas where walruses congregate on land, they occasionally panic and stampede to the water when approached by one or more polar bears or for reasons that are sometimes not apparent, with the result that sometimes pups or young animals are trampled to death or separated from the adults in the rush, thus leaving them vulnerable to the bears. In areas where large numbers of walruses haul out, some animals may die of natural causes. Sometimes bears of all sizes and ages may scavenge on the same carcass.

Similarly dramatic, though less common, is the situation in which beluga whales (sometimes called white whales) become entrapped in a small pool of water surrounded by solid ice, with no escape route to open water. Such an entrapment is known as a *sassat* in Greenlandic. Such events are a fairly regular occurrence in several parts of the Arctic. In this circumstance, large adult male bears may harass the whales when they surface to breathe, eventually tiring them sufficiently to be able to seize one with their teeth and claws and drag it onto the ice, where several bears can then feed at the same time. In one spectacular example, during an aerial survey over the pack ice in the northern Bering Sea, biologists from the State of Alaska found a place where polar bears had dragged over forty beluga whales onto the ice. In a similar small entrapment in Jones Sound in the Canadian High Arctic, polar bears killed 20-30 whales by exhausting them to the point where a large male was to able to grab hold and pull the weakened animal out onto the ice where it could be killed. Many bears and gulls came to scavenge on the abundance of carrion.

Throughout the Arctic, beluga whales enter the mouths of rivers in summer, where they use

However, harbour seals are not abundant in most areas inhabited by polar bears, and probably do not account for much of the bears' annual energy requirements.

In some places, such as along the west coast of Alaska, in the Bering and Chukchi seas, and in the Canadian Arctic islands, polar bears also kill walruses, both on the pack ice or in areas where

the rough gravel bottom to rub off their sloughing skin. In some of these areas, such as Cunningham Inlet on the north coast of Somerset Island in the High Arctic (Figure 8), the water can be quite shallow, especially at low tide, with the result that occasionally, an unwary whale may be stranded for several hours until the next high tide. In nine years of observations of belugas through the summer in Cunningham Inlet, Tom Smith and his colleagues recorded 10 incidents of stranding, sometimes with as many as three whales simultaneously. Had bears been present, these whales would have been completely vulnerable to predation.

During the same period, Smith's group also witnessed four unsuccessful attempts by bears to stalk belugas in shallow water and two successful kills, out of three attempts, by the same large male bear hunting from drifting ice pans. In both cases, the belugas caught by the bear were young calves, estimated to be 200-250 cm (79-99 in) in length. The bear caught them by lying at the edge of an ice floe until the calves swam close enough for him to be able to jump onto them, then hang on well enough to drag them out onto the ice. On another occasion, during aerial survey of another High Arctic estuary, Tom also sighted eight polar bears and several whales from a helicopter. The bears had captured five belugas and four narwhals, including a calf. Two of the adult female narwhals were still alive and had been dragged 150-200 m (490-660 ft) inland, presumably to prevent them from being able to escape back into the water. These fascinating observations make it clear that a few bears, probably large males, are capable of learning to capture belugas and occasionally narwhals, given the right circumstances.

However, despite the predictable occurrence of belugas at estuaries such as Cunningham Inlet at the same time every year, it appears that few bears have learned to take advantage of the situation. In nine summer seasons of observations, Tom and his colleagues recorded only 24 bear sightings, of which several were young animals that were not large enough to successfully kill something as large as a beluga. The small number of times that successful predation on belugas or narwhals have been reported throughout the Arctic over the years, and the fact that the only two successful hunts of whales in water were made by the same large adult male, probably indicates that in most circumstances, these whales are simply too large for most polar bears to be able to capture on a regular basis.

The most valuable contribution made by whales to the diet of polar bears is more likely

made by animals that periodically die of natural causes and wash up on the beach where polar bears of all ages and sizes can scavenge with equal success. Larger whales such as bowhead, sperm, minke, and fin whales can provide a windfall of abundant food for local bears, a supply that sometimes lasts for as long as a year or two.

Diversity in the diet of polar bears in different areas

Over the years, a large amount of information has been accumulated from the collective observa-tions of Inuit hunters, explorers, scientists, eco-tourists, and others about what species of marine mammals polar bears feed on. Furthermore, from anecdotal observations of hunting bears, as well as interpreting events from their tracks in the snow, we have also learned a fair amount about how the bears capture different species. However, although we knew the bears kill a variety of prey in different areas, until recently it has not been possible to assess how valuable a contribution to the diet each species might make, although it is generally accepted that ringed seals are the most

A group of belugas in a sassat (entrapment in the ice with no escape).
© Sue Flood

POLAR BEARS: The Natural History of a Threatened Species

important prey.

In a series of recent studies, Greg Thiemann analyzed the fatty acids stored in the body fat of polar bears to make several exciting new discoveries about how variable the diets of polar bears of different age and sex classes can be, as well as differences between bears from different geographic areas. It has been known for some time that, depending on the species, many of the fatty acids contained in an animal's adipose (fat) tissue are derived directly from whatever it eats. Polar bears are about 97% efficient at digesting fat so, although the methodology is complicated, the simple concept was that by analyzing what fatty acids are deposited in the fat one could determine what the bear had been eating. In addition, it is possible to estimate the size of the dietary contributions from each of the different species available. Since bears store fat on different parts of

their body, it was essential to first determine if fat sampled from different parts of the body gave the same results. It was a relief to find that no matter where the sample was taken, the results were the same. That result made it possible to analyze specimens collected from bears immobilized for research as well as those that were killed by Inuit hunters, which in turn allowed for larger sample sizes and a wider representation of age and sex classes.

By analyzing fat samples from polar bears from several different areas, Thiemann was able to confirm not only what species the bears were eating but assess the relative importance of each, both between areas and in different seasons (Figure 11). The generalization of ringed seals being the most important prey species holds true for all the areas illustrated here, and also in those surveyed but not included here. However, there is fairly

Left: A polar bear approaches the sassat to investigate the belugas.
© Sue Flood

The bear tries for a beluga but it escapes.
© Sue Flood

Wounds on the belugas from bear attacks.
© Sue Flood

Above: Glaucous gulls scavenge as the bear feeds on a beluga it has caught.
© Sue Flood

Large male polar bear feeding on a beluga in pack ice. It is possible he caught it in the water between the floes.
(© Stefan Lundgren)

wide variation in the importance of other species, including bearded seals in different regions. The relatively high importance of belugas in some areas suggests there are still some things to learn about the relative contributions from direct hunting by the bears themselves and how much might originate from scavenging naturally dead whales or carcasses left over from Inuit hunting.

The greatest prey diversity of any of the areas studied was Davis Strait. Not surprisingly, harp seals were more important there because of their large population size (>six million) and because they concentrate in large numbers to give birth to their pups in predictable areas in spring. Not surprisingly, harp seals accounted for about a third of the diet of the bears. Even in winter however, when harp seals are more widely dispersed at much lower densities, they made up about 15% of the diet which was still higher than anywhere else recorded. Harp seals are also taken

the Greenland coast where they are unavailable to polar bears. Overall, hooded seals comprised only about 2-3% of the diet and were much more important in spring than in winter. However, the clear inclusion of hooded seals in the bears' diet indicates that many of the bears know where and when the animals are available and how to make focused use of them for a short period of time. Both adult male and female hooded seals are large and very aggressive, so to be killed mainly by large male bears. The pups are weaned in an unbelievably short period of time—only four days. After that, they are on their own and completely unafraid of predators on the sea ice. Thus, it seems likely that bears of all age and sex classes selectively hunt pups, which are extremely fat and highly vulnerable following weaning.

In Foxe Basin, where walruses are particularly abundant, Thiemann's work clearly showed they were still less important to the bears than all four species of seals in the area. Ringed seals were still the most important prey species. In other areas where walruses are available, such as Baffin Bay, Davis Strait, and Lancaster Sound, they only accounted for small portions of the diet, which is consistent with the observation that for the most part, polar bears have difficulty killing them. It is likely that a large proportion of the walrus inclusion in the bears' diet comes from scavenging dead animals.

Although not illustrated here, in both the northern and southern Beaufort Sea, the ubiquitous ringed seals are by far the most important prey, followed by bearded seals and little else. Interestingly, bearded seals are more important in the southern Beaufort Sea than in the northern areas, which may indicate their greater abundance because of the greater availability of their preferred habitat of pack ice overlying the shallow water of the continental shelf.

Watching bears hunt

Although we learned a lot about how and what bears hunt from anecdotal observations, looking

by polar bears in the pack ice north of Svalbard in summer but what proportion of the diet they make up is not known.

In Canada, hooded seals are only available to polar bears in Davis Strait when they aggregate on the ice to give birth to their pups in two relatively small areas for a few weeks in March: off the coast of southern Labrador and near southeastern Baffin Island. After the pups are weaned, the whole population remains mainly pelagic along

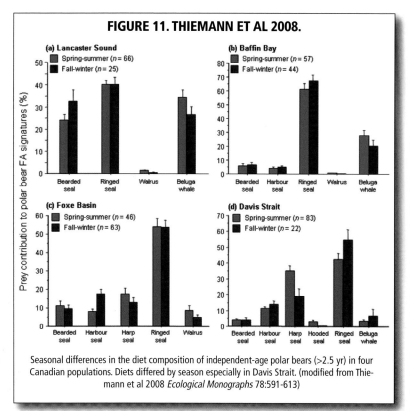

FIGURE 11. THIEMANN ET AL 2008.

Seasonal differences in the diet composition of independent-age polar bears (>2.5 yr) in four Canadian populations. Diets differed by season especially in Davis Strait. (modified from Thiemann et al 2008 *Ecological Monographs* 78:591-613)

impression of being oblivious to their surroundings. Given a choice, bears usually move into the wind, or across it, which probably enables them to detect a distant seal by its smell. Periodically, a bear will stop to look around or raise its nose to test the wind before plodding on. Despite the apparently casual appearance, little passes unnoticed. Their eyesight is about the same as that of a human but it is their prodigious sense of smell that they rely upon for information. Scent, like an invisible code, identifies a place to hunt on the ice, tells them if other bears are upwind, if there is a seal carcass to scavenge on, or maybe just something interesting that warrants investigation. The longer one watches, the more one realizes there is absolutely nothing casual about these animals. Their entire existence is built around hunting and the conservation of energy; taking in energy as efficiently as possible when an opportunity presents itself and then expending it as parsimoniously as possible between meals. Their actions and what they do through a day, or a week, if you have the patience to watch for long enough, will tell you what it means to be a polar bear.

A bear may pick a spot to hunt because it has seen a seal basking on the surface of the ice, heard one breathing nearby, or because its amazing sense of smell confirmed a place where a seal breathed recently. Seals have strong fishy breath which likely leaves a trace on the snow or ice and it appears that a bear can tell by smell that a seal breathed there recently. Because of the constant threat of predation, ringed seals usually have a choice of several breathing holes or different locations along leads or in pools of open water where they may breathe. During our long-term observations at Radstock Bay, we observed that ringed seals often breathe several times at the same place but then move to another, presumably to make their movements less predictable to a bear. Sometimes, when a bear passed a spot soon after we knew a seal had just been there, it stopped to hunt, apparently recognizing a place where there might be an improved chance a seal

at their tracks in the snow, and talking to Inuit hunters and other scientists, nothing provided more insight that simply watching undisturbed bears hunt, 24 hours a day, for weeks at a time. I used to term this as just sitting back, watching, and letting the animals tell you about themselves, in their own time. At Radstock Bay (Figure 8), more than anywhere else, we developed an understanding of how bears used sea ice, what they cued on, how long it took to catch a single seal, how many different sorts of hunting patterns there were, the importance of scavenging, and a host of other things that, together, make up the life of a free-ranging wild polar bear.

Hunting seals on the sea ice in summer

In summer, prior to break-up, bears wander along leads or across broken pack ice, looking for a seal hauled out on the sea ice or at breathing holes, until they identify a place worth trying to hunt. Their great heads swing gently from side to side as they walk, giving the completely misleading

might surface to breathe once more before moving on to another location. Prior to actually watching bears choose a place to hunt in this manner, we were often quite baffled when we came along in a helicopter and saw a bear lying hunting at what appeared to us to be a very unlikely spot such as along the edge of a wide lead.

Polar bears apply variations on two fundamental methods when hunting seals on the sea ice in late spring or early summer, prior to break-up:

stalking and still-hunting. The best-known method, and certainly the most exciting to watch, is the stalking of a seal hauled out on the surface when both the bear and its intended prey are fully visible. Stalking is usually only seen when the weather is above freezing and seals haul up to bask on the surface of the ice. A bear's planning for a stalk begins when it first notices a seal lying on the ice, usually at a distance of a few hundred metres. Instantly the lackadaisical ambling stops

A polar bear scavenging a beluga carcass. The cause of the whale's death was unknown.
(© Mark Freedman)

and the bear freezes, sometimes in mid-step like a bird dog on point. It stands motionless, peering intently at the seal. Sometimes it will stand for several minutes, apparently evaluating how to get close enough to make a final charge. Once the bear begins to stalk the seal, it lowers its head and walks slowly and steadily in as straight a line as possible toward the seal, sometimes in a semi-crouched position as it gets closer. Ringed seals are normally on high alert when basking on the ice and constantly raise their heads to look around for predators. When an Inuk hunter is stalking a seal, if it raises its head, the hunter will remain motionless until the seal puts its head down again. Curiously, a polar bear doesn't do that. It simply keeps slowly but steadily moving toward the seal in as straight a line as possible, while holding its head low, a posture which probably makes its dark nose and eyes less visible. When the bear gets within about 30-40 m (100-130 ft) from its prey,

it suddenly charges, at quite incredible speed, while the horrified ringed seal bolts for its hole in complete panic. Ringed seals usually haul out alone at a breathing hole. It is easy to see why. If there are more than two seals by a single breathing hole, which is sometimes the case in the late spring when a female may still be accompanied by her pup, they can get in each other's way when trying to escape a charging bear. This gives the polar bear the split-second advantage it needs to get its claws or teeth into one of them. After grabbing a seal, the bear bites its head many times rapidly before dragging the carcass away from the hole, sometimes 100 metres or more (330+ ft), before beginning to eat it. This behaviour ensures both that the seal is truly dead and that it cannot possibly escape back into the water.

A few bears specialize in what I have called the aquatic stalk. Like the bears that stalk seals across the surface of the ice, they seem to memorize the route to the seal before they slip into the water. There are two kinds of aquatic stalk. In one, the bears dive and swim underwater between holes in the ice or along the edge of an ice floe. They surface to breathe so stealthily that only the tip of the nose breaks the water between dives as the bear moves closer to the seal. The longest dive I timed between breathing holes was 72 seconds. Finally, the bear reaches the last available breathing hole before reaching the seal and slips out of sight again. After an eternity of suspense-filled seconds, the water in front of the seal explodes as the bear suddenly uses its powerful forelimbs to vault itself up onto the ice after its prey. Despite this imaginative approach, more

often than not the seal manages to evade the lethal claws and reach the water where it can easily outswim the bear. In one instance, I watched a bear stalk a bearded seal from a distance of over 300 m (985 ft), only to miss it by less than a metre in the last seconds. The seal may have seen him coming up through the water because it began to appear nervous as if it was already getting ready to dive off the ice as the bear surfaced. However, adult bearded seals are large and powerful, so most are probably capable of spinning and escaping once into the water, even if a bear has a partial hold on them.

I sometimes think about this type of aquatic stalking in relation to a question I was once asked

The bear lying still-hunting in this open area probably smelled that a seal had hauled out or breathed beside the ice edge.
(© Mark Freedman)

An adult female holding her head low as she stalks steadily toward a seal, using the walking stalk approach.
(© Ian Stirling)

by an Inuk hunter in northern Québec. He wanted to know if I had ever seen a "sea bear." When I asked what they looked like, he said they appeared the same as any other polar bear but they were such good hunters that they grew too huge and fat for their legs to still be able to support them as they walked on the ice. Thus, they had to remain in the water all the time, hunting along the edges of leads. There, according to the hunter, such a bear is apparently able to surface suddenly and seize an unsuspecting seal with its long forepaws. He told me sea bears are very dangerous and this was why one should not to camp close to the edge of the open water. With memories of many aquatic stalks in my mind, I assured him I would not.

Another type of aquatic stalk involves the use

of the water-filled channels that form on top of the sea ice as it melts during the summer. These channels are about 25-50 cm (1-1.5 ft) deep. Again, the bear stands and studies the route to its intended dinner before lying flat in the channel and sliding along almost completely out of sight. Occasionally, bears used channels so close to the base of the cliff below our camp that we could look straight down and clearly see the black snout and small dark eyes, barely above the surface of the water, as the bear silently slid along. Because the channels are usually fairly shallow, the bear propels itself with its paws and lower legs extended to the side, rather than underneath, in order to keep its profile as low as possible.

Several years ago, one adult female had a hilarious individual modification to using the aquatic

stalk in the channels of the summer sea ice. She lay with the front half of her body flat in the water, but kept her rear legs straight so that her whole rear end towered over the ice. From a distance, it looked like the seal was being stalked by a small iceberg! Curiously, this slow-moving white object did not appear to unduly alarm the seals, until it got very close. Several years later, I saw another bear exhibiting the same pattern of behaviour at Radstock Bay and wondered if it was the same female, or whether one of her cubs had learned the same inimitable technique from watching her mother.

One particular aquatic stalk will always stand out in my memory because of what it shows about the ability of a polar bear to remember a plan. It took place during the summer, about a kilometre from our camp on the top of the cliff so that through the telescope, we had a clear view of what happened. Like most other bears, this female was plodding across the ice, seemingly unaware of her surroundings. When she spotted the unmistakable dark outline of a seal lying on the ice, she froze instantly and, for several minutes,

A bear stealthily entering the water to begin swimming for an aquatic stalk. (© Jenny E. Ross)

A large polar bear completes a successful aquatic stalk on a bearded seal in this four-part sequence.
© Stefan Lundgren

peered intently at the maze of channels in the ice that led toward her quarry. Then she lowered herself into the water and glided silently off in the direction of her quarry. About halfway to the seal, she came to a fork in the channel. The left-hand channel headed toward the seal while the one on the right slowly veered away. She paused for a moment and started up the wrong channel for about a body length, and then stopped. Without lifting her head to check her bearings, she slowly backed up and headed off again along the correct channel. I was astonished.

I have seen several bears lift their heads slightly to check their bearings but I have never seen such a demonstration of conscious memory. It reminded me of my old friend, the late Jimmy Memorana, an exceptionally knowledgeable Inuk polar bear hunter from Holman. "Keep looking around when you are working on the sea ice," he once told me in his usual patient manner. "Because, if the bear is hunting, you won't see him until he comes for you."

One of the most recurrent legends about hunting polar bears is that they will cover their give-

away black nose with a paw when stalking a seal. None of the Inuk hunters who have mentioned this to me has actually seen it themselves but the story exists in the oral history of several areas. Peter Freuchen, the famous Danish explorer (and even more famous storyteller!) claimed to have seen a bear cover its nose with a paw, as did the arctic physiologist Kare Rodahl on the coast of East Greenland in 1939-40. Perhaps. All I can say is that in several thousand hours of watching polar bears hunt, no one in my group has ever seen a hunting polar bear cover its nose. If it does

happen, it certainly is not very common.

In areas such as Hudson Bay, Foxe Basin, or the eastern coast of Baffin Island, the sea ice melts completely in late summer, which forces bears to retreat to land while waiting for the sea to refreeze. In general, it seems that very little successful hunting of seals goes on at this time since ringed seals rarely haul out on land, and they are far more agile swimmers in water than polar bears. However, young bearded seals sometimes rest on sand bars near the mouths of rivers and harbour seals may rest on rocks along the

An adult bear sliding into a shallow water channel on the surface of the melting sea ice to begin an aquatic stalk. Note the small toe-prints behind the bear showing how it has been pushing itself along on its belly to keep a low profile as it enters the channel.
(© Jenny E. Ross)

coast or in rivers, where bears are occasionally able to capture them.

Hunting seals in the open water

There is one very interesting, though quite unusual, observation of a bear catching a seal in the open water. In August 1978, Don Furnell, a biologist from the Northwest Territories Wildlife Service, and David Oolooyuk, an Inuk hunter, were watching a large adult male polar bear swimming in relatively shallow water near the shoreline of Wager Bay in northwestern Hudson Bay. About 75 m (245 ft) away, a ringed seal appeared to be alternating between diving to feed and surfacing between dives near the same location each time it needed to breathe. The bear swam toward where the seal was surfacing.

When the seal came up for a breath, the bear lay motionless in the water. Finally the seal came up only half a metre away; close enough for the bear to lunge, bite it firmly in the back, and take it to shore to feed on it. A few days later they saw a large male swimming with a dead seal in its mouth though they could not confirm if was the same bear or if it had killed the seal it had with it. They speculated that a seal might surface near a motionless bear in the water because its colour made the seal think it was just a piece of ice. This is plausible. It is well known to both Inuk hunters and biologists that seals are often attracted to pieces of ice during the open water season, probably because seals feed on the invertebrates and small fish that live in the channels in the undersurface of the ice. Seals will also

often use a small piece of ice to haul out on and rest. Furnell and Oolooyuk did not know if more than one bear was hunting this way but they reported seeing a small number of other fresh seal carcasses along the beach., and it is well known that bears are quick to learn from both their own experiences and by observing other bears. Possibly, this specialized hunting behaviour may have been learned by a small number of other bears and was practiced in the local area. Even so, considering how many people frequent coastal regions throughout the Arctic for extended periods every summer, the paucity of similar reports suggests that successful hunting by polar bears in open water is rare.

Still-hunting in summer

After the snow has melted from the surface of the ice sufficiently for seal breathing holes, and narrow leads in the ice to no longer be hidden, the polar bears' main hunting technique what we call "still-hunting": the bear sits, stands, or lies motionless beside a breathing hole or at the edge of a lead while waiting for a seal to surface to breathe. Of these three approaches, lying still-hunting is by far the most extensively during summer, about 80% of the hunting is done this way, probably because the bear expends a minimum of energy while waiting for its prey. However, it was only after we had spent considerable amount of time watching bears hunting that we

An adult female doing an aquatic stalk in a shallow channel in summer sea ice. (© Ian Stirling)

realized this was the main method of hunting. Early explorers and naturalists who wrote the first anecdotal accounts of polar bear life history may have thought a distant bear lying on the ice was just sleeping, when in fact, it was actively hunting in the most efficient manner. Thus, it is probably not surprising that the spectacular nature of a stalking hunt, complete with the last-minute charge, was the most common type of hunting to be described in early written accounts and that the lying-still method was largely overlooked.

A young bear investigates a seal breathing hole that has been exposed by melting of the covering layer of snow. (© David Shaw Wildlife)

The most usual position for still-hunting is to lie on the stomach and chest with the chin close to the edge of the ice or the lip of a breathing hole. It is essential to be absolutely motionless when hunting at breathing holes. Seals are easily frightened and will go somewhere else to breathe if they hear anything at the surface. I have tested the transmission of noise through the snow-covered ice myself by putting a hydrophone in the water through a seal breathing hole and then making a graded series of disturbances. Even the slightest movement of my boat on the snow or surface of the ice immediately transmits a loud crunching or scratchy noise into the water. The sound of a person (or a polar bear) walking can be heard clearly up to 400 m (1,300 ft) away. No wonder a polar bear must remain so still!

Most still-hunts are less than an hour long although some may last for several hours, another

reason why most bears prefer to save energy by lying down comfortably wherein they are less likely to make unintended noise. Another possible advantage to lying down may be that that posture presents the lowest silhouette against the sky (when viewed from below by a seal).

When a seal surfaces to breathe, the scene of peace and tranquillity instantaneously becomes one of action. In a single movement, the bear seizes the seal's head or upper body in its teeth, flipping it out on the ice, where it wriggles about much like a trout just pulled out of a stream. The bear then bites the seal many times about the head and neck and carries or drags it several metres, or sometimes several hundred metres, away from the edge of the water before starting to eat.

Seal hunting in winter and spring before the snow melts

During the cold weather, few seals haul out on the ice, so almost all of the hunting is done by still-hunting: waiting for the seal to come to the bear. Wherever there is open water, seals will surface to breathe. Seals continue to breathe at cracks in the ice for as long as possible before these freeze over because it is easier, doesn't require the use of additional energy, and doesn't restrict their movements as much. After the ice freezes, the seals must keep their breathing holes open

Most bears quickly move a freshly killed seal away from its breathing hole to ensure no possibility of escape.
(© Sue Flood)

Clockwise from top left Ringed seal breathing holes in freshly formed ice, made by simply pushing a head through it.

Bug the seal dog sniffs out a breathing hole that was hidden by a shallow snow drift.

A snow drift over a breathing hole, deep enough for a ringed seal to dig a birth lair that was later dug out (unsuccessfully) by a polar bear.

Sometimes a seal will make its breathing hole and birth lair under an arch of buckled ice to give its pup additional protection. (© Ian Stirling)

themselves for the rest of the winter. When the ice is young and thin, a seal can just push up through it with its head. These holes are fairly exposed and easily accessible to the bears, so, not surprisingly, freshly frozen narrow leads with new breathing holes present a highly desirable situation for seal hunting. As the winter progresses and the remaining cracks freeze, the seals' movements are restricted to the area around the breathing holes which they maintain themselves by scratching the ice with the heavy claws on their foreflippers. In time, drifting snow accumulates over the cracks and pressure ridges, removing all sign of the breathing hole location. Later in the winter,

when the drifts over the breathing holes deepen and the wind hardens the snow on the surface, some ringed seals excavate small lairs, like little snow caves, to rest in above their breathing holes. In the spring, the pregnant females use these subnivean (beneath the snow) haul-out lairs to give birth to their pups, out of sight of the ever-present polar bears.

In the winter and early spring, the cold white surface of the arctic sea ice appears as lifeless as any desert one might imagine. Snowdrifts accumulate along the edges of the long pressure ridges of jagged ice that zigzag across the horizon. No seals are to be seen. Only the occasional track of

POLAR BEARS: The Natural History of a Threatened Species

a polar bear or an arctic fox reminds you that animals are even present. Even so, life is abundant if you know where to look. For a bear, though, looking is less effective than sniffing. The polar bear's extraordinary sense of smell enables it to locate ringed seal breathing holes beneath the snow from over a kilometre away upwind, although, initially, we had no idea of how impressive its ability was.

As a polar bear plods steadily across the ice, it appears oblivious to the possibility of anything else being about. Yet the bear constantly sniffs the wind as it walks. Occasionally, it stops to look about or check again for some scent it might have just caught briefly.

By the time the behaviour of a bear walking over the sea ice changes sufficiently for a human observer to notice that it has decided to investigate something, the hunter is usually only about 50-100 m (164 to 328 ft) from the point of interest. At first I thought that this distance indicated how far away a bear could detect a breathing hole under the snow and, in comparison to how poorly a human's sense of smell is developed, I was quite impressed. Then I was fortunate enough to collaborate in some studies on ringed seal birth lairs with my long-time colleague, the arctic seal biologist Tom Smith, and his incredible dog, Bug. Along with the late Jimmy Memorana, who was a walking encyclopedia of life on the sea ice, we wanted to study the relative importance of different types of ice and snow drifts used by seals. This, we thought, would help us to better understand the hunting behaviour of polar bears and how they selected habitat for hunting. Equally important, we were being asked to evaluate the importance of different sea ice habitat types for seals in order to determine how various industrial activities, such as offshore drilling in ice-covered waters or year-round shipping, might take place with minimal negative impact. At the time, no one had any idea how one might even approach such an intimidating problem in a quantitative fashion. At Jimmy's suggestion, we used a frozen seal pup that

had been killed but not eaten, by a bear, to train Bug to sniff out seals, "...like the old people used to do long ago," Jimmy said. Bug was an exceptionally intelligent and motivated Labrador retriever, so we told her the frozen seal pup was a bird, hid it in snow drifts, and then sent her off to find it. She caught on almost instantaneously. Soon, at the cry of "Go find those birds!" she tore off across the sea ice, sniffing out seal lairs and breathing holes all over the place. We were aston-

Tom Smith digs out a large ringed seal birth lair buried under half a metre of hard wind-blown snow. The extra time taken by a bear to break into such a lair allows time for the occupants to escape.
(© Ian Stirling)

ished at how many structures she found so quickly, often in relatively small areas. But most impressive of all were some of the distances at which she could smell things. Bug could detect a seal breathing hole under a m (3 ft) of snow, from a carefully measured distance of a kilometre or more! We were astonished.

I am sure that a polar bear's sense of smell, on which it depends for survival, has evolved to be at least as good as that of a Labrador retriever. The realization of how far away the dog could detect seals made it clear to us that a bear we observed as it casually walked over the sea ice, periodically testing the wind but giving no indi-

cation of being aware of anything in particular, was being anything but casual. From working with Bug, it became apparent that any bear on the sea ice must be checking a veritable smorgasbord of smells indicating breathing holes, abandoned lairs, and lairs being actively used by tasty seal pups. Although we could not tell from just watching the bears what cues they were using, it was clear they were being highly selective about exactly where they were going to hunt.

In the cold weather of late winter and early spring, most still-hunting is done by standing rather than lying down. Once a bear chooses a place to hunt, usually by smell, it creeps up slowly and stealthily to the chosen spot. Then it stands absolutely still with the toes of its hind feet closer to the heels of its front feet than would normally be the case if it was just standing somewhere. Sometimes, a bear in this posture may give the impression it is about to defecate. However, this slightly odd-looking posture appears to allow the bear to shift its weight back onto its hind feet without moving them, which would transmit sounds through the snow to a seal below. Thus, when the bear hears or smells a seal beneath the snow, it slowly takes the weight of its body on its hind legs while raising its massive forelimbs above its head momentarily before crashing down with its front paws to try to break into whatever lies beneath the snow. Sometimes the snow has become so hardened by the winter wind that even a very large bear must pound down with its full

A large male pauses to sniff the small drift ahead of him while he decides whether to hunt there or not.
(© Mats Forsberg)

An Inuk hunter in Greenland poses in traditional seal-hunting clothing, polar bear pants, seal-skin (waterproof) boots, caribou parka, and harpoon.
(© Sue Flood)

at all in breaking into a lair, it is empty by the time the bear's head can enter, which illustrates how critical the protection of a hard snow roof over the subnivean lair can be to the survival of the seals inside, and of pups in particular.

Although accounts of seal hunting in the journals of explorers and many of the early naturalists tended to focus on the stalking of seals by bears, it is clear that the Inuit hunters of long ago were more observant. In fact, they must have watched polar bears hunting seals in a variety of circumstances because several of the methods they developed for hunting seals appear to be a direct copy. The journals of explorers such as Charles Francis Hall contain vivid accounts of hunters standing motionless with a spear over a seal breathing hole for many hours in freezing temperatures in wait of a seal. It is well known to hunters that if a lair has been broken into, a seal will realize there is more light shining down into the water through the breathing hole and not surface to breathe. Once a hunter cleared the drifted snow over a breathing hole well enough to be able to harpoon a surfacing seal, he would then cover the opening with a piece of snow to keep out the light, leaving a tiny hole stuffed with a feather or a small stick. If the feather moved, it was because a seal had surfaced and breathed out, so the hunter knew exactly when to thrust his harpoon. To keep his feet warm, and thus minimize making noise during hunts that might last for many hours, the hunter would sometimes stand on a piece of polar bear fur. It also seems likely that watching polar bears stalking seals across open expanses of ice gave Inuk hunters the idea of making a screen of white cloth to hold in front of themselves. There is no way of knowing if such speculations are correct but when one thinks about how an Inuk hunter's very survival depended on his ability to notice anything that might help him be successful, it is entirely plausible they learned a lot about seal hunting from polar bears.

Polar bears break into seal lairs, right over the

body weight on its forepaws several times in rapid succession, and dig furiously, in an attempt to break through quickly enough to capture the occupant of the breathing hole or haul-out lair before it escapes. Sometimes a bear is successful at breaking through the snow on its first try, but more often it takes several smashes to penetrate the hard surface of the snow. If there is any delay

breathing hole. Sometimes, if a bear catches a very young pup with little body fat, it will kill but not eat it. One of the most fascinating things I have seen a hunting bear do (but only occasionally) when it breaks into a birth lair in a deep snowdrift, is go head-first down the hole. Sometimes the bear will still hunt for long enough in this manner to leave a clear imprint of his forearms and chin in the snow beside the breathing hole. It appears that such behaviour may prevent the sunlight from shining onto breathing hole. Inuk hunters have told me this practice may make the ever-cautious ringed seal mother think its lair is still intact and safe to return to. Sometimes, a female may come back for a quick check on her pup and gets caught. Nursing female seals are much fatter than their pups and provide much more nutrition for a polar bear.

Inuit of earlier times may have learned another quite specialized seal hunting method from the polar bear. I had the opportunity a few years ago to watch some of this now-disappearing form of hunting practiced by an expert. I was working along the coast of southeastern Baffin Island with Tom Smith and an Inuk hunter named Ipeelie Inookie. It was late in the spring and warm, so if one looked carefully along the line of a snow drift, a slight depression could sometimes be detected, indicating the sagging roof over a seal birth lair. Ipeelie approached the drift slowly, like a stalking polar bear, then took a short run and jumped. After smashing through the roof of the lair with his feet, Inookie then quickly dove in headfirst to try and seize the seal pup. If successful, he then dangled the pup in the water on a rope in case the mother came back to check on it. This method of hunting reminded me very much of a polar bear doing much the same thing, as described above.

Sometimes if a bear kills a pup and it has no fat, it will simply leave most of the carcass and hunt at the birth lair for the adult female.
(© Ian Stirling)

still-hunt. That is the signal for the cubs to lie down immediately and not move until she is finished. Usually the cubs are quite well behaved and wait patiently, but some get bored, or maybe just curious, and approach her before she is finished. When there are two cubs, it is not uncommon for them to get distracted after waiting a while and begin to play. Usually, one cub initiates things by biting or pushing its sibling, who promptly responds. Soon the two are biting, rolling over, and chasing each other back and forth across the ice. In the summer, they seem to particularly like to run through shallow pools of melt water on the ice surface. If the cubs disrupt their mother's hunt by running about or playing and chasing each other, she may show her displeasure with a sharp cuff or two, after which the cubs are on much better behaviour... for a while anyway.

The cubs eventually learn to watch their mother's every move intently and investigate any site where she hunted, whether she was successful or not, and trying to imitate her behaviour. Even so, by eighteen months of age, they still do very little actual hunting. The duration of their hunts is much shorter than that of an adult bear, and only rarely do they catch a seal. When they do, it is usually a newly weaned ringed seal pup that has not yet learned how to avoid a polar bear.

The intense interest shown by one cub in her mother's hunting was quite comical. Its mother was a master of the aquatic stalk. She would flatten herself into a water channel in the ice and then painstakingly push herself toward the seal, keeping her profile as low as possible. Meanwhile her cub stealthily stalked along with its head down, a few metres behind her, watching her every move intently, but in plain view of every seal she stalked. Needless to say, the seals went down their holes long before they were in any danger and the mother didn't appear to catch on to the fact she was being so visibly shadowed.

Sometimes single cubs get tired of waiting as well. One yearling cub I watched was particularly energetic. Often after a relatively short waiting

Learning to hunt

Polar bear cubs remain with their mothers for two and a half years, watching her hunt thousands of times in a wide variety circumstances in all seasons. Like most predators, a cub's initial learning comes first from watching its mother and later by imitating her behaviour. Cubs-of-the-year do almost no hunting during the first spring and summer after leaving the maternity den. Instead, they follow closely behind their mother, watching everything she does, and sniffing about curiously in all the same places. She trains them to instantly recognize a change in her behaviour when she spots a seal to a stalk or a place to lie down and

This polar bear broke into a seal lair and is using its body to block out sunlight while it continues to still-hunt at the breathing hole.
(© Mats Forsberg)

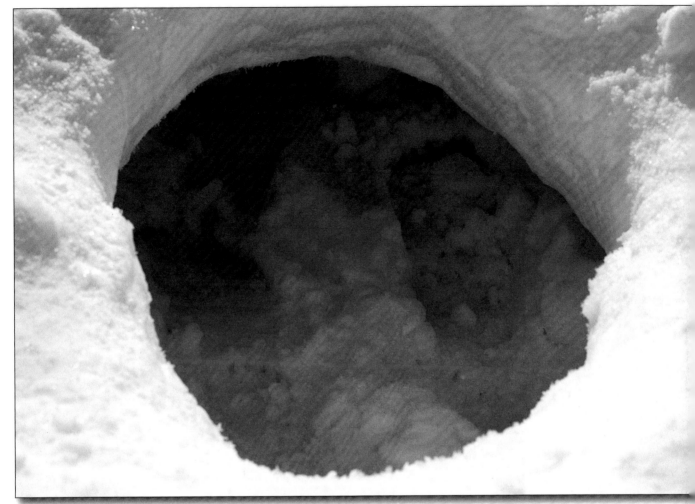

time, he amused himself by making long running leaps headfirst into melt pools in the ice, resulting in some quite spectacular splashes. Once, (I was watching him closely through the telescope), just as he was actually flying through the air toward the water, a seal popped up right in front of him and practically put its head into the bear's mouth. The startled yearling grabbed it by the head, pulled it out on the ice, and killed it. Instead of beginning to eat his kill immediately like most bears, he raced about on the ice with the carcass, throwing it up in the air and then running after it. Then he began to throw it into the water, diving in, and retrieving it. Finally the yearling's mother looked over, saw the seal, and raced over to begin eating it immediately. From the small size of the seal, it was clearly a recently weaned

pup, only a few months old, and not very wise about predators. No adult seal would have surfaced anywhere near where the cub was galloping around so energetically. The abundance of these fat but naive young seals in the late spring and summer is extremely important to young bears as they learn to hunt for themselves.

Yearling and two-year-old cubs hunt about 4% and 7% of the time respectively, while their mothers spend from 35-50% of their total time hunting. The yearlings we observed caught only one seal per 22 days of hunting, while their mothers caught one every four to five days in summer and one every two to three days in April and May. Even though two-year-olds did not hunt very much, they caught an average of one seal every five to six days when hunting in July, after they

The inside of a birth lair where a bear has been still-hunting while blocking the light with its body. Note the imprint of both forearms on the floor of the lair, claw marks visible on the right, and imprint near the top of image where the bear's chin rested in the snow near the edge of the breathing hole (not visible). (© Ian Stirling)

An Inuk hunter dangles a seal pup in the water of a former birth lair to try to attract the mother back. The same technique, used at intact birth lairs, was probably originally learned from watching polar bears kill a young pup, not eat it, and stay hunting at the lair.
(© Ian Stirling)

hunt when the female lies down to still-hunt, they do likewise, more less where they were standing when the female stopped moving. There is little independence of choice involved in picking a hunting site. By contrast, two-year-old cubs still with their mothers follow behind them up to 1-2 km (0.6-1.2 mi) and choosing their hunting sites independently. By the time a cub is two and a half years old, it has learned to hunt reasonably well but does not appear to be motivated to spend a large amount of time practicing, possibly because its mother is still supplying it with food. More simply put, the cub is probably lazy. During the early spring, yearlings and two-year-olds do almost no hunting. They are likely just too small and light to be able to break through a hard snowdrift fast enough to catch a seal. Part of the reason polar bear cubs remain with their mothers for so long may be that they need extra time to grow large enough to hunt successfully during the winter and early spring.

Feeding behaviour

Immediately after a polar bear captures a seal, it drags the prey away from the edge of the water, bites it several times about the head and the neck to make sure it is dead, and usually drags it several more metres from the water. Sometimes a bear may drag its kill several hundred metres away before starting to consume it. The bear that killed the seal then begins to eat it immediately, holding the carcass down with a forepaw, biting into the body, and then ripping upwards. Initially it rips pieces off and swallows them with a minimum of chewing. This rapid and voracious initial feeding is important because whenever a bear kills a seal, any other bears downwind will soon catch the scent and come to investigate. Adult males are particularly quick to approach the kill of another bear as the chance is good of being able to take it away and get a free meal—a fact which underscores how important it is for a younger bear, or a female with cubs, to eat as much as possible, as fast as possible. Subadults

had been weaned and become independent, indicating they had learned a great deal more during the additional year of tutelage.

Another factor which probably influences the number of seals killed by cubs of different ages is the way in which they choose places to hunt. Cubs-of-the-year and yearlings tend to stay close behind their mother, watch her movements closely, and imitate them. If these younger cubs

may also investigate a kill quickly but it appears they usually approach to see if there might be a chance to do a bit of scavenging. When the seal is small, and the bear that killed it is adult, there will not be much left over for subadult scavengers, who if they attempt to get too close, are quickly threatened and chased off.

When the kill is a ringed seal, skin and fat are eaten first and sometimes in a very exacting manner. Fat is the preferred part of the seal but the skin is fairly thin and easily devoured along with the fat. As the meal progresses and most of the skin is gone, one can sometimes see the bear delicately using its incisor teeth, almost like shears, to snip away fat lying over the torso while taking a minimum of meat. Bearded seal skin, however, is thick and apparently not as appetizing to most bears. Often, it is peeled away from the fat but not much is eaten. Near the west coast of Banks Island, I once found the complete hide of a bearded seal, which had been totally removed from the carcass and spread out hair-side down on the ice. All the fat had been shaved away as neatly as if a hunter's wife had done it with her ulu (a special crescent-shaped skinning knife, with the handle positioned like a "T" above the middle of its curve, used only by women).

Polar bears are incredibly clean animals and washing is an integral part of their feeding behaviour. In the summer, after an initial feeding period

Two cubs get tired of waiting while their mother hunts so they start playing and imitating some of her hunting behaviour.
(© Jenny E. Ross)

Two four-month-old cubs sit motionless as their mother hunts for a ringed seal pup in its birth lair and disappears beneath the snow with only her feet showing. (© Per Michelsen)

of 20 to 30 minutes, a bear will normally go to a nearby melt pool where it will alternate between rinsing and licking its paws and muzzle. Most bears we watched washed for up to 15 minutes after finishing feeding. In the winter, when water isn't available, a bear substitutes by rubbing its head and in the snow and rolling about for several minutes at a time. Back in the days when bears fed at the Churchill dump, some became so dirty they looked more like black bears, so they periodically walked a kilometre to the bay to swim about until they were relatively clean again.

We have handled several thousand polar bears over the years and found very few to be dirty or to have any discernable odour. When one considers how greasy seal blubber is, that is quite a testimony to how clean polar bears like to be. If one comes across a bear that smells bad, which is very unusual, it is likely to be a sick animal, unable to keep itself clean.

When uninterrupted, a bear may feed for an hour or more. If the kill is small or the bear is large and hungry, it may eat most of the carcass, but usually there is some fat and meat remaining for scavengers. Unlike brown bears, polar bears do not cache the remains of their kills to feed upon later. Occasionally, they will make a few scratching motions in the snow, reminiscent of a dog burying a bone, but most bears simply depart the kill, leaving the remains on the ice. These carcasses are then scavenged by other bears, particularly subadults, which rely on this source of food while they are learning to hunt for themselves. During our long-term observations of individual bears at Radstock Bay, we were able to confirm that although a few bears returned to the site of their own recent kill to scavenge, such behaviour was not common. In the case of young bears, or

females with cubs that may have made the kill in the first place, not returning to the side may also reduce the risk of attack by a larger bear.

Scavenging and competition over kills

Scavenging provides an important source of nutrition for many polar bears, particularly subadults and newly weaned two-and-a-half-year-old cubs on their own for the first time. When a bear investigating a seal kill (or the remains of one smelled from a distance) finds a bear of similar size feeding on it, it probably will not fight. Bears are well armed with large teeth and short, sharp, strong claws, making the chance of mutual and serious damage from a non-essential fight too great. Instead, the two bears may threaten, or possibly bluff-charge each other once or twice, but ultimately end up feeding side by side, sometimes pulling on opposite ends until the carcass becomes severed. Each will then consume its own piece.

An adult female with cubs will usually avoid adult males on a kill, possibly because of the threat of predation on the cubs, although she may push a younger bear off its kill. If she has a kill and is approached by an adult male, she will usually leave rather than defend it. However, a female who has gone a long time without a kill may not be so easily dominated. One adult female I watched, accompanied by a two-and-a-half-year-old cub, met adult males double her size on two occasions while she was feeding on seals she had killed. In the first case, she had already been feeding for 78 minutes and simply left when the male appeared. She and the cub had probably eaten most of the seal already and the remains were not worth the risks involved with trying to defend it. We were able to keep her under continuous observation, and it was a full five days before she caught another seal, despite many attempts. Nine minutes later, a large adult male arrived and briskly walked toward the female and her cub as if he expected her to simply leave. This time however, rather than leave her

This partially eaten adult ringed seal illustrates how carefully the bear has removed the fat and skin only from the carcass. (© Ian Stirling)

While feeding, a bear often walks to a clean patch of snow or ice and rolls around to clean fat and blood from its fur.
(© Jenny E. Ross)

kill, the female charged the male. He lowered his head and charged to meet her. When they separated a few seconds later, she was bleeding freely from a wound on her right shoulder and the male was bleeding from his rib cage. The female then charged him again but he did not move. She stopped before reaching him whereupon he made a similar bluff charge. Again, they did not come into contact. After standing looking at each other for about another 30 seconds, the male, the female, and her cub all began to feed on the carcass together. After 21 minutes of feeding, the female and cub left to wash in a nearby pool. When they returned to the carcass, the male chased them away and continued feeding. Meanwhile, a subadult arrived and circled cautiously, waiting for an opportunity to scavenge. After a few more minutes, the male stopped feeding to go and wash. The cub then approached the carcass. The male turned and ran toward the cub, at which

point the female charged him again. He retreated and then all three bears fed on the carcass again. Finally, the female and cub departed. After a while, they lay down while the cub licked the female's wound. When the male finished feeding, he followed the female and cub but she would not let him get close. After two hours of steadily following her, he went off in another direction.

A side benefit to remains of polar bear kills on the ice

Another well-known scavenger of sea ice is the arctic fox. During the winter, fox tracks may be seen following polar bears for many km far out on the sea ice. Remains of most old kills are scavenged by arctic foxes and sometimes one will see a dozen or more of them at a time at one feed. The foxes are also not shy about trying to help themselves before the bear is finished. As bits and pieces of seal meat begin to be spread about on the ice, foxes dart in to share the booty. During the summer near land in places like Radstock Bay, foxes venture out on the ice to scavenge as well and take pieces back to their pups in nearby dens. In summer they must compete with birds like glaucous and ivory gulls, which, like vultures, land within minutes after a seal is killed. Usually, the bears ignore the foxes but occasionally one will make a short charge at a particularly audacious animal that is trying to help itself too soon.

Efficiency of polar bears hunting ringed seals

From our small observation cabins at Radstock Bay, we were able to watch polar bears of all ages and sex classes hunting ringed seals for extended periods, sometimes for several 24-hour periods in a row when the weather cooperated and the bears

didn't disappear around a distant corner. That made it possible to document the durations of hunts, the methods used, and the success rates of bears of different ages and sex classes through the two most important periods of the year, spring and early summer. During spring (April and May), the windblown winter snow drifts are still hard and the ringed seal pups are born into their hidden subnivean birth lairs where they are nursed, and accumulate fat, for about six weeks. Leads, if there are any, and the floe edge are very important hunting sites because subadult and older seals concentrate in these areas where they can breathe, and are accessible to hunting bears. By summer (late June and July), the snow is melted, leaving bare ice, many leads, and melt holes of various sizes. Seals haul out on the ice in large numbers, especially around old breathing

Instead of fighting and risking injury, two bears of similar size pull a seal carcass apart so each has a piece to feed on.
(© Norbert Rosing)

An arctic fox scavenges on the remains of a ringed seal carcass.
(© Mats Forsberg)

holes and narrow leads, to bask and moult. There are many fat, recently weaned, young ringed seal pups that are not yet as wise as adults about predators. After the ice breaks up and melts by late July or early August, the seals become pelagic and largely unavailable until after freeze-up in late October or early November.

Even at the best time of year for hunting, the long-term capture rate, averaged over bears of all ages and sex classes was three full 24-hour days in spring and over five days in summer just to catch one seal, and this was in an area that has one of the highest densities of ringed seals anywhere in the Canadian Arctic (Table 2). While the rates in summer were fairly similar between years, it is particularly interesting to note how

much variation there was in hunting success in spring. Although the long-term average was about three days of hunting per seal captured, the range was from 1.72 days to over 16. The astonishingly low kill rate in 1976 was not just an aberration of a small or unrepresentative sample size because the total accumulated observation time that spring was the second highest we recorded. Thus, it seems the very low capture rate suggests the possibility of either a reproductive failure (few pups born) that year, which we have documented a couple of times in other parts of the Arctic, or a large change in distribution in that area for that year alone, which seems less likely.

There was also considerable variation in the amount of time spent hunting by bears of different ages and sex classes in summer. Cubs of all ages, from a few months to two and a half years old, did almost no hunting at all in spring while adult females accompanied by cubs-of-the-year and yearlings hunted 18.5% and 19.6% of their time respectively and adult males about 24.7%. I suspect the young bears were still too light to be able to break through the roofs of the seal lairs. However, by summer, there was no covering of snow and the cubs of all ages began to hunt a bit more actively.

Table 3 summarizes some data on the amount of time that bears of different age and sex classes spent hunting during summer and the rates at which they captured seals. Not surprisingly, the cubs-of-the-year did very little hunting and, of course, caught no seals. Even yearlings and, two-year-olds spent only 4.3% and 7.3% of their time actually hunting in summer, though both were successful. (Mind you, the seal the yearling caught was the one referred to earlier that practically put its head in the yearling's mouth while it was diving in the water.) It is interesting to note that even though the amount of time two-year-olds spent hunting was a small percentage, they caught two seals and it only took them about 50% more time

An ivory gull scavenges on the remains of a ringed seal carcass. There is some concern that the high contaminant levels in seal fat may have a negative effect on some scavenging gulls.
(© Mats Forsberg)

A ringed seal lifts his head to look nervously over the ice for polar bears. (© Ian Stirling)

their mothers to be successful, which illustrates how much they learned and put into practice in the year since they were yearlings. The amount of time spent hunting by females accompanied by young is astonishing. Those with yearlings and two-year-olds hunted about 35% and 37% of their total time respectively, while females with cubs-of-the-year were over 50%. Clearly, the responsibility for providing both seals and milk to growing cubs places a high demand on a mother bear to spend a lot of time hunting. The need for females with cubs-of-the-year to hunt more than those with older cubs may relates to their need to continue to replenish body condition after ma-

ternity denning the previous winter, giving birth to cubs, and nursing them up to a size large enough to follow her onto the sea ice. When we capture females with cubs-of-the-year in spring, they are usually very lean. The mothers, besides providing milk to cubs that have the fastest growth rate of young polar bears of any age, are trying to replenish their own body condition as well. Adult males also lose a certain amount of condition because of the high rate of activity during the breeding season in spring (with an accompanying lower amount of time hunting at 25%). Thus, late spring and summer is also a vital time for large males to re-build body stores before the open water season of late summer and fall, followed closely by the cold temperatures and more difficult hunting conditions of winter.

For the various categories of bears, there are some similarities in the patterns of how much time they spend hunting and the duration of their still-hunts in summer (Table 4). Interestingly, the yearlings and two-year-olds are quite similar (20-25 minutes) and a third to a half shorter in time than their mothers (34-40 minutes) while adult males averaged about 68 minutes per hunt. There are probably several other factors that can be interpreted from these numbers. From Table 3, the highest kill rates were those of the females, mean-

ing that, on average, if a seal is going to surface where a bear has decided to hunt, most will do so within 40 min or so. It is also possible that hunts of females with cubs are shorter than those of adult males because their hunts are interrupted more often by cubs, or occasionally by approaching single bears.

One really only sees hunting by stalking on a regular basis in late spring and summer. This technique is infrequent before the weather warms up. Before that, it appears to be warmer for the seals to remain in the water. It is interesting to compare the relative effectiveness of the two methods. In one summer sample of 288 hunts,

Bearded seals will often haul out on the smallest floes possible in summer to reduce their risk of predation by polar bears. (© Ian Stirling)

TABLE 2. SUMMARY OF THE TOTAL NUMBER OF "BEAR DAYS" OF HUNTING FOR EACH RINGED SEAL CAPTURED AT RADSTOCK BAY, NUNAVUT, IN SPRING AND SUMMER

Month and Year	Number of bear days Of observation	Number of seals observed killed	Number of bear days hunting for each seal killed
April and May			
1975	38.81	12	3.23
1976	32.11	2	16.06
1977	13.42	5	2.68
1980	13.72	6	2.79
1990	27.53	16	1.72
Subtotal	**125.59**	**41**	**3.06**
Late June and July			
1973	25.04	5	5.01
1974-76	90.51	17	5.32
Subtotal	**115.55**	**22**	**5.25**

(Courtesy: Ian Stirling)

65 (22.6%) were done by stalking and 223 (77.4%) were by lying still-hunting and waiting for a seal to surface. The success rate was 1.5% for still hunts and 1.8% for stalking. No wonder it can take several days of hunting, even at the best of times, to catch a seal. Bears that use a lot of stalking are using more energy for a similar catch rate as those that still hunt, which, helps to explain why so many more hunts are done by waiting for the seal to come to the bear.

How polar bears have influenced the evolution of ringed seal behaviour

For hundreds of thousands of years, arctic seals have been hunted by land predators. The polar bear is the most recent, and likely the most important, but there have also been foxes, wolves,

TABLE 3. AMOUNT OF TIME SPENT HUNTING BY BEARS OF DIFFERENT AGE AND SEX CLASSES DURING SUMMER AND THE RATES AT WHICH THEY CAPTURED SEALS

Polar bear age and sex class	Total minutes of observation	Minutes spent hunting (% in brackets)	Number of kills made	Summer kill rate (days/kill)
Cubs of year (COY)	13,646	14 (0.1)	0	0
Yearling	31,133	1351 (4.3)	1	21.62
Two-year-old	15,733	1140 (7.3)	2	5.46
Adult female with COY	5,896	3,130 (53.1)	1	4.09
Adult female with yearling	23,401	8,222 (35.1)	8	2.03
Adult female with two-year-old	13,066	4,844 (37.1)	2	4.53
Adult male	27,462	10,952 (39.9)	3	6.35

(Courtesy: Ian Stirling)

probably a few grizzly bears, and in more recent time, indigenous humans. In contrast, the seals that occupy the same sort of habitat in the Antarctic have never had a predator on the surface of the ice.

The presence or absence of terrestrial predators has had a profound effect on the behaviour of seals, especially those that live on and under the landfast ice. The ringed seal of the Arctic is one of the smallest seals, averaging only about 60-70 kg (130-150 lb) while adult Weddell seals in the Antarctic regularly exceed 400 kg (880 lb). Both wean their pups in about six weeks, despite the large difference in body size.

Both must maintain their own breathing holes when the ice freezes in the winter. The ringed seal scratches the newly freezing ice with the heavy claws on its foreflippers; the Weddell seal abrades it with its large canine teeth. Both situate their breathing holes in the last cracks to freeze, but that is where the similarities end. Each ringed seal maintains three to four individual breathing holes. If it only had one, and a polar bear was waiting above it, the seal would face certain death when it had to surface to breathe. In contrast, several Weddell seals may share the maintenance of the same breathing hole. In an area where feeding is good, Weddell seals may have many breathing holes concentrated in a small area and several seals may haul out at a single hole. Ringed seals are widely distributed at low densities and, most

TABLE 4. AVERAGE LENGTH OF LYING "STILL HUNTS" DONE BY POLAR BEARS OF DIFFERENT AGE AND SEX CLASSES DURING SUMMER

Category of bear	Number of lying still hunts in sample	Average duration of hunts (in minutes)
Yearling	44	25.07
Two-year-old	49	20.20
Adult female with COY	61	36.52
Adult female with yearling	162	40.36
Adult female with two-year-old	115	33.52
Adult male	137	68.22

(Courtesy: Ian Stirling)

commonly, only one seal hauls out at a single hole. More seals at any hole means they may not all be able to escape a charging polar bear. Individual breathing holes are usually more than 200 m (650 ft) apart.

When ringed seals bask on the ice near a breathing hole, they appear restless, raising their heads every few seconds to look around for possible predators. They retreat to the water at the slightest disturbance. When Weddell seals haul out on the ice, they fall into a deep sleep and move so little that sometimes the outline of the seal's body becomes melted into the ice. Ringed seals almost never defecate onto the ice, probably because the odour would attract predators. Weddell seals commonly do so. In the open water season, if no ice is present, Weddell seals haul up on land to rest, since there are no terrestrial predators.

Ringed seals are born with a white coat for camouflage as protection from predation.
(© Mats Forsberg)

Ringed seals don't haul out on land at all but remain pelagic until the water freezes again, although there have been reports of ringed seals hauling out on land when a pod of marine hunting killer whales approached.

When Weddell seals haul out along a crack in the landfast ice, they appear to be willing to haul out anywhere, regardless of the width of the lead. If there is a choice, ringed seals choose to haul out on sections of the crack that are no wider than their bodies. This may protect them from being caught by a charging polar bear making a last second dive into a lead just as they were escaping.

The pressure of surface predators on arctic seals has been so great that in most species, the young are born with a white coat to camouflage

them from their enemies as they lie helpless on the ice. Antarctic seal pups are all born with dark coats. An interesting anomaly is the bearded seal of the Arctic, which gives birth to a pup with dark hair. However, there are white blotches on its head, back, and rear flippers, as though it were currently in the process of evolving a white coast for the pup.

In the landfast ice where ringed seals are born, the constant threat of predation by polar bears means that if pups were simply born onto the surface of the ice, they would be extremely vulnerable. The pups are hidden, however, in the small birth lairs dug in snowdrifts above the breathing holes. In fact, probably one of the main reasons that ringed seals have remained so small is so that

Newborn bearded seal pups have white patches on a dark coat at birth, as if they are evolving a protective white coat for camouflage.
(© Ian Stirling)

they can continue to use this unique habitat under the snowdrifts to provide some protection from polar bears while resting and giving birth to their pups. If ringed seals were larger, like harp or bearded seals, the snowdrifts in most places would simply not be deep enough to hide them and they would be vulnerable to much higher rates of predation, likely too high for them to continue to live and reproduce in the stable landfast ice.

Because ringed seals are so spread out under the ice, a territorial male can probably control access to no more than two or possibly three females in overlapping territories. The sex ratio of adult males to females is even. In contrast, one Weddell seal male can exclude his competitors from a single breathing hole when it is being used by several females and there are more adult females than males. In this case, polygyny can develop and the sex ratio in breeding areas is about six to eight females to one male.

Taken together, the differences described provide at least a partial explanation of how important the pressure of predation by polar bears has been in moulding the ecology and behaviour of the arctic seals.

Chapter 9

LIFE AND DEATH

As Charles Darwin pointed out in *The Origin of Species*, intense competition for survival is a daily fact of life. This is as true for polar bears today as it was when Darwin wrote it over 145 years ago, regardless of how tranquil the bears may appear. From the time that each year's crop of cubs leaves the den to begin life in the wind and snow of a cold arctic spring, weaker individuals

A young bear buries the remains of a seal kill in the snow.
(© Stefan Lundgren)

continue to fall by the wayside. Because most bears probably die out on the sea ice and their bodies sink to the bottom of the ocean, actual observations of dead polar bears, for which one could attribute the cause of death, are rare. However, like detectives, we can gain considerable insight by carefully sifting through the accumulated wealth of anecdotal and scientific information.

Mortality of cubs

For cubs, the struggle for existence begins immediately. Some cubs do not live long enough to leave the dens they were born in. A few are born dead or die shortly after birth. In years when productivity of ringed seals is low, so is survival of polar bear cubs born that year. However, polar bears have evolved to live a long time and produce cubs at a low but steady rate. That way, more than enough cubs are produced to replace the bears that die each year. Thus, over the life of a female, if the cubs produced over a few years do not survive, it is not detrimental to the long-term maintenance of the population. In fact, the survival of the adult females is paramount, so if a cub dies shortly after birth, the best strategy for the female to maximize her own survival is probably to eat

A 4-month-old cub that died en route to the sea ice with its mother after leaving the maternity den. The cause was unknown.
(© Doug Allan)

POLAR BEARS: Ecology and Conservation of a Threatened Species

A thin andult female that likely starved in the previous winter.
(© Sue Flood)

it. If she then mates again in spring, and produces another litter the next year when her condition or environmental circumstances may have improved, so will her chance of raising strong, healthy cubs.

Although strong enough to leave the den with their mothers, a few cubs are still too small and weak to compete with their siblings in the harsher environment outside. The mortality rate of cubs in their first year of life varies between 30% and 50% in different populations. This rate is even higher when ecological circumstances are diffi-

cult. The date that polar bear families leave their dens for the sea ice has probably evolved to coincide with the period when female ringed seals have their pups in birth lairs. These dens are located beneath the snow, over the seals' breathing holes. This seasonally abundant food supply greatly increases the female bears' chance of hunting successfully. In fact, this food supply is probably the most important, single, significant factor in determining the cubs' chances of survival in its first few months on the sea ice.

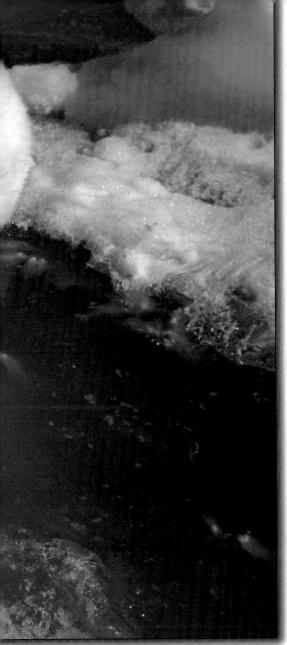

than Western and Southern Hudson Bay, where dens may be up to 80 km (50 mi) or more inland, families expend little energy returning to their hunting habitat.

Polar bears are also creatures of habit that have a high degree of fidelity to specific areas in different seasons. Females with cubs return in spring to places where they have hunted successfully before. However, shifts in the distribution of seals may take place between years, or the numbers of pups born may be greatly reduced, sometimes with dramatic consequences for newborn cubs. For example, in the spring of 1974, the production of pups in the eastern Beaufort Sea fell dramatically, probably by at least 80%, and some polar bears were threatened with starvation. We caught two emaciated adult females soon after they had left their dens. They had been unable to catch any seals and had simply lost their cubs. Another female had cubs with her that were so thin that one could barely walk. The following year, ringed seal pup production fell even lower and did not increase again for a year or two after that. As a result, bears of most age and sex classes were significantly lighter in 1974-75 than they were in 1971-73 and the survival of cubs born from 1974 to 1976 plummeted. Some of the adult females were in such poor condition that they failed to have cubs at all. The cohorts of cubs born from 1974 to 1976 survived poorly and, as a result, were underrepresented in the age structure of the population for a decade.

Occasionally we have been able to directly observe the effects of environmental variations at work. When females leave their maternity dens with their cubs to hunt seals on the sea ice, they have usually exhausted most of their stored fat reserves. Catching a seal soon after the family reaches the ice, or possibly finding the remains of a kill that can be scavenged, is critical to her survival, and the survival of her cubs. In most areas, the maternity dens are within a few km of the landfast ice along the coast. Thus, in areas other

Mortality of subadults

The most difficult period of a polar bear's life is probably between the first year after it is weaned and the age of two and a half years when it is forced to become independent. From then until they become successful adults at five or six years of age, they are subadults, the teenagers of the polar bear world, with polar-bear insecurities not unlike those associated with human adolescence. They are fairly inexperienced at hunting and do not kill seals as often as adults. Worse, when a subadult does make a kill, it has a significant chance of losing it to a bigger bear. I have often seen subadults forced off their own fresh kills. They were then reduced to scavenging sometime later on the scraps left by the dominant bear. Although we have caught a lot of healthy subadults over the years, we have not caught many really fat ones. In particular, younger animals often go into winter in poorer condition than adults; their greatest mortality factor is probably starvation. This is why such a high proportion of so-called problem bears that haunt human camps and garbage dumps are subadults. They are more likely to be thin and hungry.

It is unusual to find dead bears in nature, although I know of two subadults that died naturally. They were found tucked in behind pressure ridges in the spring, curled up in a ball and frozen solid the way they died. Autopsies showed them to be little more than skin and bone with no body fat, losers in the continuous and unforgiving struggle for survival.

Longevity of adults

Once polar bears reach maturity, they seem virtually immortal. Annual survivorship of adults in a healthy population exceeds 95%. Adults have no natural enemies, except humans and occasional predation by adult males. Mature bears have learned an efficient annual cycle of hunting, seasonal movements, and fasting in their home range; in other words, how to make a living there. The importance of this learning cannot be overemphasized, especially when one considers how different environmental conditions and the availability of different prey species can vary between areas, such as, for example, Western Hudson Bay, the Beaufort Sea, or Svalbard and the Barents Sea.

Survival is still a constant struggle, no matter how canny a bear may become. The battles between adult males for reproductive privileges produce scarred heads and broken teeth, providing strong testimony to the intensity of competition.

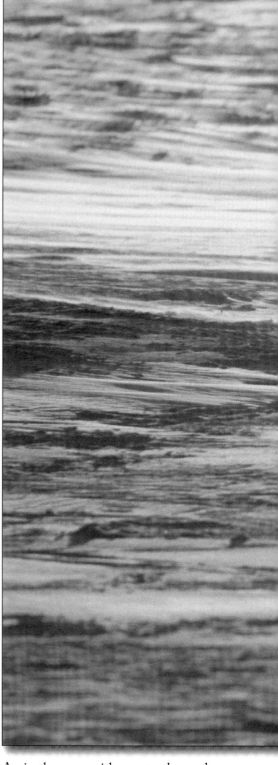

As is the case with most other polygamous species, the intense competition between adult males is probably the main reason they have a higher annual mortality rate than females. The

average age of adult bears in a healthy population is around 9 or 10. In general, only a relatively small proportion of them live past 20 years. Most adult females cease having cubs by their mid- to late 20s, although a few of these older bears manage a single cub.

The oldest polar bears we have found in the wild were both 32-year-old females. One was

An adult female attacks
an adult male to
protect her cub.
(© Dan Guravich/
PolarBearsInternational.org)

A healthy adult male cannibalises a yearling it has captured and killed.
(© Jenny E. Ross)

from the James Bay islands at the very southernmost part of their range. We don't have much information on these bears but there seems to be a relatively high proportion of old-timers. This may be because: they are relatively isolated from humans, they fast on the islands during the open water season, and, during the winter, they travel far out on the ice of Hudson and James Bays into areas that hunters seldom access. The oldest male we have from a wild population, aged 28 years, was also from James Bay.

I will never forget the other 32-year-old female. Tom Smith, his Labrador retriever Bug, and I were continuing our seemingly incessant search for seal breathing holes and birth lairs in different habitats all over the Arctic. This time, we were at Radstock Bay, on Devon Island, where we have made many of the behavioural observations on polar bears. It was mid-April, cold but clear with a light wind—beautiful weather for that time of year. I was climbing through some large pressure ridges close to the shoreline when I saw a polar bear lying in the snow about 2 m (6.5 ft) away. You don't stop to think at such moments, and in an instant, I was well out on the sea ice. At that point, I had time to think about what I had just seen. Something in my subconscious told me that the bear's behaviour in those pressure ridges was unusual. Also, it was strange that it had not stood up to peer out at us. Cautiously, I crept back into the ice blocks and drifted snow until I was only a few metres from the bear again.

She appeared small and at first I thought she was a subadult. Then she lifted her head and slowly looked in my direction, with eyes that no longer had the sparkle and alert intensity of a normal polar bear. She had a medium-sized frame but appeared small because much of the former muscle mass over her body had wasted away. Every bone pushed up under her hide, making it appear as if her hide had been draped over a skeleton. The hair over the worn muzzle was missing in a few places. Only then did I realize the bear was not a subadult. She was a very old adult female in the last stages of starving to death (dying of old age some might say). She could neither attack me nor try to escape. She couldn't even stand up.

Although I have seen thousands of polar bears and studied them for forty years, that moment was especially poignant. There, in an arctic snow drift, this ancient matriarch was ending her long, experience-rich life. Much of it had probably been spent within 160 km (100 mi) of where she now lay dying. I had probably watched her hunt seals and nurse her cubs on sunny summer days in better times. As she rested her head on the snow, I watched her quietly and thought about the life she must have led. Then I backed away quietly and left her to die undisturbed.

There was a blizzard the next day, and we couldn't find her carcass in the new snow drifts afterwards. We relocated her remains on the beach and collected her skull the following summer. When we determined her age from one of her teeth, we found she was 32 years old.

Although finding old polar bears in their last months of life is uncommon in most areas, we see one or two on the western coast of Hudson Bay each autumn. They are usually ancient males, fairly inactive, minding their own business, and largely ignored by other bears. Occasionally, these walking skeletons die on land and we find their remains curled up in a clump of willows or behind an esker along the beach. From the teeth we have aged, it appears that most are in their early to mid-twenties. Even so, the majority of these thin old males seem to survive long enough to make it back onto the ice, but we often don't see them after that. That we find so few old bears dead along the shoreline suggests to me that most die out on the sea ice in winter.

Polar bears enjoy a much longer life in captivity, than they do in the wild. The oldest polar bear I know of was a 42-year-old female named Debbie that died at the zoo in Winnipeg, Manitoba, in 2008. It had been captured as an orphaned cub in the Russian Arctic in 1966. Debbie was a full 10 years older than the oldest female I have personally encountered in the wild. She had six cubs that survived during her time in captivity. Another female in the London Zoo lived to the age of 41 and several females in other zoos live past 30 years. A male in the Milwaukee zoo reached 34, as did Debbie's companion Skipper, who died in 1999. At least 14 polar bears are known to have lived more than 30 years.

Considering that few wild female polar bears reproduce much after their early to mid-twenties, some of the ages at which captive females have had cubs are quite impressive. In 1935, a bear at the Milwaukee zoo gave birth to her last cub at 24 years. Katherine Latinen from the Detroit Zoological Park reported that females aged 34, 36, and 37 all gave birth to live cubs. The 36-year-old female successfully reared her cub while that of the 37-year-old died after about a day. The fact that bears in zoos appear to have a maximum longevity—about a third longer than their counterparts in the wild—gives us some insight into how much stress is involved with survival in the wild.

Cannibalism

In general, females with newborn cubs just out of the den tend to seek out habitat not favoured by adult males. Later however, they move into habitat that may be occupied by bears of all age and sex classes. Regardless, females with dependent cubs of all ages avoid contact with males whenever possible, probably because males sometimes kill and eat cubs. Males sometimes kill older bears as well, so, in general, smaller bears of all ages simply avoid large males. After several thousands of hours watching polar bears on the sea ice at Radstock Bay over a number of years, we have observed many encounters between single bears of different sizes and encounters between adult males and family groups. We have watched adult males follow these family groups, sometimes for hours at a time, without being able to get any closer than the female was willing to tolerate. However, we witnessed no predation, or direct attempts. Large adult males are well insulated, slow moving, and overheat quickly when they run. In comparison, young bears and females can run for longer periods without overheating. Thus, if a young bear can spot a male at any distance, it seems unlikely it would be caught. On the Hudson Bay coast in fall, females with cubs generally avoid males, but we have also seen instances where they attack and dominate males.

Occasionally, an adult male might surprise a family that is sleeping or feeding. Such an encounter can be dramatic. In such circumstances, the male is sometimes able to make a rush and capture a cub or yearling. When this happens, the female might try to defend the cub, risking death in the process. In two separate incidents during the open water season in the Canadian Arctic, adult males in good physical condition were found feeding on the fresh carcass of an adult female while her yearling cubs watched from a distance. In both cases, biologists thought the female had likely died in defence of her cubs. Unfortunately, in the last few years, polar bears have become nutritionally stressed in some populations, due to the negative effects of climate warming on sea ice. In these circumstances, sadly, cannibalism by large but thin males has become more frequent. This trend is discussed in greater detail in the chapter on climate warming.

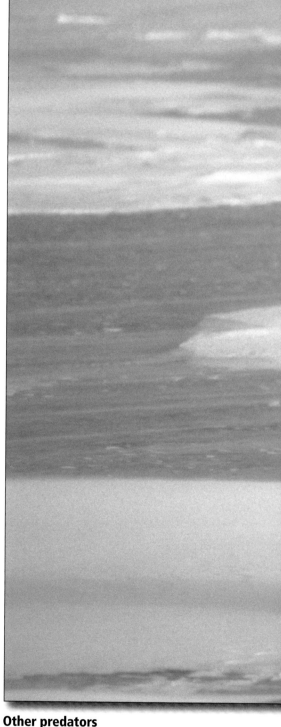

Other predators

I have stressed that polar bears are intelligent carnivores that learn things quickly and that each animal in fact is an individual with its own accumulated set of experiences and learned skills. Of course, this applies to other carnivores as well. In a few instances, wolves have learned

to prey on bear cubs of various species. In 1983, the late Malcolm Ramsay and I found evidence of a pack of wolves in the Churchill denning area that had learned to kill polar bear cubs when they were on their way to the sea ice from their maternity dens. Tracks in the snow revealed that some wolves would worry and dis-tract the mother while another seized a cub and apparently escaped with it. The cubs were devoured completely. In more recent years, wolf numbers appear to have increased since the area south of Churchill became a national park. Here, we have again seen tracks indicating predation of bear cubs by wolves. Evan Richardson

An adult female stands on her hind legs while nervously watching a nearby adult male. (© Dan Guravich/PolarBearsInternational.org)

An adult male walrus with the remains of a ringed seal he has almost finished eating.
(© Mats Forsberg)

also documented another instance of successful cub predation on sea ice just off the northwest coast of Banks Island in the Beaufort Sea.

In most areas, the distributions of polar bears and wolves do not overlap very much. However, where they do, some wolves are learning, to become successful predators of polar bear cubs, though it is probably not a common behaviour.

The significance of another arctic marine predator, the Greenland shark, is unknown but intriguing. These sharks are abundant around Svalbard, Iceland, and southern Baffin Island. One of the largest specimens measured was 6.4 m (21 ft) long and weighed 1,022 kg (2,250 lb) although the average range for adults is 3.5-5 m (11-16 ft). Although these sharks appear to feed primarily on fish, evidence of predation on seals has been confirmed in waters off shore from Baffin Island, Iceland, and Svalbard. In a recent study near Svalbard, led by Christian Lydersen from the Norwegian Polar Institute, the stomach contents of 45 sharks weighing between 136-700 kg (300-1,540 lb) were examined. Of these, 40% (18) had eaten seals, suggesting that although some may have been scavenged, others may have been actively preyed upon. Since it appears that seals can swim more quickly than sharks, the scientists speculated that since seals sleep soundly at the surface, the sharks may be able to stalk and catch them while they're asleep. That said, one shark caught near Iceland also had part of a polar bear leg in its stomach, though it is not known whether the shark killed the bear or scavenged on a carcass. It seems unlikely that a slow-swimming polar bear could outmanoeuvre a Greenland shark so, for the moment, whether or how often these sharks prey on swimming polar bears is an open question.

Although polar bears prey on young walruses both on land and ice as opportunity permits, the tables are turned in the water. Walruses can be very aggressive, especially when one has been wounded by a hunter. Some have even attacked small boats. It is not surprising then that there are a number of anecdotal accounts of bears that were suspected to have been killed, or received broken bones from walrus attacks in water.

I once watched a group of walruses mount a coordinated attack on a five-year-old female polar bear in the Dundas Island polynya in northern Nunavut. There were a few walruses hauled out around the edge of the polynya and as the bear approached each one, it retreated to the water. Suddenly, a group of about 20 walruses in the water charged toward her, churning up the water in the process. When almost at the ice edge, two large walruses at the front of the group suddenly made a rapid forward rolling motion and smacked their hind flippers on the water. The resultant sounds were like gun shots and immediately afterward, there were 45 walruses milling in the water. The bear immediately ran from the polynya as fast as it could until it was at least 100 m (328 ft) away. It then slowed down and continued to walk away until out of sight.

It is unknown how the walruses coordinated the attack, though the use of underwater vocalisations is most likely. However, it was clear they knew what the polar bear was and were prepared to attack from the water at least. Had the bear gone into the water, it would likely have been killed.

There is another linkage between the ecology and distribution of walrus and polar bears: male walruses prey on ringed seals and young bearded seals. Consequently, numbers of these seal species are low in areas frequented by walruses. Polar bears visit the small polynyas in the Canadian High Arctic and occasionally kill subadult walruses. However, the bears do not remain for long in areas where walruses are feeding, probably because there are usually few ringed or young bearded seals remaining in the immediate vicinity.

Chapter 10

THE POLAR BEAR CAPITAL OF THE WORLD

A yearling cub checks out his toes.
(© Daniel J. Cox/NaturalExposures.com)

The most famous polar bears in the world live in western Hudson Bay. Every fall, polar bears assemble along the coast only a few kilometres from the town of Churchill while they wait for the ice to re-freeze so they can return to hunting seals. Here, you can watch polar bears at fairly close distances in circumstances that are safe for both bears and people. Not surprisingly, several thousand visitors

A large adult male on the coast of Hudson Bay awaits freeze-up near Cape Churchill (© Robert and Carolyn Buchanan/ PolarBearsInternational.org)

POLAR BEARS: The Natural History of a Threatened Species

are attracted there from all over the world every year. Over the decades, the Churchill bears have starred in dozens of television programs and untold millions of photographs have been taken by photographers. The result has been the development of a global interest in the bears and the branding of Churchill as the "Polar Bear Capital of the World."

For most people, the initial sheer excitement of simply seeing these magnificent bears soon gives way to desire to know more about them. Some of the most frequently asked questions include: Why are the bears on the coast near Churchill every fall in the first place? Have they always been there? What do the bears do for the rest of the

year, where do they have their maternity dens? And more recently, what will the effects of climate warming be for these bears? My response to the frequent query about whether there is anything particularly special about the polar bears in Western Hudson Bay, is that yes, this population has contributed more to our knowledge of the biology and ecology of polar bears than any other. For that reason alone, the polar bears of Western Hudson Bay merit a chapter of their own.

A brief introduction

Polar bears have been recorded in the Churchill area since the first white man arrived there, but were known to the First Nations and Inuit of the

A polar bear feeding in the Churchill Dump, which is now closed.
(© Jenny E. Ross)

An aggressive adult female with cubs charges another female with cubs along the Manitoba coast in the fall while waiting for freeze-up.
(© Jenny E. Ross)

region long before that. The first European to spend the winter in western Hudson Bay was the Danish explorer Jens Munk. He spent the long, cold winter of 1619-20 near present-day Churchill and reported the killing of a polar bear there in September. In 1684, the York Factory trading post of was established by the Hudson's Bay Company at the mouth of Hayes River, about 190 km (120 mi) southeast of Churchill. York Factory became the hub of the fur trade in the area. The first Hudson's Bay traders to sail into the mouth of the Churchill River did so in 1686. They didn't establish a trading post there, until 1717. (Churchill Factory, later Fort Prince of Wales). Although York Factory remained the main trading post for Hudson Bay and much of Western Canada for many years, in 1870 it was downgraded to a coastal trading post and continued as such until it was finally closed in 1957. The local environment apparently was not able to support the demand for furs and regional fur returns became marginal. However, polar bear hides continued to be traded there well into the twentieth century.

The presence of the maternity denning area north of the Nelson River and south of Churchill was well known to the local native trappers of the area. According to Hudson's Bay records from York Factory, hides from females and cubs, which probably came from the nearby denning area, were traded there. Bears were also harvested by native trappers for dog and human food by those who travelled on their traplines.

In 1930, the Province of Manitoba passed an

encounter polar bears. It is also likely that bears were attracted to the base's garbage dumps in fall. There is no record of how many bears may have been killed by military personnel in self-defence, for protection of property, or for a souvenir hide, but judging from the numbers quoted in unsubstantiated rumours, it seems the overall total was probably substantial. In those years, however, polar bears rarely came into Churchill in the fall, as they would in later years, at least in part probably because of human-caused mortality.

It is often difficult to confirm a cause-and-effect relationship when trying to reconstruct the past. Nonetheless, it seems likely that three events significantly reduced the number of polar bears killed along the coast and in the denning area between the Churchill and Nelson rivers. In 1957, the Hudson's Bay Company closed York Factory and the native trappers who lived around the post were moved inland. From 1952 to 1957, an average of 17 polar bears were taken in the area annually but since then, almost no bears have been reported killed in the denning area to the northwest of York Factory. In 1964, the Canadian Army withdrew from Fort Churchill. After that, soldiers returned only occasionally for specific training exercises, often in winter when there are few bears on land. In 1968, quotas were established for Inuit settlements in Nunavut and females with cubs and bears in dens were protected. Altogether the total bear population probably increased because fewer bears were being killed in Western Hudson Bay overall, and because of the added protection given to females in their main maternity denning area in Manitoba.

Increasing numbers of polar bears were seen each autumn along the coast east of Churchill through the 1960s . They became regular visitors to town and, by the middle of the decade, were constantly seen at the town's three garbage dumps. In November 1968, up to 40 polar bears were recorded in one of the dumps at the same time. People came to view the bears, to feed them and, regrettably, sometimes to provoke them.

act protecting the dens of all fur-bearing animals while upholding the rights of Aboriginals to hunt polar bears for their own use. A system of registered traplines was established in the area of York Factory area in the early 1950s and trappers were encouraged to limit their polar bear kills. In 1954, new wildlife regulations were passed that made it illegal for non-Natives to hunt polar bears and for anyone to trade or barter in polar bear hides.

The polar bear presence along the coast of western Hudson Bay, in both Manitoba and Nunavut, did not attract widespread attention until sometime after the establishment of a military base at Churchill in 1942. Military land training took place on the tundra east and south of Churchill and out to the coast during summer and fall, when and where they were most likely to

A helicopter moving a problem bear away from Churchill. (© Jenny E. Ross)

polar bear tracks through an area of stunted spruce trees and undulating rocks near his school. He had separated from his companions to follow a separate set of tracks when he suddenly stumbled onto a sleeping polar bear. The startled animal leaped to its feet, chased the boy, and caught him almost immediately. The boy's friend heard his screams and ran for help. The local Royal Canadian Mounted Police attempted a rescue but could not get a clear shot without endangering the boy or onlookers crowding around the spot. A shot was fired over the bear, whereupon it ran about 25 m (80 ft) with the boy in its jaws before dropping him and then rearing up on its hind legs. At this point, the bear was shot and the boy was rushed to hospital, where he died shortly afterward.

There was both concern and confusion about the increasing numbers of bears and the subsequent encounters between bears and people. While it was clear things had changed dramatically, people were less certain about why and what to do. Why were the bears coming to Churchill in the first place? Was the bear population increasing, and why were there more bears in some years and not in others? Did the same bears keep coming back year after year? Did all the bears in the population come to town or only some of them? If it was only some of the bears, which ones were they and why did some but not others show up? How dangerous were they? What could be done to reduce the threat to humans? Did feeding on garbage have a detrimental effect on the bears? Could the danger to humans be reduced to an acceptable level without killing all the bears?

These fascinating questions were good enough reasons to study the polar bears at Churchill. But there were also significant non-biological considerations: easier logistics and reduced cost. Instead of being spread over thousands of square miles of ice, far from camps or fuel supplies, the whole Western Hudson Bay population was ashore for four months during the ice-free period and concentrated within about 250 km (160 mi)

People and bears sometimes scavenged side by side in the dump. Bears often wandered into inhabited areas to feed on garbage and occasionally broke into buildings where food was stored.

Not surprisingly, the number of encounters between people and polar bears increased. People were attacked, but not killed, in 1966 and 1967. However, on 17 November 1968, a 19-year-old Inuk boy unwisely set off to follow a fresh set of

of Churchill. Through most of that period, there is no snow on the ground, making the white bears easy to see. Long days and warm temperatures through summer and fall make outside work efficient and comfortable (except when bugs are rampant). Churchill itself is less costly to travel to than most locations in the Arctic. Equipment and specimens can be shipped by rail, which is far more economical than shipment by air. The combination of these factors still make Churchill one of the best places in the world to study polar bears.

These were the circumstances and issues that ushered in a new era of research on polar bears in the Churchill area. Initially, many of the studies focused on issues related to the management and conservation of the bears. Before long

though, it was apparent we needed considerably more understanding of their basic biology to conserve them more effectively. Over the past forty years, more research on the basic biology of polar bears has been conducted in Manitoba than anywhere else in the world. The results have been fascinating, useful, sometimes surprising, and often applicable to polar bears in other parts of the world. Taken together though, the research undertaken in the area clearly justifies calling Churchill, "The Polar Bear Scientific Research Capital of the World."

Why do polar bears congregate along the Manitoba coast of Hudson Bay in the fall?

It is necessary to understand why polar bears occur along the Manitoba coast of Hudson Bay

A large male polar bear finds a rock to be a nice pillow while he rests on the Hudson Bay coast. (© Jenny E. Ross)

Young adult males participating in ritualised non-harmful play fighting.
(© Jenny E. Ross)

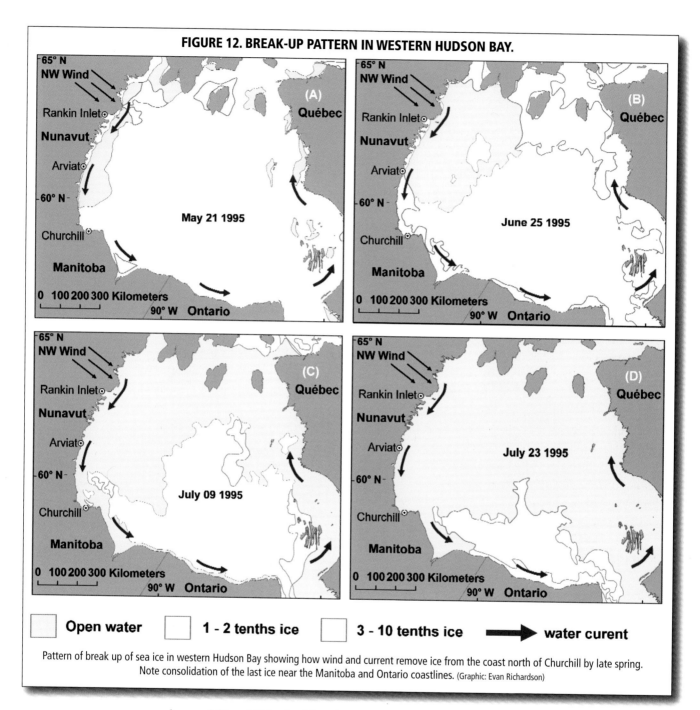

FIGURE 12. BREAK-UP PATTERN IN WESTERN HUDSON BAY.

(A)
65° N
NW Wind
Rankin Inlet
Nunavut
Arviat
60° N
Churchill
Manitoba
Québec
May 21 1995
0 100 200 300 Kilometers
90° W Ontario

(B)
65° N
NW Wind
Rankin Inlet
Nunavut
Arviat
60° N
Churchill
Manitoba
Québec
June 25 1995
0 100 200 300 Kilometers
90° W Ontario

(C)
65° N
NW Wind
Rankin Inlet
Nunavut
Arviat
60° N
Churchill
Manitoba
Québec
July 09 1995
0 100 200 300 Kilometers
90° W Ontario

(D)
65° N
NW Wind
Rankin Inlet
Nunavut
Arviat
60° N
Churchill
Manitoba
Québec
July 23 1995
0 100 200 300 Kilometers
90° W Ontario

☐ **Open water**   ☐ **1 - 2 tenths ice**   ☐ **3 - 10 tenths ice**   ➡ **water curent**

Pattern of break up of sea ice in western Hudson Bay showing how wind and current remove ice from the coast north of Churchill by late spring. Note consolidation of the last ice near the Manitoba and Ontario coastlines. (Graphic: Evan Richardson)

and around Churchill in the fall in the first place. We must know this before we can more fully appreciate their present-day ecology in that region and, later, understand why they are being so negatively affected by a steadily warming climate (see chapter on climate change for details). The most important factor is the pattern and timing of sea ice break-up. Although Hudson Bay is completely covered by ice from late fall through winter, its ice breaks up and melts completely in July and doesn't refreeze until November or early December in most years. However, as illustrated in Figure 12, it is the pattern of break-up and where the last ice floes eventually melt in the late spring and early summer that determines where the bears in the Western and Southern Hudson Bay populations go ashore. Here, on land, they will wait out the open water period of summer and fall. Freeze-up then begins around Cape Churchill and north along the coast which explains why polar bears accumulate along the coast south of Churchill in the fall, and some move farther north along the coast into Nunavut.

Using satellite records from 1995, Figure 12 illustrates the pattern of sea ice break-up in Western Hudson Bay. The combination of a southerly current along the northwestern coast of Hudson Bay, and strong prevailing winds from the northwest, produces open water by early spring along the coast of Nunavut to the north of Churchill (Figure 12A). Through the late spring and early summer, the open water near the coast widens and the remaining ice moves south, eventually consolidating in the southwest corner of the bay (Figure 12 B, C, D). Not surprisingly, the bears remain with the ice hunting seals for as long as possible. Thus, by the time the last remaining ice melts, most of the Hudson Bay bears are off the coastlines of Manitoba and Ontario, so that is where they go ashore for summer. Consequently, in most summer there are very few bears north of Churchill along the coast until you get close to Southampton Island. Although bears from Manitoba, Ontario, and southern Foxe Basin sometime mix on the sea ice in winter while hunting, and from genetic studies there appears to be some interbreeding, each group remains remarkably faithful to its summering area and there is surprisingly little mixing between populations during the ice-free period.

As the bears come ashore, they segregate by age and sex class, with adult males most commonly found along the coast where it is coolest. Pregnant adult females and most females with dependent cubs go inland, in part to avoid the danger of predation by adult males. Subadults are found both inland and along the coast in between areas where adult males concentrate.

When the ice re-freezes in early winter, it does so first along the coast from Cape Churchill and to the north. Thus, by early October, bears that were widely spread out along the Manitoba coast and inland through the summer begin to move north in anticipation of returning to the sea ice. The northward movement of bears in fall is well known from as far south as York Factory and Kaskattama (Figure 13). As more bears accumulate along the coast, the largest and most dominant animals tend to congregate on points of land or small islands near the coast, while family groups, subadults, and non-pregnant females occupy intermediate areas, such as that between Churchill and Cape Churchill. This largely explains why bears accumulate to the east of Churchill in fall where bear-watching activities are concentrated. As fall wears on and freeze-up approaches, progressively more bears accumulate along the coast. Many continue to walk north from Churchill, toward and past Arviat in Nunavut, where the first ice often forms. From this brief overview, it is clear that the main reason bears occur near Churchill in fall is simply because the town is in an area where bears normally aggregate in anticipation of freeze-up, or pass through as they move farther north along the coast in search of newly frozen sea ice.

Defining the boundaries of the population

At first, of course, very little was known about the polar bear population at all. Therefore, the first tasks were to develop safe techniques for capturing and tagging individual bears. Then, several basic aspects quickly became apparent from recapturing tagged bears in subsequent years, getting tag returns from Inuit and Indian hunters, and tracking bears with radio collars. The bears around Churchill and along the Manitoba coast in summer were found to have a high degree of seasonal fidelity. In other words, regardless of where they travelled to hunt seals in winter, they still returned to the Manitoba coast in summer. The southern boundary of the population was, conveniently, at about the Ontario border, while the northern boundary lay in the vicinity of Rankin Inlet in Nunavut. Very few bears originally caught in Manitoba have ever been captured or shot anywhere else. Similarly, only a tiny number of the many bears tagged in Ontario or farther north in Foxe Basin or Davis Strait have been recaptured in Manitoba. Taken together, this information confirmed that the bears we saw around Churchill and along the Manitoba coast comprised a separate subpopulation. Thus, by using the information from tagging and the radio-tracking of movements, the boundaries of the Western Hudson Bay population could be defined for management purposes (as illustrated in Figure 13), and appropriate management and conservation could be developed.

Initial management of dumps, humans, and problem bears

Prior to the polar bear ecotourism boom, the main concerns about the polar bears in the Chrchill area focused on human safety, minimizing damage by bears, and estimating sustainable harvest levels for Inuit hunters in Nunavut. From the time the first bears were tagged, it was clear that many individuals returned to the Churchill dump in subsequent years. Some females tagged there as cubs later returned with their cubs, which in turn brought their cubs. Several individuals were caught there two, three or more years in a row. Meanwhile, it did not require more than common sense to recognize that Churchill's garbage was a primary attractant. Meetings were held to find ways to reduce the problem and public education programs were initiated. Garbage sites near town were closed, an incinerator was built (but later shut down because of operational problems) and, most recently, garbage was shipped south on the railway for eventual disposal elsewhere. New plans are now afoot which include compaction and landfill in the Churchill area.

Some problem bears were sent to zoos in the south as a way to avoid killing them, but a few repeaters were euthanised. Polar bear viewing as a tourist resource was also suggested in the late 1970s, but didn't really begin until the 1980s.

In 1969, Manitoba assigned conservation officers to patrol the town and chase out problem bears. The initial around the clock cost was $20,000. In 1970, the 24-hour polar bear patrol cost $35,000. By 1983, when they responded to 191 calls, the cost doubled. Now it is well over $400,000 annually. Nevertheless, what is now known as the Polar Bear Alert Program is, despite its expense, a visionary conservation program which dramatically reduces the number of bears killed in defence of life and property in the Churchill area each year.

One solution to a problem bear in town is simply to relocate it. Between 1971 and 1975, 40 potentially dangerous problem bears were moved by air from Churchill to distant points to avoid having to shoot them if they became too dangerous. Although benefits were limited since many returned in a short time, we learned a certain amount about the bear's movements and fidelity to the Churchill area. A side benefit was that the "bearlift" gave rise to some hilarious newspaper cartoons, many depicting bears in the Churchill airport waiting to catch flights. Three males released at the Kaskattama air strip near the Ontario border in 1971 (see Figure 13) made the journey back to Churchill (480 km or 300 mi along the coast) in 14, 15, and 24 days respectively. In 1974, it took an adult female with two female cubs-of-the-year just 18 days to return. In all, 13 of the 40 bears removed were recaptured in the Churchill area, indicating that the bears knew where they were and still had a high degree of fidelity to Churchill. However, many of those that were released to the north of Churchill, which is the direction they would normally be moving in the fall, did not return in the same season. As a result, problem bears flown out of Churchill and released back to the wild these days are all moved north rather than south.

What bears used the dump and why?

Not surprisingly, the first problems that needed to be studied related to bears around the dump and those that threatened human life and property. We knew from our initial aerial surveys and tagging program that there were at least several hundred bears in the population, and probably more, but the great majority of them *did not* come to the dump. This left obvious questions of which bears went to the dump, why, and what might be done about it. It was also apparent that even though the bears came ashore by about the end of July, and the dump was available then, few were seen in Churchill before early to mid-October. Why did bears that knew about the dump not come in to feed as soon as they came ashore? We wondered if the dump could be an important

supplemental food source to some bears or whether, in an ecological sense, it was simply convenient for some bears but not actually vital to their eventual survival and reproductive success. If the overwhelming majority of the bears in the population were never even seen in the vicinity, what did those outside the Churchill area do when they came ashore to spend the summer on land?

When we began to capture bears outside the Churchill area, we found there were many large males around Cape Churchill and along the coast to the south that rarely, if ever, came into town, although some subadult males did. Even more interesting was the capture of several adult males that had first been caught at the Churchill dump as cubs with their mothers, or

Typical maternity den dug into frozen peat below black spruce trees along a raised bank by a stream bed. This den is probably only a few years old. (© Ian Stirling)

Old, well-used maternity den site with activity going back several decades. The gap in the trees above the bank is where all the roots died and the den that was once there collapsed and filled in. Later dens were dug to the left. (© Ian Stirling)

as lone subadults. Some had been repeat visitors, caught as often as three or four years in succession, and then not seen near town again. We had often wondered what happened to them but, suddenly, there they were, fat and healthy, along the coast. They had simply stopped visiting the dump, even though they obviously knew it was there. Adult females with a history of vis-

iting the dump never came in the year they were pregnant, although several returned with their young cubs the following fall. Clearly, it was time to study whether feeding at the dump was of ecological importance or simply a photographic distraction and management concern.

Through each fall, from 1981 to 1983, Nick Lunn drove out to the dump every morning at

POLAR BEARS: The Natural History of a Threatened Species

To determine whether bears that fed at the dump received any significant benefits that those not feeding there missed out on, we compared bears of the same age and sex classes from both groups. Besides observing the bears in the dump, we tried to do comparative studies of the behaviour and activity budgets of bears of the same age and sex classes that did not go there. This was complicated by the fact that most of the families were far inland in wet and more heavily vegetated habitat that was difficult or impossible to access. However, we were able to make comparative behavioural observations in more open areas nearer to the coast and we could compare things like body weights, litter size, and survival between dump bears and non-dump bears from captured animals.

Every bear that came into the dump was caught as soon as possible after it was first seen. It was then tagged, measured, and weighed. Of 207 individual bears captured, 67 (32%) were recaptured there at least once after the year of their original capture. Several adult females returned repeatedly over a period of 10 or more years.

When bears first began arriving at the dump in fall, there were no significant differences between their weights and those of bears of similar age and sex classes that did not go to the dump. Before freeze-up, when the bears returned to the ice, we recaptured as many individuals from both groups as we could find to see if they had gained or lost weight. Bears outside the dump lost 0.3-0.4% of their body weight per day, whereas most of those that fed at the dump gained 0.1-0.6% of their initial body weight per day. For an adult female nursing her cubs-of-the-year away from the dump area in the fall, this meant an average loss of 34 kg (75 lb), while a similar female with cubs feeding at the dump through the same period might gain as much. Statistically, that was a significant difference. However, when we compared the survival and reproductive success of the two groups of bears, there were no significant differences. Clearly, in the early 1980s at least, by the

dawn, parked his truck a few hundred metres away, and recorded everything the bears did until dark. After a while, he became almost as much of a tourist attraction as the bears themselves. Visitors and tour buses stopped regularly to get the latest information on what bears were around, what they were doing, and anything else that might be interesting.

time the bears came ashore in summer, they already had enough fat stored on their bodies to survive the open water period and did not need additional feeding opportunities.

One female, first caught in the dump as a yearling in 1967, kept coming back with successive litters of cubs until 1985 when she was 19. Another female, first caught at the dump as a cub with her mother, was recaptured there with her own cubs several years later. Up to 1983, 33 individual adult females had brought 57 litters (totalling 101 cubs) to the dump. After weaning, 21% of those cubs were known to have returned to the dump. These examples clearly demonstrate the importance of cubs learning from their mothers. However, we had not expected to find that subadult males that fed in the dump until they were four to six years old, were rarely seen in the area again. In contrast, male black and brown bears that have learned to feed in dumps continue to do so as adults.

The structure of dominance hierarchy varies greatly between polar bears in the dump and their black and brown bear cousins, and polar bears hunting on the sea ice. At the Churchill dump, adult females with cubs, not males, were the dominant animals. The few adult males that came to the dump kept out of their way. Usually there was a dominance hierarchy between the family groups as well, with some families staying well out of the way of others. One year there was a remarkable deviation from this pattern of mutual avoidance and occasional aggressive interaction. A 10-year-old female with twin female cubs-of-the-year and an 18-year-old female with twin yearlings fed, walked to and from the dump area and rested together for over a month. At no time were these females aggressive toward each other, although they were to other family groups. The four cubs sometimes played together while one mother watched over them and the other fed at the dump. We have never seen anything like this before or since. I have often wondered if the younger female was the daughter of the older one,

which might possibly explain their unusually relaxed manner with each other. Unfortunately, they were both first caught as independent adults before we started to routinely bank specimens for future genetic studies, so the possibility of their being related remains a mystery.

There were also some detrimental side effects to feeding at the dump and around nearby settled areas. For example, one bear was found dead, apparently poisoned by eating part of a car battery. Another subadult almost certainly died of kidney failure after he was chased away from near a building where he had drunk several litres of old transmission fluid. Bears that feed in the dump, and later wander into town may lose some of their natural fear of humans. A significantly higher proportion of subadult males with a record of being in the dump were shot as problem bears. Similarly, becoming used to humans around the dump may make polar bears less wary of Inuit settlements along the coast to the north of Churchill. Of tagged bears shot by Inuk hunters along the western coast of Hudson Bay, a higher proportion of subadult males with a record of having been at the dump were shot than subadult males that had not been recorded there. Throughout North America, it has been shown over and over that acclimation of bears to dumps and humans result in strongly negative effects for the bears. In summary, the same was true in Churchill. Now that the dump in Churchill is permanently closed, that attraction is no longer a concern. However dumps and carrion still attract polar bears to some of the small Inuit settlements and hunting camps to the north along the Nunavut coast of Hudson Bay.

The polar bear jail

In 1981, as part of their developing program to minimize the killing of problem bears in the Churchill area, the Manitoba Department of Natural Resources built a "polar bear jail" capable of holding at least sixteen individual bears and four family groups. The idea was that as soon as

A typical pit dug down to the permafrost at the edge of a lake. (© Ian Stirling)

POLAR BEARS: Ecology and Conservation of a Threatened Species

A collapsing maternity den in the bank of a small lake after a forest fire destroyed the trees and root mat that previously supporte the roof.
(© Ian Stirling)

a bear showed up at the dump or in town, it would be captured, locked up immediately and held there until freeze-up, at which time it was released back onto the sea ice. That way, a bears would get a positive reinforcement for going into town, in the form of food. Furthermore, the bears were not fed in jail because our research had demonstrated that, in the 1980s at least, the bears on land during the open water period were able to sustain themselves on their stored fat reserves without feeding until the ice formed again. Thus, they did not receive a reward for going to jail, in the form of food, which might make the jail an attraction or further acclimatize bears to humans. The bears were given water however, or snow when the weather turned cold, although they

bears released 10-20 km (6-12 mi) to the north of Churchill returned that season.

Although this program has become very expensive, it has largely succeeded in preventing polar bears from spending much time around the settled areas where they might be killed. Visitors see fewer bears near town these days but, more important, it means it is safer for both bears and people. In 2009, conservation officers responded to almost 300 occurrences of bears in the Churchill area. Close to 60 bears were subsequently captured and held for variable periods of time in the polar bear jail. Overall, the program has been so successful at reducing kills of problem bears (while keeping the area as safe as possible for people), that the facility was completely upgraded and modernized in 2010, including installation of a cooling system for bears held there during the hot weather in late summer. Overall, it has been one of the most creative and successful programs undertaken in polar bear conservation anywhere in the world.

Behaviour of bears along the coast during the open water season

Much of the Manitoba coast of Hudson Bay consists of raised beaches, small ponds, clumps of willows, and grassy flats, interspersed with long gravel ridges called eskers, left from the last glaciation. One of the best known coastal locations, Cape Churchill, is an almost flat esker extending north into a sand spit stretching into the shallow tidal flats of Hudson Bay, about 49 km (30 mi) east of Churchill (Figure 13). The Cape is located at the point where the east-west orientation of the coast leading out of Churchill suddenly bends southward again to form the western coast of Hudson Bay. The lack of geographic relief can give the impression of bleakness or isolation on an overcast, windy day as the roaring waves of Hudson Bay pound on the beaches. The coastal plain in this area is treeless; the four-foot-high willows around some of the small lakes are the tallest plants. The remaining vege-

probably didn't need it.

If the jail filled up, and more bears kept coming into town, the inmates that had been there longest were flown several kilometres north along the coast because studies of their movement patterns indicated they are more likely to walk north than south in the fall. Radio-collared bears that went onto the ice first headed northeast. Few

tation consists largely of sedges, grasses, and a few flowers and mosses. In fact, the place can seem decidedly unremarkable except that by late fall, large numbers of bears still gather there, and on other points and small offshore islands, as they wait for freeze-up.

We knew that the bears were spending several months on land during the open water season but we didn't know a lot about what they did during this period. From an observation tower we established at Cape Churchill in 1976, Paul Latour quantified the behaviour and activities of the bears there in October and November. To a large degree, he found they did not do a lot of anything. Adult and subadult males were inactive 79% and 74% of the time respectively, while subadult females were inactive 56% of the time. Few females accompanied by dependent cubs frequented the area, probably because of the presence of so many large males. Apart from a bit of grass and some kelp washed up along the beach, there is little to eat along the coast, so it was not surprising to find that the bears only fed for about 1.25% of their total time. This, in turn, also explained the reason the bears were so inactive. Basically, they needed to metabolize their stored energy reserves at as low a rate as possible in order to make them last until freeze-up when they could return to the sea ice to hunt seals again.

These results from the autumn were similar to what Brian Knudsen found several years earlier when he observed polar bears spending the summer on North Twin Island in James Bay. Bears of all ages and sex classes there spent about 87% of their time inactive and 2-5% of their time feeding, mainly on grass, kelp, and crowberry, along with occasional Canada geese, although in total it appeared that very little was actually eaten.

Social behaviour of bears along the coast

Despite the apparent inactivity and lack of social structure among bears along the coast, a certain order is still discernable. As the density of bears along the coast increases through the fall, there is segregation between the adult and subadult males. On the Cape, and at other locations along the coast, the large older males prefer the points or small islands near the coast, often forming groups of four to 10 or more in close proximity to each other. On average, males that aggregated in groups were about 60 kg (132 lb) heavier that those that were not in aggregations, though their average ages were similar. Although such aggregations of the largest and most dominant males seem a bit surprising in what we usually think of as a solitary species, it is also the time of year when their testosterone levels are at their lowest. Probably because of their low testosterone levels, and the lack of females or food to compete for, the large males are able tolerate each other at close distances at coastal points that may be most suitable for waiting out the open water season, because it is cool by the sea and no additional energy is wasted going further inland.

In general, subadults maintain a greater distance from the adult males than the adult males do between themselves, which probably indicates nervousness on the part of the subadults. As the fall wears on, however, all bears begin to walk around a bit more and interact more frequently than they do in summer. Whether this occurs simply because the weather becomes cooler, or because they are anticipating freeze-up and a return to the sea ice is uncertain. Regardless, young adult and subadult males spent 3-4% of their total time in social interactions which primarily consisted of ritualized wrestling matches in which none of the participants was usually hurt. This behaviour is much loved by the ecotourists who come to see and photograph the tussling bears. During the play fighting, the males come into body contact as if in serious combat, but without injuring each other. These ritualized bouts are usually about three to four minutes in duration but sometimes last considerably longer. A pair of 365 kg (800 lb) males pushing each other around and wrestling is an awesome sight! Each is capable of inflicting terrible wounds on the other, and yet they do not. There are several repeated behavioural patterns such as mutually rearing up on the hind legs with the forelimbs partially folded into the body, mouth open and head angled down, but making no contact with the partner. Sometimes this is followed by mutual pushing with the forepaws on the neck or chest of the opponent in an attempt to force him down. In another common posture, the males appear to be holding each other's arms as if dancing. Facial contact is common; the bears may touch noses and then one may rub the other's neck just behind or below the head. Facial contact may suddenly give way to a bear lunging toward its opponent and pushing him on the neck or chest with the forepaws. Inhibited bites take place, in which one male grips an opponent's neck or shoulder by the teeth but doesn't take advantage of its purchase to cause serious damage. Much of the jousting seems oriented toward trying to put the opponent off balance. But even when this is done, and a male has pinned his rival, the bites and pushes are still inhibited so as not to cause serious wounds. Bouts usually end with the loser walking or running away. Interestingly, it was the bears with whom fights were started that most often terminated the encounters by fleeing. This suggests polar bears are able to assess the size and strength of potential opponents so they don't start fights with animals they are less likely to be able to dominate. In this situation at least, bears usually initiate encounters with bears of a similar or slightly smaller size. Sometimes, a third huge male will stand and watch the protracted combat of two of his compatriots, refraining, like a gentleman, from joining in. Once the scrap is over, he may then challenge the winner but he does not join in punishing the loser as dogs sometimes do.

The high frequency with which this behaviour occurs suggests it has an important biological function, most likely the continued development of an ability to assess the strength of opponents and the development of motor skills for serious fighting, both of which could be critical to reproductive success when competing for receptive females during the breeding season. The biggest, oldest, and most scarred adult males do not normally participate in the stereotyped fighting. Subadult females spent up to 8% of their time in social interactions, but to a large degree, their behaviour consisted largely of moving away when approached by males of all ages. Subadult females did not engage in the ritualized fighting.

Behaviour of bears in the inland areas

Although it was not practical to conduct long-term observations on adult females with young after they moved inland for the summer, it appeared from those that were carrying radio collars that they moved away from the coast fairly quickly. Once in a location of their choosing, they remained in a relatively restricted area and, like the males, were largely inactive in order to conserve their energy. Pregnant females moved inland shortly after coming ashore, selected a den dug in the frozen ground and, if not disturbed, simply remained at the same den site through the winter.

Being able to enter a cool, shaded den early and remaining largely inactive there is probably helpful to their overall conservation of energy. Although such behaviour was most common with pregnant females, some bears of other age and sex classes did this for shorter periods as well. Polar bears are designed to be comfortable in cold temperatures. When the temperature rises to 20-30°C (75-85°F) during July and August, bears must cope with heat stress. Keeping cool is made very difficult by the fact that the bears must carry a large layer of fat just under the fur to survive on through the open water period and through the winter as well in the case of pregnant females; it seems like the worst of both worlds!

Some bears, primarily subadults and family groups, showed signs of having fed to some degree on vegetation when they were captured. Based on a sample of 748 females aged 8 months to 29 years, and 436 males aged 8 months to 25 years, we confirmed feeding on vegetation of some sort in 34% of adult females accompanied by cubs and 31% of females that were alone, which was not significantly different. Of those that ate vegetation, about 81% had fed on blueberries and crowberries, while trace amounts of other vegetation, such as grass or moss, was documented as well.

To assess whether the intake of terrestrial food could be contributing significantly to the total diet, Keith Hobson worked with us to analyse stable isotopes from blood samples collected from fasting bears. This method can be used to determine whether energy from terrestrial as well as marine sources is being stored in body tissues. There was no evidence that any intake from terrestrial sources was significant enough to be detectable. In a subsequent study to further test whether berries could be important, we analysed CO_2 from the breath of 300 immobilized polar bears, some of which showed evidence of feeding on berries while others did not. The results indicated that bears which fed on berries while fasting on land received an insignificant amount of energetic benefit in terms of their total annual requirement.

The uniqueness and antiquity of the inland denning area

The main denning area for the polar bears of the Western Hudson Bay population, to the south of Churchill (see Figure 13), is unique. This is because, in most years, suitable snow drifts for maternity denning, such those used by pregnant females in most other parts of the Arctic, have not yet formed in northern Manitoba. Thus, pregnant females are forced to dig their maternity dens in the frozen ground. Counting both those in current use, and the myriad of old and long-abandoned dens, there are likely a few thousand sites that have been used throughout the area at some time in the past, making it one of the densest denning areas in the world. Peter Scott led our group in a detailed analysis of not only what the

specific requirements were for maternity denning but also, the antiquity of some of the dens and their history of prior use.

Within the overall denning area, the bears have remarkably specific ecological requirements for maternity denning sites. The region is one of discontinuous permafrost. However, in a highly selective fashion, pregnant females dug

their terrestrial maternity dens almost exclusively into banks of frozen peat, 150-300 cm (5-10 ft) deep, in inland areas along the edges of lakes and stream banks where the peat is deepest. The peat needs to be deep enough for a den, while still being high enough so that water does not seep in at the den bottom. Dens dug into the banks are located beneath clumps of black spruce that commonly occur along the bank edges. The denning females depend on the established root systems of the spruce trees to maintain the stability of the earth in the den's roof (which does not remain frozen), thus preventing it from collapse. Additionally, the dimensions of the maternity dens dug in the frozen peat are very similar to those of dens dug

A typical pit dug down to the permafrost at the edge of a lake.
(© Ian Stirling)

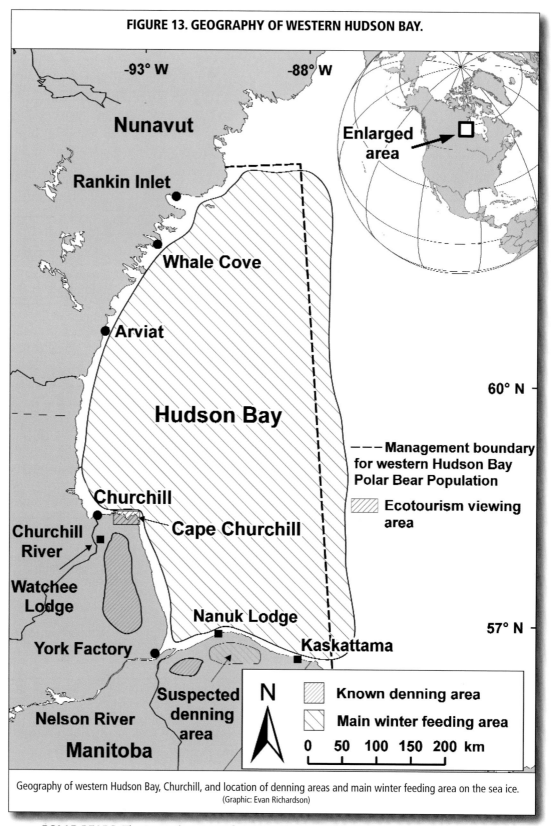

FIGURE 13. GEOGRAPHY OF WESTERN HUDSON BAY.

-93° W   -88° W

Nunavut

Enlarged area

Rankin Inlet

Whale Cove

Arviat

60° N

Hudson Bay

- - - Management boundary for western Hudson Bay Polar Bear Population

///// Ecotourism viewing area

Churchill

Cape Churchill

Churchill River

Watchee Lodge

Nanuk Lodge

57° N

York Factory

Kaskattama

N

Suspected denning area

Nelson River

Manitoba

Known denning area

Main winter feeding area

0 50 100 150 200 km

Geography of western Hudson Bay, Churchill, and location of denning areas and main winter feeding area on the sea ice.
(Graphic: Evan Richardson)

in snow banks in other parts of the Arctic. This suggests that in order to maximize the efficiency of use of fat reserves to maintain some minimum temperature inside through the winter, thus maximizing the use of stored energy for nursing cubs, there is an optimal size for den construction.

From tagging studies, it is clear that female polar bears in this population show a high degree of fidelity to the denning area, although not necessarily to specific dens. Movements of radio-collared females show that even when they leave the ice in a different area of the coast, they often return to the same general part of the denning area.

How long it takes to dig a den in the permafrost is unknown but, from anecdotal observations of some partially dug dens, it appears that at least some may require more than one season to construct. Possibly because of the effort required to dig into frozen ground, most dens are reused many times over the years, which conserves stored energy the pregnant female can redirect to supporting herself and her cubs while fasting.

Much about the pattern and long-term duration of reuse is recorded in damage to the roots of the trees over the den. When a female selects an old den for re-use in the fall, she excavates old peat that has melted or fallen down on the inside and generally freshens up the site. In the process of re-excavation, her claws scar the roots of the trees above the den. By examining the annual rings in the roots, in relation to the annual rings in the main truck, it is possible to determine much of the previous history of use of individual dens. The results were fascinating!

We examined 617 disturbances from 72 trees sampled at 31 den sites, and found that prior use of 12 of the sites dated back over 100 years. The oldest tree damage that we attributed to a bear occurred in 1795, but our ability to go further back that far in most areas was limited by the relatively young age of most trees. We found that despite a large choice of existing dens and locations for construction of new dens, 57% of freshly used dens were reused within two years. Between periods of use, or reuse, den sites then remained undisturbed for at least 10 years prior to being reused. It is possible that the vulnerability of pregnant females or females with newborn cubs, to predation by other bears or wolves may explain why dens are only used for a few years at a time. If use of such locations is too predictable, it might increase the vulnerability of the occupants.

Because of the antiquity of many of the dens, the chronology of their use provides an added perspective to speculation about reasons for the apparent increase in size of the Western Hudson Bay population through the 1960s and 1970s. From 1900 to 1920, as many as 50 polar bear hides were traded at York Factory, near the southern end of the denning area. Many of those were likely adult females. Because we know that females tend to show general fidelity to parts of the denning area, it is likely that those with a history of denning in the southern portion were more vulnerable to harvest. During the 1900 to 1920 period, dens we examined at Skidmore Lake, the closest site to York Factory in our study, showed no sign of being used, while those at the greatest distance away had the highest and most consistent levels of use. Similarly, through the 1900s, as hunting polar bears in Manitoba declined, York Factory closed, and the aboriginal community moved inland from the coast, the overall rate of disturbance of dens in the sample increased fivefold. Taken together, this strongly suggests that the overall reduction of legal hunting of polar bears in Manitoba, along with the departure of the Army from Churchill, resulted in a marked improvement in the survival of adult females. Consequently, their productivity and the survival of their cubs to reproductive age, probably increased substantially, resulting in an overall increase in population size.

Over the years, there have also been forest fires in the denning area, and these may become more common as the temperatures rise in summer and dry out the vegetation. The locations which are most vulnerable to burning are also those that are most important for denning: the thin bands of spruces along the tops of the frozen stream and lake banks. Studies of lichen regeneration indicate that it takes about 100 years or more for the tundra and its vegetation to regenerate following a fire.

Other structures

Two other structures are common. Pits dug on the surface of the ground, are often found on beach ridges along the coast and near the edges of inland lakes. These areas are exposed to wind which may function to both cool the bears and to reduce insect harassment. The bears also use large excavations we term "shallow dens." These relatively simple structures are often simply semi-circular excavations in the side of a bank, usually not even beneath trees, suggesting that a roof secured by roots was not as essential as it is for a maternity den. Permafrost lines the back of freshly dug, or re-excavated shallow dens,

suggesting that part of their function may be related to keeping cool in warmer weather. In one sample of 14 bears captured from maternity dens over a two year period, 11 (79%) were lone (suspected pregnant) adult females, 2 (14%) were subadult males, and one was an adult male. In a sample of 17 bears caught in shallow dens, 15 (88%) were lone females, 1 (6%) was a subadult male, and 1 (6%) was an adult male. Of 15 bears occupying pits, 2 (13%) were lone females, 2 were females with cubs-of-the-year, 1 (7%) was a subadult male, and 10 (67%) were adult males. Of 64 bears recorded captured in pits over an 18-year period, 43 (67%) were adult males and most were caught in August and September. Over that same period, of all bears caught while using a pit or den in August, 35 of 49 (71%) were in pits; while of those caught in September, 127 of 140 (91%) were in dens. Use of pits declines by late September as the weather cools, and later, in October, even many of the large adult males retreat from the beach ridges to dense patches of willows to escape direct exposure to strong, cold wind.

Chapter 11

SOME HIGHLIGHTS OF CONSERVATION, PAST AND PRESENT

Five fat bears scavenge at night on leftovers from Inupiat whalers at Kaktovik, Alaska. (© Daniel J. Cox/NaturalExposures.com)

A brief history of polar bear hunting

Polar bears were hunted by aboriginal peoples throughout the Arctic for hundreds, if not thousands, of years prior to the encroachment of modern civilization into their previously isolated world. Since indigenous people possessed only primitive weapons, the tactical advantage lay with the polar bear and most were probably killed with spears or arrows while swimming, or through holes cut in the snow roof of a maternity den. Even so, there are still many vivid stories in

HIS SITUATION WAS NOW ONE OF EXTREME PERIL, IN SPITE OF THE KNIFE.

tions. The journals of these explorers displayed melodramatic wood cuts of hunting exploits and threats from bears. My favourite is from *The Realm of the Ice King*, originally published by the Religious Tract Society in 1874. The book recounts the adventures of one of the officers hunting polar bears at Magdalena Bay, Svalbard, in June, 1818. The man shot a large bear which then fell down, but when the officer approached and hit it on the head with the stock of his musket, the bear jumped up and seized his thigh. At this point, the officer was allegedly on his back with only his knife. The woodcut, reproduced here, gives the ultimate Victorian understatement, "His situation was now one of great peril, in spite of his knife." He was saved by his shipmates. However, the melodrama of the woodcut is emphasized by a foreboding night scene with a lantern and stars, even though 24-hour daylight prevails in June. Nevertheless, no good story should lose anything in the telling.

Although the number of bears killed by explorers and aboriginal hunters in North America in the 19th century probably ran into the hundreds in the North American Arctic alone, it is unlikely the total had any significant effects on polar bear populations. However, with the establishment of commercial fur trading posts and the invasion of the whalers, humans began to have a much larger impact. In his review of polar bear harvesting in the Canadian Arctic, James Honderich estimated approximately 15,500 hides were traded through Hudson's Bay Trading Posts from the late 1800s up to 1935. Polar bear hides continued to be traded through local trading posts and fur auction houses in North America and Europe for decades after that and continue to be traded in some countries, albeit at reduced numbers.

Whalers hunting bowhead whales in the Beaufort Sea but especially in Davis Strait, Baffin Bay, and Hudson Bay shot and purchased increasingly large numbers of polar bears from Inuit, to maintain revenue for voyages, especially as the stocks of bowhead whales began to be depleted by the

Inuit oral history of bears being killed on the open ice by incredibly brave men armed only with spears and aided by their dogs. However, with stone-age weapons, even unlimited hunting of breeding adult females did not threaten the survival of any polar bear subpopulations.

All that changed when the Arctic was invaded by Europeans seeking new trade routes or resources to exploit. Cumulatively, the journals of non-native polar explorers in the Canadian Arctic from the early 1600s through to the Ttwentieth century report substantial numbers of bears being killed, both for sport and food, by most expedi-

late 1800s. Whenever bowheads were not captured in sufficiently large numbers, the whalers shifted much of their attention to seals, belugas, walruses, and polar bears. By the mid-1800s, whaling stations that were originally designed to be overwintering harbours only became full-time trading posts. Some were in places the Hudson's Bay Company had not yet tapped, such as on eastern Baffin Island. Polar bears, readily attracted by the smells from whale and seal remains, were especially vulnerable to being shot. Honderich reported that 50-100 polar bear skins were traded annually in these areas. In one specific example, he noted that in 1909 and 1910, Dundee whalers alone obtained 234 and 242 hides respectively from whaling stations around eastern and southern Baffin Island. He also tallied a total of 1457 bears taken on 66 voyages in the Canadian Arctic between 1831 and 1913, an average of 22.1 bears per trip. Obviously, some ships took more bears than others, but when one considers that historian Gill Ross documented over 6,500 whaling voyages in Davis Strait, Hudson Bay, and Baffin Bay between 1719 and 1916, it is clear that a very large number of bears were killed and that the harvest could have had a negative impact on the polar bear populations in some of those areas at the time.

Commercial hunting and trade in animal products in the European Arctic, was more extensively developed considerably earlier than anything similar in North America. By the seventeenth century, Russian hunters and trappers were active in Svalbard and several trading ships sailed there each year. In the winter of 1784-85 for example, a single Russian crew at Magdalena Bay, in northern Svalbard, killed 150 bears, and similar, less well documented, harvests were taken in subsequent winters. After reviewing available documentation, the late Russian polar bear scientist Savva Uspenski suggested that the annual harvest could not have been less than 150 to 200 bears through the entire eighteenth century. In the nineteenth century, the volume of the

Russian fur trade decreased, but Norwegian polar bear hunting increased at the same time. Estimates based on admittedly incomplete information indicate that between 1875 and 1892, the average annual Norwegian harvest at Svalbard was 144 polar bears, increasing to 415 between 1893 and 1908. The kill averaged 355 per year from 1924 through 1939 and, after World War II, dropped to 324 per year from 1945 to 1970.

A Norwegian trapper's polar bear hides drying in Svalbard in the 1960s. (© Thor S. Larsen)

An example of the unsporting polar bear hunting from a ship in the pack ice that helped arouse world concern for polar bear conservation.
(© Thor S. Larsen)

Altogether, over 22,000 polar bears were killed during this period.

Uspenski summarized the annual harvests in the archipelago of Franz Josef Land as follows: in the 1800s, not fewer than 100; from 1890 to 1909, 100-150; from 1910 to the end of the 1930s, 150-200; and in the 1940s and early 1950s, not fewer than 50.

There is an even longer history of marine mammal hunting in the area of Novaya Zemlya, where there are records of polar bear hides being exported as early as 1556. In the winter of 1835, there were 80 vessels in the area, with over 1,000 hunters on board. Although they were mainly hunting walruses, most ships took polar bears as well whenever they had the opportunity. In other areas, polar bears were also taken regularly but in lower numbers, although

POLAR BEARS: The Natural History of a Threatened Species

the accuracy of the records is poor.

Interest in harvesting polar bears increased again in the first half of the twentieth century. In the Soviet Union, bears were taken all across the north at weather stations and hunting camps. Overall, Uspenski estimated that more than 150,000 polar bears have been killed or captured in Eurasia since the beginning of the eighteenth century—quite an impressive record.

Most of these (60-65%) were taken in the western parts of the Barents Sea including the archipelago of Svalbard. Twenty to 25% were estimated to have been killed in the Chukchi Sea, and only 10-20% in the Kara, Laptev, East Siberian, and Bering seas.

International concern about polar bears

Through the 1950s and particularly during the 1960s, the recorded number of bears killed rose quickly, largely because of the rapidly increasing value of their hides in North America and Europe, and a growing number of non-native hunters seeking the opportunity to kill a polar bear. The ubiquitous availability of high-powered rifles and the extensive use of oversnow machines, aircraft, and ships, also facilitated unprecedented increases in the numbers of polar bears reported killed, especially in North America. In Alaska, for example, the trophy kill alone increased from 139 in 1961 to 399 in 1966. The recorded harvest between 1953 and 1964 in Canada, fluctuated between 350 and 550, while in 1967 it suddenly jumped to 726. Worldwide, the recorded harvest of polar bears rose from about 700 in 1960 to 1400 or more in some years by 1970. However, the records are incomplete in all countries, so we will never know the actual numbers of bears killed.

Besides concerns about the rapidly escalating numbers of bears being killed from a total population of unknown size, there was also worldwide public outrage that many polar bears were being legally hunted in very unsporting ways. In Alaska, bears were being hunted down with the aid of small aircraft capable of searching vast areas of the offshore pack ice of the Beaufort and Chukchi seas, well beyond the territorial limits of Alaska and certainly inaccessible to shore-based native hunters. Between 1950 and 1972, trophy hunters in Alaska accounted for 85-90% of the kill.

Similar in its lack of sportsmanship, but less frequent in occurrence and less publicized, was

A large male bear lies dead in the snow, shot by a set gun in Svalbard.
(© Thor S. Larsen)

the shooting of polar bears by tourists on board Norwegian tour ships near Svalbard. Some of these bears were helplessly swimming in the water when shot. Also, on Svalbard, many polar bears were taken by Norwegian trappers at un-manned trap sites. At these "set guns," as they were called, a bait was attached to the trigger of a loaded high-powered rifle aimed just above the lure. When a polar bear came to investigate the site and pulled the bait with its teeth, it shot itself, usually in the head. The set-guns indiscriminately killed or wounded any bear that set them off, re-gardless of age or sex class. In Canada and Green-

land, there were no restrictions on the number of bears that could be killed and the recorded harvest tripled through the 1960s. Only in the USSR, after many years of heavy hunting pressure, was the legal killing of polar bears prohibited com-pletely, beginning in 1956. Clearly, there was a need for a coordinated conservation plan for polar bears throughout the Arctic if healthy popula-tions were to survive into the future.

Events leading to the coordination of international concern

In response to the growing concern about the

numbers of polar bears being killed each year, and the absence of information that could be used to regulate the harvest within sustainable limits, the United States Secretary of the Interior, Steward L. Udall and Senator E.L. Bartlett, called for "an international conference of Arctic Nations to pool scientific knowledge on the polar bear and to develop recommendations for future courses of action to benefit this resource of the Arctic region." This initiative led to the First Scientific Meeting on the Polar Bear, held in Fairbanks, Alaska, in September, 1965. Representatives of all five "polar bear countries" (Canada, Denmark/ Greenland), Norway, the United States of America, and the Union of Soviet Socialist Republics) attended.

After much discussion, agreement was reached on the following points.

1. The polar bear is an international circumpolar resource.
2. Each country should take whatever steps are necessary to conserve the polar bear until the results of more precise research findings can be applied.
3. Cubs, and females accompanied by cubs, should be protected throughout the year.
4. Each nation should, to the best of its ability, conduct a research program on polar bears within its territory.
5. Each nation should exchange information freely and the International Union for the Conservation of Nature (IUCN) should function to facilitate such exchange.
6. Further international meetings should be called when urgent problems or new scientific information warrants international consideration.
7. The results of the First International Scientific Meeting on the Polar Bear should be published.

The IUCN was asked by the five nations to act as an information centre and to coordinate the exchange of research results on polar bears. The Conservation Foundation in the United States became the catalyst for the next stages of development. In 1967, the Foundation funded Dr. Richard Cooley of the University of Washington

to organize another meeting of polar bear scientists. After Cooley met with key persons in each of the five polar bear nations, the IUCN, hosted the first meeting of Polar Bear Specialists at its headquarters in Switzerland in 1968.

Travel funds for an invited group of scientists were provided by the Conservation Foundation. Besides discussing a number of scientific questions and management needs, the scientists also organized themselves into what is now known as the IUCN Polar Bear Specialists Group of the Survival Services Commission. Initially, the group met every two years, from 1968 to 1972, to discuss the coordination of research and management of polar bears. But, most importantly, with the active support of their governments, they successfully negotiated an agreement on the objectives and text of a ground-breaking document that was simply named the "Agreement on the Conservation of Polar Bears". Although the document is sometimes also referred to as "The International Agreement on the Conservation of Polar Bears and Their Habitat", this is not the technically correct title.

The Agreement on the Conservation of Polar Bears

On 15 November 1973, the Agreement on the Conservation of Polar Bears was signed in Oslo, Norway (see Appendix I for the complete text). It was ratified by three countries (the minimum number required) on 26 February 1976 and came into effect three months later. The remaining two countries ratified the Agreement shortly thereafter, making formal support unanimous. After completion of the trial period of five years, the Agreement was unanimously reaffirmed for an indefinite period in 1981. From a political point of view, one of the most significant aspects of this remarkable Agreement is that it was the first time the five arctic nations successfully negotiated a framework for addressing a unique circumpolar concern. The proceedings of the first meeting on polar bears, held in Alaska in 1965, and all subsequent meetings of the Polar Bear Specialists Group up to the present, except for the politically sensitive meeting of 1968, which has never been released, are freely available to be downloaded in PDF format from the website of the IUCN Polar Bear Specialist Group (http://pbsg.npolar.no). Taken together, they represent a detailed record of the history and progress of polar bear research and management, nationally and internationally, from its inception.

Of particular significance, from a biological perspective, is that the Agreement is fundamentally sound scientifically. It is not simply a protectionist document, which would have contributed little of substance. Although the Agreement allows for taking polar bears (which includes hunting and capturing), it sets out specific conditions under which those activities may take place. These are: for *bona fide* scientific purposes, to prevent serious disturbance to the management of other resources, by local people exercising traditional rights, and for protection of life and property. All the countries agreed to conduct national research programs on polar bears, with particular emphasis on the conservation and management of the species and to exchange data from those studies.

From the viewpoints of either ecological soundness or overall conservation, Article II is probably the most profound part of the Agreement and the one which will, if acted on by all nations over the long term, be of the most significant benefit. It states "Each Contracting Party shall take appropriate action *to protect the ecosystems of which polar bears are a part* (my emphasis), with special attention to habitat components such as denning and feeding sites and migration patterns, and shall manage polar bear populations in accordance with sound conservation practices based on the best scientific data." Clearly the original intent was to protect polar bear populations from becoming endangered as a result of either overhunting or the detrimental effects of humans on the en-

vironment. Equally clear is the recognition that the conservation of a large and potentially dangerous carnivore requires a flexible management plan. Since the original development of the Agreement, the unforeseen but now overarching threat of climate warming and its negative effects on sea ice and polar bears have

come to dominate our concerns about the long-term survival of the species. The urgent conservation need for polar bears now is to respond to climate warming in a way that protects their habitat, as agreed to in Article II of the Agreement, and committed to by the signatories in 1973.

Legal protection of polar bear habitat

Largely stimulated by the negotiation of the Polar Bear Agreement, there was a great burst of new research projects through the 1970s and 1980s. As data accumulated, several new areas of polar bear habitat were given varying degrees of legal protection in different countries. The following

Polar bear skeletons showing indiscriminate and excess harvest from hunting with setguns in Svalbard. (© Thor S. Larsen)

examples are not exhaustive list, but give an indication of the extent of international efforts.

Approximately 40% of the land area on Svalbard was protected by Royal Decree in June, 1973. This included three national parks, two nature reserves, and 15 bird sanctuaries. In 1976, the Northeast Svalbard Nature Reserve was made into a Biosphere Reserve under UNESCO's Man and the Biosphere program. Because of this, most of the denning areas and important summer sanctuaries in that region are now completely protected. Even entry by scientists to do research on polar bears is allowed by permit only.

The National Park of North and Northeast Greenland, which includes a lot of good polar bear habitat, was established in 1974. Subsistence hunters from neighbouring Ittoqqortoormiit/Scoresbysund are allowed to hunt there but may only use small boats or dog sleds for access. The vast majority of the polar bear hunting in this area by Greenlanders is carried out during spring by dog sled which limits their hunting range considerably. Furthermore, since the late 1970s, polar hunting activity in the National Park has decreased significantly. Part of Melville Bay in Northwest Greenland—another important area for polar bears—was established as a Nature Reserve in 1981. Hunting in this area, and all other travel, is totally prohibited. All identified denning areas in Greenland now receive protection up to 200 nautical miles out to sea.

In 1976, Wrangel and Herald islands, which have some of the most important polar bear denning areas in the USSR, were designated as state reserves. Managers of reserves can stop or restrict all human activity within their boundaries, including research, and visitors are not allowed.

In Canada, Polar Bear Provincial Park was established along the Hudson Bay coast of northeastern Ontario in 1970. It is a wilderness area that contains important maternity denning habitat in winter and summer sanctuaries for bears of all age and sex classes during the open water period in summer. No motorized transport is permitted. In Manitoba, the Cape Tatnum and Cape Churchill Wildlife Management Areas were established in 1968 to give managers the ability to regulate activities, including research, along the coast. The areas are fairly large and include most of the important denning areas and summer sanctuaries along the western coast of Hudson Bay. In 1996, Wapusk (Cree for polar bear) National Park was established and included the majority of the maternity denning area, Cape Churchill, and much of the Manitoba coast where bears fast during the summer. In southeastern Baffin Island, Auyuittuq National Park, primarily established for its spectacular scenery, contains a small amount of polar bear denning and summering habitat in the fiords in the northern areas. On Bathurst Island in the Canadian High Arctic, Polar Bear Pass National Wildlife Area was established in 1986 to protect wildlife and habitat. It is not a high-density polar bear area but some animals migrate through the pass seasonally and a few females den there. Subsequently, and of greater importance, several new National Parks were established in areas where polar bears have maternity dens or spend the summer during the open water period, in Nunavut, Northwest Territories, and Yukon. In recognition of the traditions of local Inuit, and to obtain their support for the creation of the parks, their hunting privileges continue within the borders of many.

In the United States, the Alaska National Wildlife Refuge (ANWR), established in 1960 and enlarged in 1980, includes part of the Beaufort Sea coast near the Canadian border in which a significant portion of the polar bears from the southern Beaufort Sea den. In 2009, the US Government set aside 200,000 square miles of Alaskan coastline and adjacent waters as "critical habitat" for polar bears, under the authority of the Endangered Species Act. Under this regulation, government agencies are prevented from authorizing activities that could hurt recovering species, which would include some activities associated with hydrocarbon exploration and production.

Responses to international concern: Initial progress and some ongoing concerns

In the years immediately following the first international meeting in 1965, the total size of the recorded polar bear kill throughout the Arctic continued to increase. Consequently, the countries involved with harvesting could not afford to simply wait until the results of long-term research studies were completed, or an international agreement was negotiated, before taking action. Simple recognition and acceptance of the reasons for international concern, and our obvious collective inability to harvest polar bear populations sustainably, provided abundant justification for action.

In 1968, for the first time, the Northwest Territories of Canada imposed quotas on all its villages from which polar bears were hunted. In the absence of scientific information on the distribution or size of any polar bear populations, the average of the previous three years' harvest was calculated separately for each settlement and a slightly lower value was set as the quota. At the time, it was explained to the Inuit hunters that this was an interim measure and that quotas would be revised, up or down, in response to population studies when they were eventually completed.

Soon afterward, two important committees were formed in Canada, to create a framework to facilitate the use of all sources of scientific and Traditional (i.e., aboriginal) Ecological Knowledge (TEK), sometimes also termed Local Ecological Knowledge (LEK), as the basis for management of polar bears and planning future research. The Polar Bear Technical Committee is supposed to consist of the research biologists from each jurisdiction that has responsibility for managing polar bears (four Provinces, two Territories, and the Federal Government), knowledgeable representatives of Inuit hunting groups, and invited experts, in relevant areas such as population modelling, physiology, and so on. They meet annually to discuss the research done in the past year, evaluate priorities, plan new studies, and consider the application of new research results to management and conservation goals. The Polar Bear Administrative Committee then evaluates the recommendations of the Technical Committee, directs the biologists to undertake research on areas of concern, makes decisions on the management of polar bears on a nationwide basis, and coordinates Canadian activities with other countries as needed. In theory, this allows for the direct application of new research results in a timely manner. Although, as with most things, politics sometimes gets in the way and slows things down, this system continues to serve the overall conservation of polar bears in Canada reasonably well.

In 1971, Alaska ceased the unlimited harvest of polar bears once allowed to residents for their own use and established an annual limit of three bears per person. The number of sport-hunting permits was restricted in 1971 to 210 for the western area and 90 for the north area. However, in 1972, the United States passed the Marine Mammal Protection Act (MMPA) and all hunting of polar bears ceased, except by native people for subsistence purposes. It also became illegal to import polar bears or parts thereof (including hides) into the United States, except for bona fide scientific purposes. However, major shortcomings of the Act included that it provided no restrictions on the number of bears that could be killed by subsistence hunters, there was no longer a closed season of any kind, and there was no protection for bears in dens or females with cubs. Although the total kill was reduced in Alaska, in terms of legal protection for polar bears, some of the provisions of the MMPA set the United States back to some degree, at least as far as polar bears were concerned. In the first decade and a half after the passing of the MMPA, a significant proportion of the kill was, legally, concentrated on the most valuable portion of the population: the reproductive adult females.

Meanwhile, restrictions on the harvest were established in the European Arctic. In Norway, an

Two adult males interact near Cape Churchill in Wapusk National Park.
(© Jenny E. Ross)

"Act on the Protection and Harvest of Polar Bears" was introduced in 1957 to provide a legal basis for regulating the catch in Svalbard. The shooting of polar bear cubs and females was prohibited in 1965. In 1967, it became illegal to use oversnow machines, boats, or aircraft to pursue or kill bears and, in 1970, the number of permits issued for killing polar bears on Svalbard was limited to 300. These were divided between residents, trappers, weather crews, sealers, and tourist hunters. Finally, in 1973, the Norwegian government established a five-year moratorium on the hunting of polar bears in Svalbard. The moratorium was not lifted. In 2001, the Svalbard Environmental Protection Act was introduced, under which all species are protected unless specific reg-

Greenland. However, in 1976, this regulation was changed so that only cubs up to one year of age and their mother were completely protected throughout the country. In 1988, the regulations were amended again to prohibited taking of cubs up to two years of age and their mother everywhere in Greenland, except in the municipalities of Upernavik and Qaanaaq (i.e. north of 72° N in NW Greenland) and Ittoqqortoormiit/Scoresby Sound on the east coast. In these three municipalities it was permitted to shoot cubs older than one year of age and their mother. Finally, in October 2005 it became prohibited anywhere in Greenland to shoot cubs still accompanying their mother, irrespective of the age of the cubs, and the mother. Polar bears in dens were protected from disturbance in May 1988. In January 1975 all bears (including family groups) became totally protected in all Greenland from June 1 until August 31. In 1976 this was changed to July 1 until 31 August in all Greenland. In 1978 this was changed so that the period of total protection became August 1 to September 30 in the Tasiilaq municipality in SE Greenland.

Although there were no quotas, the recorded harvest by Inuit hunters was 100 to 150 polar bears annually and that simply continued. By the late 1990s, it became clear from satellite tracking of individual bears that the populations they were harvesting from in West Greenland were shared with Canada. In 2006, an arbitrary total quota of 150 (100 in West Greenland and 50 in East Greenland) was established. In 2007, the total was further reduced to a total of 139. However, that number is still not part of a coordinated estimation of total sustainable harvest by both countries, based on the results of a scientific study of population size and it is likely the Baffin Bay population is still being harvested unsustainably.

The USSR had already declared complete protection of polar bears in 1956 and the ban on hunting was well enforced. However, following the break-up of the USSR and the formation of the Russian Federation, significant economic dif-

ulations allow for a harvest. No harvest of polar bears is permitted.

General regulations applying to all Greenland for the harvest of polar bears were first introduced in 1974 and took effect in January 1975. According to these regulations cubs up to two years old and mother bears accompanied by cubs up to this age were completely protected throughout

ficulties were experienced by people living in remote areas of northern Russia and subsidies for societal needs including food, fuel, and jobs created serious basic needs. Enforcement of wildlife regulations suffered and bears were killed for food, as threats to life and property, and for illegal commercial purposes. Although it is difficult for obvious reasons to accurately document the extent of poaching, estimates based on interviews in local villages indicated a range of 70 to 300 bears killed annually in Chukotka. Clearly, illegal hunting has become a serious and continuing problem in Russia at the moment.

The first co-management agreement

The polar bear population of the Southern Beaufort Sea is shared between the United States (Alaska) and Canada and the bears there are hunted by both the Inuvialuit of Canada and the Inupiat of Alaska. In Canada, following the establishment of quotas in 1968, there were enforced regulations governing quotas, closed seasons, and protection of females with cubs and bears in dens. In Alaska however, following the passage of the Marine Mammal Protection Act (MMPA) in 1972, it became legal for native people to kill polar bears for subsistence purposes without restriction. The Federal Government could not take over management and conservation until the population was legally declared to be depleted. There was no coordination of a total harvest level between the two countries. Even if the bears killed in Alaska, harvested for subsistence purposes only, contributed to an overharvest situation, harvesting would have been legal under the MMPA until such time as the population was declared depleted. That didn't make much conservation sense.

Clearly, there was a need to do something more quickly than was likely to be possible through government agencies. However, if the Agreement between the United States and Canada on the conservation of the Porcupine Caribou Herd, which took more than ten years to negotiate, was

any example, it could take decades to negotiate an intergovernmental agreement that would likely not even be possible without making significant changes to legislation such as the MMPA. Regardless, the Inuit hunters of both areas remained concerned because the bears continued to be of cultural and economic importance, albeit in different ways, and they were aware of how much negative publicity might be aimed at them if the population became depleted as a result of overhunting. In response, the Alaskan and Canadian Inuit, with the technical assistance of polar bear biologists from both Canada and Alaska, successfully negotiated an unofficial "user to user" agreement between themselves with which to safely manage the polar bears of the southern Beaufort Sea. In two short years, they concluded a formal agreement, signed in Inuvik, Northwest Territories, on 29 January 1988. The hunters used all the scientific information available, and heeded the technical advice of the scientists while still retaining many of their own views on several aspects. However, the most significant point was that they voluntarily took on the leadership role to conserve the bears. Although the Agreement itself had no basis in the legal systems of either country, that would be relatively unimportant so long as both groups abided by it's terms. This was a landmark development in polar bear conservation, and demonstrated the capability of native people to take a direct leadership role in wildlife management in the Arctic.

A detailed assessment of the success of the first ten years of the Agreement, led by Charlie Brower from the North Slope Wildlife Management Department and the late Andy Carpenter from the Inuvialuit Game Council and several colleagues, was completed in 2002. They concluded that, while there was room for improvement in a number of areas, the overall goals of the Agreement were being achieved. Consequently, they recommended that the Agreement remain in effect, which it has. In the course of that review, it was also noted that, at the time the Agreement was first negotiated, the ongoing harvest levels were at about what was estimated to be sustainable. Thus, no reductions of harvest levels were needed, and no difficult negotiations required to equitably share a smaller harvest than people were used to. However, a more rigorous test of the longer-term efficacy and robustness of the Agreement may be coming up relatively soon because the population now appears to be declining in response to the negative effects of climate warming. If a continuing downward population trend is confirmed, then the sustainable harvest will have to decline, possibly precipitously, which in turn will require making much more difficult decisions if the Agreement is to survive.

Further evidence of the overall importance of the Southern Beaufort Sea Polar Bear Agreement and its achievements was that, in later years, it served as a model and partial inspiration for similar user-based conservation agreements. Agreements are now in place on conservation of the beluga population shared between Canada and Alaska, polar bear populations shared between the Inuvialuit of the Beaufort Sea and the Inuit from Kugluktuk (Coppermine) and Cambridge Bay in Nunavut, and more formalized population-based Memoranda of Agreement between the Government of Nunavut and the communities that hunt them.

Guiding of non-resident sport hunters in Canada

When Canada ratified the Agreement on the Conservation of Polar bears in 1976, it also submitted a Memorandum of Understanding to clarify that hunting polar bears was a traditional right of Inuit and Indian peoples and that, "the local people in a settlement may authorize the selling of a polar bear permit from the sub-population quota to a non-Inuit or non-Indian hunter, but with additional restrictions providing that the hunt be conducted under the guidance of a native hunter and by using a dog team and be conducted within Canadian jurisdiction."

This economic opportunity provided by guiding non-resident hunters (mostly Americans) greatly emphasized the importance of being able to demonstrate that hunted populations were being managed sustainably, which in turn generated considerable support for ensuring scientifically-based sustainable harvest levels. At no time did the guided sport hunt increase the number of bears taken; the tags issued came out of the quota that had already been established for each village. The use of mechanized vehicles such as snowmobiles is not allowed for hunting, although they are used for taking supplies to camps. The hunt is supposed to be conducted by dog team. The potential economic benefit to the Inuit, however, is significant because, instead of receiving $1,000 or so for a hide, a guided hunt may sell for $20,000 or more. Guides, helpers, and others in the community providing other services share in the benefits. In a cash-poor economy with few opportunities for diversification, the income from guiding hunters for several species of wildlife in the Arctic can be extremely important.

Initially at least, there was an additional conservation benefit to the bears from the guided sport hunt. Each village has an allotment of polar bear tags assigned to it and the resident Inuit hunters have all winter to get them. Thus, as long as conditions are favourable for travel, it is unusual not to fill the quota. However, the tags assigned to guiding non-resident hunts were actually paid for and owned by the individual hunters. If the hunt was unsuccessful, the tags were not returned to the Inuit hunters. Since not all sport hunts are successful, several tags were not used each year. Thus, although the economic benefits of an unsuccessful still went to the local Inuit, fewer polar bears were killed in total. Although that rule still applies in the Northwest Territories, unused sport hunt tags are now returned to the Inuit hunters in Nunavut, thus eliminating that small incidental benefit to the bears.

The opportunity to spend up to two weeks

travelling by dog team on the sea ice and experience some aspects of the life of an Inuk hunter first hand is a rare one. To me, just going on such a trip would be more rewarding than taking a polar bear hide home for a trophy. In fact, with the steady rise in ecotourism in polar regions, it is quite likely that undertaking similar trips with the primary objective of seeing wild polar bears and learning about their habitat and ecology will soon become more important than hunting for trophies. There is a significant economic opportunity that, for the most part, has not yet been taken up in North America or Greenland, through ecotourism to see polar bears is thriving and economically significant in Svalbard. .

Following passage of the MMPA in 1972, it was not legal to import polar bear hides from legally guided sport hunts in Canada, so most non-resident hunters came from countries such as Germany, Japan, and Mexico. However, in 1994, the U.S. Congress amended the MMPA to allow importation to the United States of legally taken hides from "qualified populations" (i.e. those that met several criteria including that the legal harvest was sustainable and based on scientific studies, quotas were enforced, and that there was a management agreement in place between the user groups and government agencies that ensured a sustainable quota). The southern Beaufort Sea polar bear population was one of the five populations that qualified, largely because of the proactive efforts of the users themselves to ensure harvest levels were sustainable, and to establish a signed co-management agreement between the two user groups. Following this change, the proportion of tags allocated to sport hunters in the southern Beaufort Sea increased markedly, as it also did in the other approved populations. However, following the classification of polar bears as "threatened" by the United States in 2008, importation of hides from Canada was no longer permitted, thus removing the incentive for US hunters to participate in guided hunts.

Comment on the International Polar Bear Agreement

In the more than 35 years that have passed since the first international meeting on the conservation of polar bears was held in Alaska in 1965, there has been an impressive amount of progress. Even though there are still large gaps in our knowledge of polar bears, an enormous amount of research has been completed. Much of this information has already resulted in sig-

nificant changes and management actions throughout the Arctic. Because of the unique degree of cooperation between the circumpolar nations, The Agreement on the Conservation of Polar Bears and the IUCN Polar Bear Specialist Group continue to promote research and coordinate their management. In an age when new species are becoming endangered ever more frequently, and environmental degradation continues on a global scale, the interna-

tional coordination of research, conservation, and management, represents a considerable success in conservation, although significant issues, both new and old, still need to be addressed.

In his book, *International Wildlife Law*, Simon Lyster noted, "The Agreement has proved very successful as a legal conservation instrument ... and ... has undoubtedly contributed to the establishment of protected areas for bears, to restrictions on hunting, and to the

A polar bear scavenges on the remains of a bowhead whale in the Alaska National Wildlife Refuge.
(© Daniel J. Cox/ NaturalExposures.com)

An Inuk-harvested polar bear hide drying on a beached schooner named Polar Bear, in the Canadian Beaufort Sea.
(© Ian Stirling)

substantial amount of scientific research that has been carried out in recent years." He also noted weaknesses in the Agreement: especially that the terms are not enforceable in any country and there is no infrastructure to oversee compliance. However, as Lyster went on to note, "The fact that Parties are not required to hold regular meetings to recommend ways of making the Agreement more effective has not yet been a serious hindrance, but it may make it easier for Parties to ignore the provisions of the Agreement if they prove to be a serious stumbling block to future industrial development in the Arctic."

Although not formally required, the IUCN Polar Bear Specialist Group continues to meet every four years or so to exchange data on research and management, identify and coordinate new research into priority areas for conservation, and pass resolutions on the most

POLAR BEARS: The Natural History of a Threatened Species

serious research and management issues of the day. The requirement to protect polar bear habitat has been most rigorously addressed by the Norway and the United States. In Canada and Greenland, polar bears and denning areas occur in several national, provincial, and territorial parks but the degree of protection afforded is highly variable. Details of research and management programs of all countries over the decades are available in the proceedings of the Polar Bear Specialist Group meetings since 1970, available as PDFs, that can be downloaded free from www.pbsg.npolar.no.

Facing the overarching threat of climate warming

The significance of climate warming to polar bears will be dealt with in a later chapter, but suffice it to say that the severity of this threat overrides all other concerns. Although there are still substantial numbers of polar bears in the Arctic today, it is clear that is changing and likely to continue to change both more rapidly and significantly in the foreseeable future if the climate continues to warm as is projected.

In 2008, Mr. Dirk Kempthorne, the Secretary of the Interior of the Government of the United States, classified the polar bear as vulnerable under the Endangered Species Act. It was a courageous decision, one he did not undertake lightly. The US Fish and Wildlife Service had asked the US Geological Survey to undertake a review of everything that was known about polar bear populations, which it did in great detail and presented in a series of seven reports. (As a disclaimer here, I note that I authored one of those reports and was a junior co-author on two others.) The overarching conclusion was that climate warming had already been documented with significant negative effects in three of the 19 circumpolar populations and, while there were likely effects in other populations as well, the available data were inadequate to support or reject that hypothesis. One of the seven reports predicted, with strong quantitative support, the likelihood that two-thirds of the world's polar bears could be gone by the middle of the century if current projections of climate warming and loss of sea ice are realized.

The reports from the USGS were formally presented to Secretary Kempthorne, whose responsibility it was to make the decision, in September 2007. Early in 2008, he decided to list polar bears as vulnerable, and a few months later assembled all the scientists involved in the reports on a conference call to thank them for their work. Then something happened that especially impressed me. Secretary Kempthorne frankly told us that at the beginning of the review process he did not think "vulnerable" would be the likely outcome of the review. Further, he said that some of his political colleagues had indicated to him that such a decision might not be a career-enhancing decision. However, he told us he had personally read all the science, talked to scientists and others who were not involved with the review, and come to his own conclusion: the science was thorough and the overall conclusions were correct. "Vulnerable" had to be the final listing. Rarely have I been as impressed with a politician's courage to make a decision which, though correct in my judgement, would clearly not have been popular with many members and supporters of his own political party.

In June 2007, ahead of the announcement of the listing classification for polar bears by the United States, a meeting of the signatories to the Polar Bear Agreement was held in Shepherdstown, West Virginia, USA, in accordance with the provisions of the Agreement, including Articles VIII and IX (see Appendix), to discuss concerns about polar bears, including the influence of climate warming. It was agreed that meetings of the Range States, under the Agreement should be held on a biennial schedule or otherwise as agreed to by the parties. The attendees also issued the following statement: "Climate change has a negative impact on polar bears and their habitat and is the most important long-term threat facing polar bears. Action to mitigate this threat is beyond the scope of the Polar Bear Agreement. Climate change affects every nation on the earth and reaches well beyond the five parties to the Agreement so the parties look to other fora and national and international mechanisms to take appropriate action to address climate change." The Range States met two years later (2009) in Tromsø, Nor-

way, to discuss how to move forward with polar bear conservation. It remains to be seen what the long-term influence of these meetings will be, but they did two important things, among others. First, they clearly and unequivocally confirmed "that impacts of climate change and the continued and increasing loss and fragmentation of sea

ice—the key habitat for both polar bears and their main prey species—constitutes the most important threat to polar bear conservation." and that "long-term conservation of polar bears depends upon successful mitigation of climate change." Second, they formally adopted the IUCN Polar Bear Specialist Group to be their technical advisors and requested them to develop an outline of topics that should be included in all national plans for action. It is too early to determine how this initiative will develop but it is starting out in the right direction, especially with respect to identification of what is clearly now the primary conservation issue.

As the sea ice polar bears depend on in several populations is melting both earlier and for longer, females must care for their cubs on land without feeding for longer periods.
(© Sue Flood)

Chapter 12

ENVIRONMENTAL CONCERNS

Environmental threats to polar bears

Initially, the major threat to the survival of viable populations of polar bears was perceived to be hunting or, more accurately, excessive hunting. It is certainly true that substantial numbers of polar bears have been killed especially in the last hundred years or so, for both commercial and subsistence use, and that some populations were overharvested. However, from a technical perspective, resolving issues to do with overharvesting is probably one of the most straightforward

The Molikpaq, a drilling rig built to remain
in the ice on a year-round basis.
(© Ian Stirling)

conservation issues to deal with, in a technical sense at least. Once sufficient resources have been provided to scientifically quantify as much as is practically possible about a population, such as its size, distribution, reproductive success, and age-specific survival rates, it is relatively straightforward to use computer models to estimate the relative degree of risk associated with the application of different levels of harvest, which can be monitored and adjusted as required. Of course, regulation of sustainable harvesting can only deal with legal hunting. Although poorly documented, illegal hunting of polar bears in Russia appears to have become a serious issue in recent years. However, like legal harvesting, the solution simply involves the political will to enforce the law, though sometimes that may be more easily said than done.

The most serious environmental issues for polar bears relate to the consequences of large-scale human industrial activity because they affect not only the bears themselves, but also the entire ecosystems of which they are a part. These include offshore exploration and production of hydrocarbons in seasonally ice-covered waters, widespread contamination of the environment by harmful industrial chemicals, extended season or year-round shipping in the Arctic and, the elephant in the room, anthropogenic climate warming. Making progress on any of these issues requires large commitments from industry and governments at all levels.

Exploration and production of oil and gas

By the 1970s, interest in offshore exploration for oil began to increase in several areas of the Arctic, including the Beaufort and Bering seas, the western coast of Greenland, Svalbard, the Canadian High Arctic Islands, and Hudson Bay to name just a few. Elaborate plans were and are being developed, for year-round drilling in ice-covered waters, large-scale production fields, year-round shipping in special ice-reinforced tankers, and inter-island and sub-sea

pipelines to take oil from the Arctic to southern markets. For example, in the summer of 2010, new subsea hydrocarbon deposits were located during exploratory drilling offshore from Greenland in Baffin Bay. If this discovery is to be developed, it will require a whole network of new support facilities, aircraft, and settlements. Offshore exploration and production activities have given rise to a new suite of concerns for the welfare of polar bears and other arctic marine mammals. These include possible detrimental effects on polar bear habitat, damage to key parts of the food chain (seals in particular), and direct injury or death to the animals themselves.

Up to a point, physical activities such as drilling or ship movements that take place during the open-water period would, initially, probably have limited immediate negative effects on the bears. However, that could change dramatically in the event of a sub-sea blowout of oil, especially one that continued into the winter. When one considers how difficult it seemed to be to close off the damaged well head causing the massive British Petroleum blowout in the ice-free waters of the Gulf of Mexico in 2010, under warm weather conditions, it is pretty clear that a blowout under the ice in the Arctic would have little chance of being stopped at all and would probably become an ecological disaster on a scale never before even imagined in arctic waters. Simply put, the technology does not exist for cleaning up an oil spill under ice-covered waters.

In most arctic areas, the greatest potential ecological problems are likely to occur between freeze-up in the fall and break-up in the spring, in areas where prime polar bear habitat (annual ice) overlaps with proposed or extant offshore drilling and oil-production sites. In both the Alaskan and Canadian areas of the Beaufort Sea, the preferred seal hunting habitat for polar bears is characterized by the system of shore leads that run parallel to the coastline over water depths of about 20-50 m (60-150 ft). Besides being some of the highest quality seal-hunting habitat for the bears, a migration route for seals and whales, these lead systems are also the main seasonal migration route for polar bears moving back and forth between their summering areas and winter hunting habitat. Individual bears may travel up to several hundred km back and forth along the lead system within or between years. Consequently, a substantial portion of the population is likely to pass near any particular point during the course of a winter if it happens to be in an area suitable for hunting seals. Unfortunately, this area of prime polar bear habitat overlaps significantly the area that apparently has the greatest potential for oil production. Hopefully, the chance of a "worst-case scenario" occurring is low, but it is clear that an uncontrolled oil blowout under the ice during the winter could be devastating. The westward flowing currents would probably carry oil under the ice from the point of origin and affect seals and bears far from the original problem area.

A second possible source of large-scale oil pollution is spills from ice-breaking tankers, should year round shipping of oil becomes a reality. Smaller spills originating from support vessels working around offshore rigs, from cargo ships using the Northwest Passage for regular shipping, or from breaches in undersea pipelines are likely to occur just in the course of normal operations. Because lead systems and polynyas probably offer easier passage for ships when the sea is ice-covered, it seems likely that those moving oil will eventually travel through them during the winter, thus raising the risk level.

In general, polar bears prefer to stay on the sea ice so that they can continue to hunt. Thus, anything that pollutes or otherwise impacts the ice, compared to the open water, has a greater potential to immediately negatively affect the bears. Steve Amstrup, George Durner and colleagues from the USGS in Alaska conducted a unique study, in a relatively small geographic area, to model the possible risks to polar bears near two oil production facilities on the north coast of Alaska. Using 15,308 satellite locations from 194 radio-collared polar bears, and almost 2,000 highly variable modelled oil spill trajectories, they simulated how many polar bears might come into contact with a spill of 5,912 barrels (the maximum thought probable from a pipeline breach) at two production sites. They compared the vulnerability of the bears during the open water season in September (when some bears are on the beach) and October, when there are mixed ice conditions. The estimated number of bears to come into contact with oil in September ranged from 0 to 27 compared to a range of 0 to 74 during October. At the site which was furthest offshore near the active ice zone, 75% of the trajectories affected 20 or fewer bears compared to 9 or fewer at the site closer to the coast. Although limited in scale and specific to certain sites, and only the product of theoretical modelling, this study clearly illustrates how much more at risk bears are to spilled oil if there is ice present.

Local habitat modification

In recent years, ingeniously engineered structures have been developed to facilitate offshore drilling for oil through the winter when the sea is covered with ice. In relatively shallow waters, artificial islands, made of gravel deposited at the drill site, have been used to drill from. However, much of the marine area of interest for hydrocarbon exploration in the Arctic is too deep to consider drilling from artificial islands. Thus, there has been considerable interest in developing rigs that can keep working while in ice-covered waters through the winter. One of the most interesting was the mobile arctic caisson known as the *Molikpaq*. This structure was designed for drilling to depths of up to 6,000 m (19,685 ft) in 20-40 m (65-130ft) of water. It was used in the Canadian Beaufort Sea in the late 1980s, where it remained in position throughout the winter as the drifting annual ice passed by on either side. Polar bears were seen in the vicinity of the *Molikpaq* throughout the winter, although most did not remain in the area for long. There was one significant exception, however. In late winter, during the coldest weather periods, most of the cracks in the sea ice that polar bears hunt beside froze over. At such times, the flow of annual ice from east to west, past semipermanent sites such as the artificial islands or the *Molikpaq*, resulted in local habitat modification. Cracks in the ice with open water formed on the downstream side of the structure and sometimes became quite sizeable. There was always at least some open water on the downstream side of the structure because of the constant passage of ice. The cracks close to the rig were used routinely by small numbers of seals, probably because of the easy access to air without having to self-maintain breathing holes. Sometimes up to 30 or 40 seals were present for a day or two at a time. Probably because of the accessibility of seals, polar bears were also attracted and they often hunted right at the base of the rig, where the open crack of water was. When the ice in surrounding areas remained frozen during the coldest periods of the winter, the crack by the *Molikpak* still remained open, and some bears lingered there for days or even weeks to hunt.

As one of the conditions of receiving a drilling permit, contractors are required to maintain a regular record of wildlife sightings. Because the field staff tend to be quite interested in polar bears, or afraid of them, bear sightings are recorded with a fair degree of accuracy. For example, between 26 October 1984 and 30 April 1985, the *Molikpaq* crew reported 176 polar bears. They sighted bears of all ages and sex classes except adult females with cubs-of-the-year. Twenty-eight of the bears were thought to be hunting and 17 were feeding on seals they had caught near the rig. The working platform was safe, several metres above the ice. The workers took all kinds of pictures of bears hunting and eating seals, cubs playing, and even an entertaining video of foxes scavenging from the seal kills and being run off by the bears. One adult female with a radio collar, accompanied by

a yearling cub, was observed on six different days between December 25 and January 2. Other sightings of an adult female with one cub were made on six different days between February 21 and April 10. As spring advanced and more new cracks appeared in the ice, thus creating many more locations where seals were readily accessible, the number of bears around the *Molikpaq* declined again.

Polar bears are quick to learn new tricks and

clearly it did not take them very long to realize that humans were not hunting them near either the *Molikpaq* or the artificial islands, and they soon realized there was good seal hunting habitat by the rigs. This has two quite important possible consequences. One is that some bears may become used to the presence of humans, lose their fear of them, and thus become either more dangerous to unarmed people working on the ice or unduly vulnerable to hunters. Another risk to the

bears of being attracted is that if there was even a fairly small blowout or spill, they could easily come into contact with it. In this circumstance, even small, perhaps undetectable quantities of oil could be fatal to individual polar bears.

Physiological effects of oil on polar bears

During the late 1970s, when offshore exploration for oil in ice-covered waters began to increase rapidly, several of us expressed concern about pos-

An artificial island build in the southern Beaufort Sea to facilitate drilling for hydrocarbons in the winter. (© Ian Stirling)

sible negative effects of oil spills on polar bears. Previous research on fur seals and sea otters, which also rely on their fur for a significant portion of their insulation, had confirmed that contact with oil could cause death from hypothermia. Although a polar bear receives a significant amount of its insulation from its fat layer, it primarily depends upon its fur for keeping warm.

From anecdotal observations, it not only appeared that polar bears did not avoid oil or some other unnatural chemicals, but rather that they often seem to be actively attracted. Possibly the smell of oil-based products attracts them because of some similarity to prey, or maybe they are simply curious, but no one knows the answer at this point. It has often been reported by Inuit hunters that when polar bears enter unoccupied camps, they will bite cans of oil used for snow machines or outboard motors. How much they might consume is unknown but on one occasion in Churchill, a subadult bear was observed drinking directly from a pail of used hydraulic oil. How much it consumed before it was discovered and chased away is unknown but it almost certainly died of kidney failure as a result. Polar bears regularly ingest non-toxic human garbage but may also consume lethal materials. One bear at the Churchill dump consumed part of a lead acid battery while another on the north coast of Alaska drank a mixture of ethylene glycol (antifreeze) and rhodamine B used for marking a runway. Both bears died. From these observations, it seems highly likely a bear would feed on a dead seal or bird that had been fouled with oil.

Thus, one might think that it should have been obvious that an oil spill would be devastating to polar bears but surprisingly, that was not the case. I was at several industry-government meetings in the 1970s where scientists who raised concerns about potential detrimental effects of oil on polar bears and seals were scoffed at, with the implication that we were only trying to use such concerns as a way or raising money for research. Incredibly,

one senior marine mammal administrator with the Canadian Federal Government at the time derisively told those attending one such meeting I was at that, although oiled bears, like oiled birds, would make great pictures in the newspapers, the oil would have no significant negative effects on the bears! Finally, after considerable pressure from the Canadian Polar Bear Technical Committee and the IUCN Polar Bear Specialists Group, enough funding was raised from government and industry to conduct a small number of tests on four polar bears in the lab at Churchill, under the direction of the late Nils Øritsland and some of his students.

Not surprisingly, some initial tests on polar bear hides purchased from Inuit hunters showed that oil significantly reduced their insulative value. However, the most dramatic results followed the exposure of three live polar bears to oil in a manner that simulated natural conditions in the wild, in that they entered a pool with oil on the surface. Curiously, the bears showed no aversion to the oil despite its strong unrefined smell. When they came out of the water, oil remained stuck to their fur. Although these observations applied to only three animals, they suggested that a bear would not avoid a lead with oil on the surface of the water and, that if it swam across a lead with oil on the surface, its fur would immediately become fouled and remain on the bear when it climbed out onto the ice again.

At this point, it is relevant to return to our long-term observations of undisturbed wild polar bears and their feeding behaviour. Polar bears are extremely clean animals. When eating a seal on the ice they may get fat on their fur and if they do, they clean themselves both during and after feeding. This is not surprising since fur that has become soiled by contact with seal fat will become matted and not have nearly as high an insulative value as clean fur. Thus, one almost never encounters a dirty bear and, if one does, it was probably either feeding immediately beforehand on a large carcass such as a dead whale or bearded seal and has not yet had time to clean itself; or, it is sick.

It was winter at Churchill and cold when the studies were done. The oiled bears soon began to shiver and lick the unrefined crude oil from their fur in the same manner as they lick seal oil from their fur when feeding on a seal out on the sea ice. However, unlike seal fat, oil is toxic when swallowed. Two of the experimental bears suffered kidney failure and soon died. The third was treated in the Assiniboine Zoo in Winnipeg for five months. It recovered fully and was eventually transferred to a zoo in Japan. No experiments were done on the fourth animal.

The rest, as they say, is history. Few well-designed scientific experiments in Canada have been so controversial and, sadly, their enormous significance was so little recognized at the time. When news of the deaths became public, the press vilified the scientists for weeks for their (inaccurately) perceived inhumane behaviour. The reason the experiments had to be done in the first place, and the large amount of valuable information that was obtained, were totally ignored. While we all deeply regretted the loss of the two animals that died, it was abundantly clear with hindsight that their sacrifice was hugely important to the conservation of the species and protection of their habitat. The speed of the grooming response of the bears to having their fur fouled by oil, and the immediate negative physiological consequences, left no doubt in anyone's mind about one thing: oil is bad for polar bears and, if oiled bears are left untreated, the contamination will almost certainly kill them. Saving the life of the third bear at the Assiniboine Zoo was also important because it demonstrated that it is possible to salvage an oiled bear if treatment begins soon enough. Largely as a result of this study, the danger to polar bears of an oil spill or blowout is now recognized and taken seriously when assessing the potential negative effects of hydrocarbon exploration, production, and shipping in polar bear habitat.

Toxic chemicals

About fifty years ago, the insecticide dichlorodiphenyltrichlorethane, better known as DDT, was found in the tissues of Adelie penguins in Antarctica. This finding signalled confirmation of the universal transport of toxic chemicals into the remotest reaches of the oceans of the world. Since then, many studies have reported high levels of contamination by many chemicals in the fat of mammals and birds at the upper trophic levels in polar regions. In part, this results because most contaminants are lipophilic, that is, they are primarily deposited in the fat of most species at all trophic levels, from invertebrates to mammals. Through a process known as biomagnification, as species successively prey on each other all the way up the food chain, they accumulate contaminants from the fat in the species they eat into their fat and pass it along up the food chain, at ever greater concentrations, until they reach a maximum in the top level arctic predators such as seals, polar bears, and humans. Thus, by periodically assessing the chemical concentrations in the top predators, we can directly monitor the chemical health or deterioration of the ecosystem.

In a recent review, Christian Sonne from Denmark provided an excellent summary of the levels of contamination of polar bears from long-range transported contaminants and some of the negative effects on their health. It is sobering to consider some of these findings from animals in a part of the world that most of us would still like to think of as remote and pristine. However, since the 1940s, large amounts of fat-soluble anthropogenic toxic chemicals have been transported via upper atmosphere air currents and marine currents to the Arctic, where they have become biomagnified in animals like polar bears and seals. Because the top-level arctic predators live in a cold environment, they rely heavily on storage of energy-rich fat deposits, in which the contaminants reside, for reproduction and survival. The main groups of chemicals found in polar bears include OCs (organochlorines) such as PCBs,

OCPs (organochlorine pesticides) like DDT, PBDEs (polybrominated diphenyl ethers) used as flame retardants, and PFCs (perfluorinated compounds) used as surface treatments. In addition, mercury from burning of coal (as well as mercury from natural sources) has been accumulating in the tissues, hair, kidneys, liver, and blood of arctic marine wildlife for the last century or so. Ironically, because of the patterns of atmospheric and marine long-range transport, some of the most geographically isolated polar bears in the Arctic, such as East Greenland and Svalbard, are now among the most contaminated animals in the Arctic today.

Several correlations between contaminant levels and possible effects in polar bears have been reported and the consequences speculated upon. For example, one study showed up to 70% of the total OC load in a mother polar bear's fat is transferred to her offspring during nursing. Similarly, transfer to neonatal young while still developing in the uterus is a risk. However, the possible consequences of either are not understood. Of particular concern is the possibility of negative impacts of contaminants on developing reproductive and immune systems. Studies reporting aberrations in reproductive genitalia in particular have attracted considerable attention. Up to 30 female polar bears have now been documented with an enlarged clitoris in Svalbard and East Greenland, and reduced size of reproductive organs in some East Greenland bears. In Svalbard, two yearling female polar bears were captured that also had a 20 cm penis containing a baculum (an internal penis bone). Neither of the females had a Y chromosome (carried by male mammals), so they were considered to be pseudohermaphrodites. Two other captured females had aberrant genitalia and an enlarged clitoris. Such anomalies could result from excessive production of androgen, caused by a tumor in the mother, or because of an endocrine disruption from environmental pollutants. Although, to date, there is no conclusive explanation for these findings from Svalbard, their presence in some of the most contaminated polar bears n the world is concerning.

In one particularly interesting study, Andy Derocher and colleagues compared levels of several contaminants in samples collected from polar bears in Svalbard in 1967 to samples collected in 1993-94. Although the levels of a some chemicals had declined, the levels of several others had increased, a few dramatically so. Harvest of polar bears in Svalbard ended in 1973 and it was expected that the population would soon recover from a previous over-harvest. However, the mean age of adult females in the Svalbard population remained similar to other populations where pollution levels are lower but harvest is intense. Although females older than 16 years accompanied by cubs-of-the-year are common in most Canadian populations, they are uncommon in the Svalbard population for unknown reasons. During the years that the population was expected to recover more rapidly, levels of several pollutants increased. Whether reproductive impairment of females, lower survival rates of cubs, or increased mortality of reproductive females could be related to increased levels of contaminants is not confirmed at this point, but remains a matter of concern and the subject of continuing research. As Sonne emphasized in his review, in most cases the best we can do is describe correlations which possibly may, or may not, confirm a causal relationship. Because of this shortcoming, it is especially important that, where possible, future studies include conducting controlled experimental work with other carnivore models such as arctic foxes or sled dogs and, where practical, on wild polar bears.

Chapter 13

CLIMATE WARMING: THE GAME CHANGER IN POLAR BEAR CONSERVATION

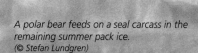

A polar bear feeds on a seal carcass in the remaining summer pack ice.
(© Stefan Lundgren)

At first glance, the status of polar bears might appear secure. They are widely distributed throughout the seemingly unlimited, ice-covered seas of the circumpolar Arctic and still inhabit the majority of their original habitat. In 2009, their worldwide abundance in 19 different subpopulations, was estimated by the IUCN Polar Bear Specialist Group to exceed 20,000 (Table 1). However, the high degree of evolutionary adaptation to life on the sea ice that has made

An adult male polar bear walks through a barnacle goose colony on Svalbard, eating eggs but ignoring the adults which he would have difficulty catching.
(© Jouke Prop)

matter (mainly spawning salmon) in their diet. Polar bears are very large animals and they too become that way by eating seals, not vegetation. In fact, it is particularly telling that the smallest black and brown bears in the world are found in the arctic tundra adjacent to the coast of northern Labrador and the Beaufort Sea, respectively, precisely because the terrestrial food resources available to them in those areas are so meager.

Sometimes there are opportunities to scavenge on the carcasses of naturally dead whales washed up on a beach, or walrus carcasses at terrestrial haulouts. While such opportunities certainly provide substantial nutritional benefits to a few bears in the short term, they are not sufficiently abundant, or predictable in their occurrence, to sustain large populations of polar bears in the longer term.

To appreciate how critical it is for polar bears to have continued access to large expanses of sea ice habitat and to be able to travel over it easily in search of prey, consider that the average bear uses a home range of at least a few thousand, and sometimes as much as a few hundred thousand, square kilometres in which to acquire its annual food requirements. On average, each bear requires approximately 43 ringed seals, or ringed seal equivalents each year to survive, though larger animals would require more and smaller ones fewer. Limited hunting of other species reduces the number of ringed seals needed, to some degree. For example, a 300 kg (650 lb) bearded seal might be considered as the food equivalent of about three or four ringed seals. However, in crude numbers, a population of 20,000 or more polar bears worldwide would require more than a million ringed seals (or ringed seal equivalents) annually. There is simply no other marine mammal in the Arctic that is sufficiently abundant, and small enough to be relatively easily killed by bears of all sizes, that could replace ringed seals for sustaining the majority of the world's polar bears. Consequently, for polar bears to survive in anything like today's total numbers depends upon

the polar bear so successful is also the very reason why it is so vulnerable to the effects of climate warming. A large carnivorous specialist such as the polar bear has few options if its habitat, and thus its access to its prey, disappears. The polar bear took tens of thousands of years to evolve from a terrestrial bear into the ultimate ice bear. That process cannot be reversed in a few generations, during which time the polar bear would once again become a terrestrial bear and revert to a diet of berries, other vegetation, and bird eggs. Although the depredations of polar bears on the eggs of ground-nesting geese or ducks may be devastating for the birds in some cases, the nutritive benefits to the bears are few. In many cases, the energy expended while searching for berries or chasing prey such as flightless geese during their molt exceeds the caloric return, even if the bears are successful. Regardless, the total energy obtainable from land-based food sources is trivial in comparison to what is obtained annually from hunting on sea ice.

Furthermore, in carefully controlled feeding experiments with captive brown bears from the coast of Alaska, researchers have confirmed that their large body size simply cannot be sustained solely by eating vegetation. To achieve their massive body size, Alaskan brown bears are dependent on large-scale access to energy-rich animal

both the continued survival of large seal populations and huge areas of ice from which the bears can hunt them.

Sea ice for polar bears in the future

The Fourth Assessment Report of the Intergovernmental Panel on Climate Change of the United Nations, published in January 2007, came to the "unequivocal" conclusion that the world's climate is warming rapidly, that the warming will continue, and that the primary cause is the long-term increase in the levels of greenhouse gases originating from human activities. What this means for polar bears, is that the large-scale loss of their sea ice habitat will continue, as will severe negative impacts on the bears' survival, reproduction, overall distribution, and total population size. Despite a superficial increase in total ice cover in the winter of 2008-2009, following the record low in 2007, the ice was thin and melted rapidly, resulting in another all-time record low in September 2009, followed by yet another in the record class in 2010.

Figure 14 illustrates the model projections of

A hungry subadult polar bear scales cliffs with Thick-billed Murres on Coats Island in northern Hudson Bay in search of eggs. The energy expended would far exceed any trivial return from Murre eggs.
(© Kerry Woo)

the amount of sea ice present in September (the time of the annual minimum) in the Arctic Ocean from 1900 to 2100. The solid black line indicates the average of the computer models that have been constructed to illustrate the changes that have taken place to date, and what the pattern of continued loss of ice is projected to be by the end of the century. As you can see, various models project both higher and lower rates of sea ice loss than the mean, but none suggests either stability or increasing amounts of sea ice into the future. However, the most dramatic

A large male polar bear leaping onto a floe after one of two bearded seals trying to escape.
(© Stefan Lundgren)

and concerning information in Figure 14 is shown by the red line. The values on the red line are not from a computer model. They are the actual annual measurements taken directly from aerial survey and photographic data in the early years and then from satellite images (which began in 1979). In cold, clear numbers, the track of the red line confirms the reality that we are actually losing ice in the Arctic Ocean more rapidly than even the most pessimistic scenario forecast by any of the computer models. That is a truly sobering conclusion.

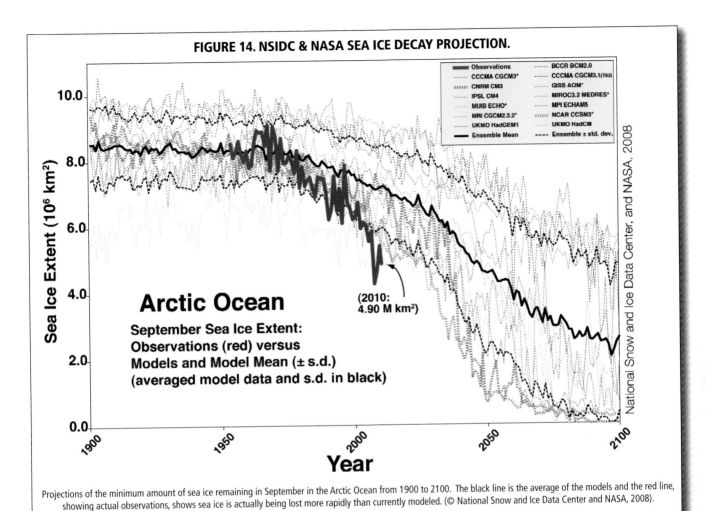

FIGURE 14. NSIDC & NASA SEA ICE DECAY PROJECTION.

Arctic Ocean

September Sea Ice Extent:
Observations (red) versus
Models and Model Mean (± s.d.)
(averaged model data and s.d. in black)

(2010: 4.90 M km²)

National Snow and Ice Data Center, and NASA, 2008

Projections of the minimum amount of sea ice remaining in September in the Arctic Ocean from 1900 to 2100. The black line is the average of the models and the red line, showing actual observations, shows sea ice is actually being lost more rapidly than currently modeled. (© National Snow and Ice Data Center and NASA, 2008).

The rapid loss of ice in the Arctic Ocean in the last few years is dramatically illustrated in Figure 15. Note the huge change between the gold line, which designates the average minimum ice from 1979-2000, and the red line which shows the new record set in 2005. Then look at the huge loss again to the minimum in 2007. The combined losses in 2005 and 2007 represent a total area greater than the whole of Greenland, in only a few years. The minimum in 2010 was similar to that of 2007.

An important point to keep in mind when looking at the graphs presented in this chapter, whether they deal with amounts of ice, break-up dates, or the condition indices of polar bears, is the importance of long-term data sets. There is usually sufficient variation between years in most of the data sets that even 10 years or so would be too short a time to be able to detect an underlying long-term trend. This underlines the absolutely critical importance of collecting and maintaining long-term data sets. Without them, we can conclude little.

Are all polar bear populations currently vulnerable to the negative effects of climate warming?

There is a remarkable amount of variation in the ecological circumstances that prevail in the areas occupied by the presently recognized 19 populations of polar bears throughout the circumpolar Arctic. Even so, there are recognizable patterns within which populations can be grouped. Steve Amstrup, formerly with USGS in Anchorage,

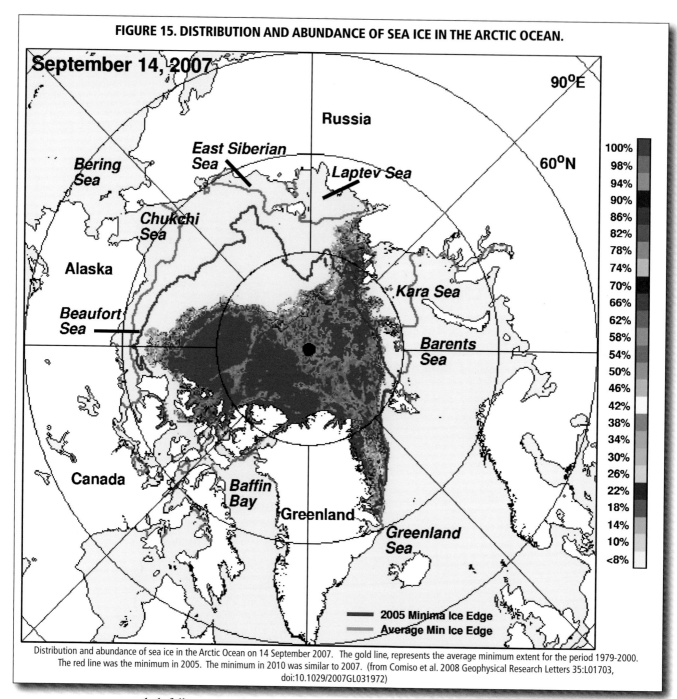

FIGURE 15. DISTRIBUTION AND ABUNDANCE OF SEA ICE IN THE ARCTIC OCEAN.

September 14, 2007

Distribution and abundance of sea ice in the Arctic Ocean on 14 September 2007. The gold line, represents the average minimum extent for the period 1979-2000. The red line was the minimum in 2005. The minimum in 2010 was similar to 2007. (from Comiso et al. 2008 Geophysical Research Letters 35:L01703, doi:10.1029/2007GL031972)

helpfully assigned populations that shared enough significant aspects of their seasonal patterns of ice melt and availability, along with forecasts of future ice patterns, into four fairly ecologically distinct "ecoregions" (Figure 16). These are: 1) the Seasonal Ice Ecoregion, characterized by the complete, or almost complete, melting of all ice for several months every year, during which time all bears depend on their stored fat reserves for survival on land until the ice re-freezes in late fall; 2) the Archipelago Ecoregion, which includes the interisland channels of the Canadian Arctic Archipelago; 3) The Polar Basin Divergent Ecoregion, characterized

FIGURE 16. POLAR BEAR ECOREGIONS.

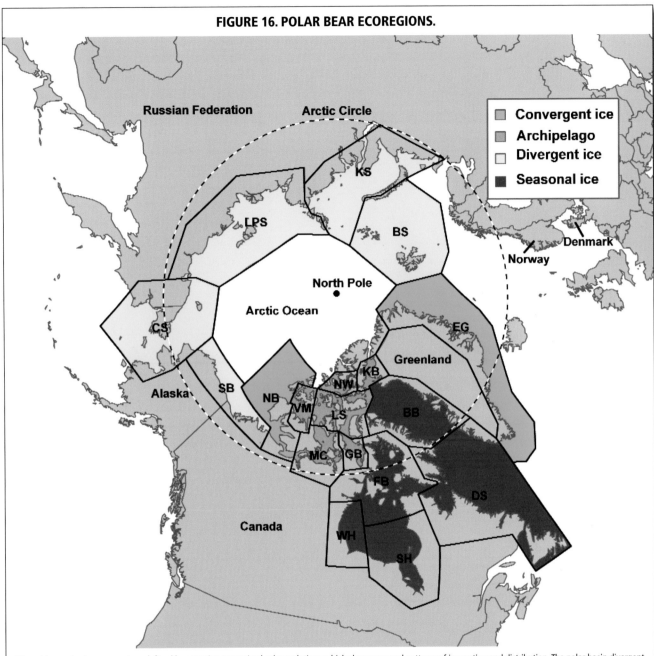

Map of four polar bear ecoregions defined by grouping recognized subpopulations which share seasonal patterns of ice motion and distribution. The polar basin divergent ecoregion (yellow) includes Southern Beaufort Sea (SBS), Chukchi Sea (CS), Laptev Sea (LVS), Kara Sea (KS), and the Barents Sea (BS). The polar basin convergent ecoregion (PBCE) (green) includes East Greenland (EG), and Northern Beaufort Sea (NBS). The seasonal ice ecoregion (red) includes southern Hudson Bay (SHB), western Hudson Bay (WHB), Foxe Basin (FB), Davis Strait (DS), and Baffin Bay (BB). The archipelago ecoregion (orange) includes Gulf of Boothia (GB), M'Clintock Channel (MC), Lancaster Sound (LS), Viscount-Melville Sound (VM), Norwegian Bay (NW), and Kane Basin (KB) (Based on Amstrup et al. 2008 *Geophysical Monograph* 180, American Geophysical Union, Washington, DC) (Graphic: Evan Richardson)

by the extensive formation of annual sea ice that typically is then advected by wind away from the coast toward the central polar basin; and 4) the Polar Basin Convergent Ecoregion, which is characterized by ice being compressed against the coastlines by the winds and currents that removed it from the divergent regions. Historically, the convergent region was also characterized by

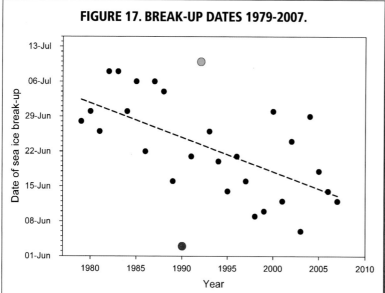

FIGURE 17. BREAK-UP DATES 1979-2007.

Figure 17. Date of break-up of the sea ice used by the Western Hudson Bay polar bear population, from 1979-2007. (From Stirling and Lunn 1999 and Lunn and Stirling unpublished data).

tween 1971 and 2003, the mean annual temperatures increased with trends varying from a minimum of 0.5°C per decade at Churchill to 0.8°C per decade at Chesterfield Inlet. During April through June, the average temperature near Churchill and over the adjacent offshore ice has warmed at a rate of 0.3 to 0.5°C per decade since 1950. In response to this well-documented warming trend, there has been a parallel trend toward progressively earlier melting of the sea ice and break-up in Western Hudson Bay. By 2000, the average date of break-up was already a full three weeks earlier than it was only 30 years previously in 1970 (Figure 17), and that trend is continuing. (Break-up is defined as the point in the annual melt when the surface cover becomes 50% ice and 50% water.)

For eight years, we tracked the movements of polar bears with satellite radio collars on the sea ice, from freeze-up through the winter until they returned to shore to fast through the open water season. Regardless of whether break-up was early or late (see the lower blue line in Figure 18), all the bears with radio collars came ashore for the summer three weeks after break-up each year (see the upper red line, Figure 18). This indicates that the disappearance of the remaining ice, following the point where it covers only 50% of the water, is sufficiently rapid that three weeks of additional hunting is the maximum available to the bears. However, the fact that the bears continue to make the most of the remaining ice for as long as they can, regardless of break-up date, clearly indicates the importance of maximizing their caloric intake before coming ashore. Thus, it is not surprising that there is a strong, statistically significant, relationship between the date of break-up and the body condition (fatness) of the bears when they come ashore to fast (Figure 19). Clearly, the earlier that break-up occurs, the poorer the condition of both adult females and males, and vice versa.

Losing body condition because of earlier break-up shortening the feeding period at the best time of the year might not seem too surprising for the

having the largest amount of multiyear ice because of the heavy rafting and compression of ice that did not melt between years.

To date, the negative effects of climate warming on polar bears have been clearly demonstrated in only one population each in the Seasonal Ice and Divergent Ice Ecoregions. While it is almost certain that similar negative effects are also occurring in other populations, unfortunately, the long-term population data needed to confirm or reject that hypothesis do not exist.

Climate warming and polar bears in western Hudson Bay

The western Hudson Bay polar bear population is one of those in the Seasonal Ice Ecoregion (Figure 16). Detailed studies of the population dynamics and body condition of polar bears in relation to sea ice ecology, based in Churchill, Manitoba, have been continuous for over 25 years and, in less detail, for more than 15 years before that. Because of the duration and robustness of that data set, it has been possible to clearly confirm the negative effects of climate warming on the polar bears and much about the mechanisms involved.

At most weather stations in Hudson Bay, be-

POLAR BEARS: The Natural History of a Threatened Species

adult females with dependent young because of the combined demands of hunting for themselves and their cubs as well as continuing to nurse the cubs. In addition, the females also have some of their kills on the ice stolen by adult males. In comparison, one might predict that adult males would be the least vulnerable age and sex class of bears to losing condition as break-up becomes earlier because they only have to hunt for themselves, they are experienced hunters, they don't have the metabolic drain of nursing cubs, they regularly take kills away from smaller bears, and they can rest undisturbed by other bears while fasting along the coast. However, although there is a bit more variation in the relationship between their body condition and break-up date than there is for the adult females, the pattern is the same and the relationship is statistically significant.

The reason that hunting seals is so critical for polar bears in the late spring and early summer is because ringed seal pups are born in early April and weaned about six weeks later. At that time, they are up to 50% fat, not very experienced with predators, and readily accessible at breathing holes and cracks in the ice, or while resting on the surface … until the last ice melts. Once the seals are in the open water, they are mainly inaccessible to polar bears. Because of the long open water season in Western Hudson Bay, bears there probably accumulate 70% or more of the energy they will need to survive for the entire year during the late spring and early summer feeding period, prior to break-up. However, because the average date of break-up is already three weeks earlier than it was only 30 years ago (Figure 17), the bears are being forced to prematurely abandon hunting seals at the most important time of the year, at progressively earlier dates, and that trend is continuing. Furthermore, in addition to coming ashore with less in the way of stored fat reserves, the bears are now being forced to fast for even longer periods because freeze-up is becoming progressively later in the fall as well.

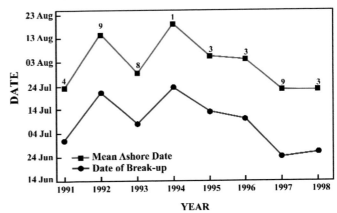

FIGURE 18. BREAK-UP AND DATE OF COMING ASHORE.

Date of break-up in the area of sea ice where female polar bears with satellite collars spent at least 90% of their time each year (blue line) and the mean dates the bears came ashore in those years (red line). (From Stirling et al. 1999, *Arctic*, 52:294-306)

Independent confirmation of the absolutely critical importance to polar bears of having an abundant supply of ringed seal pups to prey on through the spring and early summer came from simultaneous population studies of both polar bears and ringed seals in the southeastern Beaufort Sea from 1971 through 1989. Twice in those decades, ringed seal pup production plummetted by 80% or more for a duration of two to three years. In response, the productivity and survival

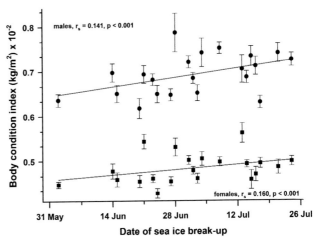

FIGURE 19. BEAR CONDITION & BREAK-UP DATE.

The relationship between the date of break-up and the physical condition of adult female (lower line) and adult male (upper line) polar bears when they come ashore to fast through the open water season. (From Stirling et al. 1999, *Arctic*, 52:294-306 and E. Richardson unpublished data)

of polar bear cubs immediately plummeted as well, and did not recover until soon after the productivity of seal pups returned to normal levels. Clearly, the most important thing to the survival of a healthy polar bear population is an abundant, and accessible, supply of fat, newly weaned, ringed seal pups.

Six bears feed on the carcass of a whale on the coast of Svalbard during the open water season when they must wait on land for freeze-up.
(© Norbert Rosing)

In other analyses of data from the polar bears of western Hudson Bay, it has also been confirmed that as break-up date became progressively earlier, the annual survival rates of cubs, subadults, and very old bears declined in response. The earliest break-up on record to date was in 1990 and

in that year, only about a third of the cubs born are known to have survived. In comparison, one of the latest dates of break-up was in 1992, and about two-thirds of the cubs are known to have survived, about double that of 1990. These differences dramatically underline the vulnerability of cubs to higher mortality rates if their mothers are unable to take on enough fat reserves before fasting through the open water season.

Throughout most of the circumpolar range of the polar bear, cubs remain with their mothers for two and a half years before weaning. Yet, for reasons that are still not understood, in the 1980s,

POLAR BEARS: The Natural History of a Threatened Species

years despite a steady loss in condition, but that will follow in due course whenever some critical point has been reached. Between 1980 and 2007, there was a significant decline of over 50 kg in average body mass of lone, probably pregnant, adult females (Figure 20). This has resulted in both smaller litter sizes and reduced cub survival. Of 118 litters of cubs leaving the denning area with their mothers in the spring in the early 1980s, when pregnant females in the fall were much heavier than they are now, 14 were triplet litters and one even had 4 cubs. Although occasional triplet litters were still seen in the late 1990s and 2000s, their occurrence is now unusual. The lightest adult female we have ever weighed in the fall, which we were able to confirm produced cubs the following spring, weighed 189 kg. Judging from the steady decline in body weight illustrated in Figure 20, if the climate continues to warm as predicted, and the ice continues to break up at progressively earlier dates, it seems pretty clear that in a few more decades, not many adult females will still be capable of reproducing in western Hudson Bay and any cubs that might be born will have difficulty surviving.

Not surprisingly, as a consequence of all these declining parametres, the polar bear population of western Hudson Bay dropped from about 1200 in 1987 to 935 in 2004, and is probably still going down. Once the population began to decline as a consequence of changes driven by climate warming, the previously sustainable harvest became an overharvest and Inuit hunting along the Nunavut coast of western Hudson Bay unintentionally served to accelerate the decline. Now, even with very little harvesting (though an increasing number of problem bears are being shot), all the parametres being monitored are continuing to decline. Computerized modelling of the population and demographic data suggests the population would probably continue to decline even without any harvesting or removal of problem bears.

With progressively earlier break-up, there has

conditions were apparently so favorable that in some years well over 40% of the one and one-and-a-half-year-old cubs on land during the open water season were already independent and survived as well as cubs that were not weaned until a full year later (at two and one-half years of age), in other parts of the Arctic. The proportion of lone yearlings in Western Hudson Bay declined from a high value of 60% in 1982, to about 15-20% by the early 1990s and very few have been recorded in the 2000s.

So far, a decline in survival has not been detected in adult males or females in their prime

also been a steady increase in the number of bears that have to be captured or removed by conservation officers at Churchill because they are threatening human life or property (Figure 21). Since earlier break-up is also significantly correlated with a decline in the bears' physical condition (Figure 19), it seems clear that many bears, especially subadults, exhaust their stored body fat well before freeze-up makes it possible for them to return to the ice and hunt seals. However, rather than lie down and die quietly like a hare or a caribou might, a large predator like a polar bear goes looking for an alternative food supply. Along the Hudson Bay coast, the most likely possible options are settlements, tourist facilities, or hunting camps, all of which have abundant attractive smells. In 2009, freeze-up was very late, many bears were thin and hungry, and there were eight known instances of cannibalism, a high number which contrasted dramatically with only about two or three such events known from the previous 30 years. Whether any of the instances observed resulted simply from scavenging on a naturally dead bear is unknown but most of the victims were probably the result of active predation. Such events in themselves are not proof of the effects of climate warming, but they are consistent with what we would predict when adult male bears exhaust their stored fat and get hungry.

Although there has been considerable variation between years, it is clear that over the long term, the number of problem bears has increased at Churchill over the past 25 years or so (Figure 21a). The lower graph (Figure 21b) clarifies why. There is a direct relationship between earlier dates of break-up of the sea ice, poorer condition of the bears, and thus an increase in the number of problem bears handled in Churchill, i.e., the earlier the ice breaks up, the more hungry bears there are in the fall that may become problems, and conversely. Similarly, over the last 20 years or so, residents of the Nunavut coast of western Hudson Bay, from Arviat to Rankin Inlet, have also reported seeing many more polar bears

around town later in the ice-free season, especially in recent years, though the degree to which this trend has been documented has been limited. There has also been an increase in the number of problem bears shot. Unfortunately, the interpretation of some Inuit hunters resident on the Nunavut coast north of Churchill still seems to be that they are seeing more polar bears because the population is increasing. However, from the cumulative documentation of population trends, reproductive parametres, and physical

condition of bears in relation to break-up dates, it is abundantly clear that the reason more polar bears are being seen in the coastal settlements along the western Hudson Bay coast (including at Churchill) is that they are hungry, and not because their population is increasing.

Other polar bear populations in the Seasonal Ice Ecoregion

A pattern of earlier break-up of sea ice in southern Hudson Bay between the mid-1980s and the mid-2000s, similar to that in western Hudson Bay, has now been confirmed. Over the same period, there has been a corresponding decline in the body condition of polar bears of all age and sex classes when they come ashore to fast through the open water season. It is highly likely that a decline in population size will likely follow, if it is not underway already. Similarly, it been demonstrated that the time of break-up of the sea ice, and the duration of the open water periods in Foxe Basin, Davis Strait, and especially in

An adult male carries the remains of a cub-of-the-year he has killed and cannibalised.
(© Daniel J. Cox/ NaturalExposures.com)

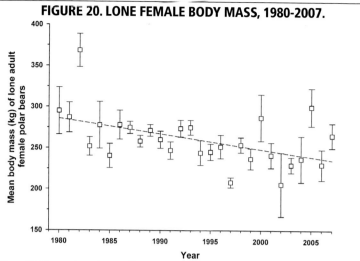

FIGURE 20. LONE FEMALE BODY MASS, 1980-2007.

Figure 20. Mean estimated mass of lone (and thus likely pregnant) adult female polar bears in the fall in Western Hudson Bay from 1980 through 2004 (dashed line indicates fit of linear regression) (from Stirling and Parkinson 2006. *Arctic* 59:261-275)

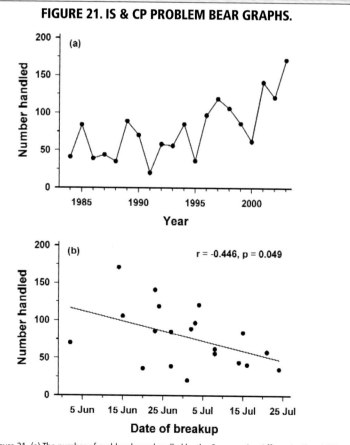

FIGURE 21. IS & CP PROBLEM BEAR GRAPHS.

r = -0.446, p = 0.049

Figure 21. (a) The number of problem bears handled by the Conservation Officers in Churchill in Western Hudson Bay from 1984 through 2003, and (b) the relationship between the date of sea-ice break-up and the number of problem bears handled (solid line indicates the statistical fit of the correlation) (from Stirling and Parkinson 2006. *Arctic* 59:261-275)

Baffin Bay, also show patterns similar to western Hudson Bay. Thus, if global temperatures continue to warm, as predicted by the IPCC, break-up of the sea ice will continue to occur at progressively earlier dates. Consequently, it is probably only a matter of time before negative effects on the polar bear populations in those areas can be confirmed from longer-term population data as well.

At present, there are indications of thinner bears and more problem animals being reported around settlements in Baffin Bay, which may also be related to less favourable trends in ice conditions. However, at the moment, there are insufficient long-term trend data of high enough quality to be able to confirm or deny possible cause-and-effect relationships between warming and negative population trends. In addition, our ability to focus on the possibility of negative effects related to climate warming and accelerated ice loss in Baffin Bay is confounded by an apparent overharvest situation that has prevailed for several years.

Claims by some that climate warming has stimulated an increase in the size of the polar bear population in Davis Strait are unsupported by data, although a recent mark-recapture study has confirmed that the population there is larger than was previously thought. However, polar bears probably became more abundant in Davis Strait over the last 25-30 years because of the combined effects of a series of cool years with heavier ice in the early 1990s, a huge increase in the harp seal population (i.e., increased food base), and a conservative polar bear harvest level, which has been in place for decades. However, more recent analyses indicate the ice is now breaking up earlier and that survival and recruitment rates of cubs may be declining. Furthermore, one of the most rapidly warming areas in the Arctic is Davis Strait. If this continues to be the case, and the ice continues to break up earlier, it is likely that the population size in Davis Strait will eventually decline in response.

Climate warming and polar bears in the southern Beaufort Sea

The southern Beaufort Sea polar bear population, shared by northern Alaska and northwestern Canada, is in the Polar Basin Divergent Ecoregion. The estimated population size appears to have declined from about 1800 in the 1980s to about 1500 in 2006. This decline has not resulted from an overharvest by aboriginal hunters because, throughout that period, the number of bears taken has never exceeded the previously estimated sustainable quota and has often been considerably lower. The major known ecological change during that period is that in an increasing number of summers, the southern edge of the remaining ice in summer has retreated farther away from the coast to the north, beyond the northern edge of the continental shelf, and the ensuing open water period has persisted for longer periods. This is important because ringed seals, which prefer water depths of about 50-150 m (165-490 ft), are considerably more abundant over the relatively shallow and biologically productive waters over the continental shelf where the depth does not exceed 300 m (985 ft). Seals are apparently still reasonably abundant and accessible to bears when ice floes to hunt from remain over the continental shelf. However, beyond the northern edge of the shelf, the water becomes much deeper, biological productivity declines, and the densities of seals drop considerably. An analysis of the movement patterns and habitat preferences of several hundred polar bears with satellite radio collars, conducted by George Durner and colleagues from Alaska, showed a clear preference for the annual ice, shore leads, and pack ice over the continental shelf. In general, the bears avoided ice over deeper water unless there was simply no ice available over shallower areas. Furthermore, as the time of freeze-up approached in late fall, bears wearing satellite collars concentrated close to the southern edge of the pack ice. This strongly suggests the bears were positioning themselves to be able to access the new young ice over the conti-

nental shelf, and the seals that live there, as soon as possible after it formed. Back in 1973, I had a unique opportunity to witness the response of bears along the southern edge of the polar pack to the sudden formation of new ice south toward the coast in late fall. I was about 120 km (75 miles) offshore, about 24 hours after the new ice first froze. There were bear tracks everywhere, all headed south. In some places, there were still areas of open water where the ice hadn't frozen yet and

A hole clawed by a bear through 45 cm of solid ice in a vain attempt to capture a seal hauling out through a breathing hole beneath a sheet of rafted sea ice. (© Ian Stirling)

A ringed seal birth lair washed away by an unseasonally early rain. The pup was dead on the ice.
(© Ian Stirling)

holes where bears had fallen through ice that was not yet thick enough to support their weight. To my surprise, I saw several seals that had been caught at their exposed breathing holes, even though the ice appeared so thin that it looked as if the seals should be able to discern a bear above them before surfacing to breathe. I wondered if, after a period of not being hunted, the seals might have become less wary than normal.

To assess the possible significance of changes in the duration and extent of open water on polar bears along the southern coast of the Beaufort Sea, Eric Regehr and colleagues defined the "ice free" period as the time when the southern edge of the pack ice was further offshore than the northern edge of the continental shelf; in other words, when polar bears were restricted to an area where the densities of seals

POLAR BEARS: The Natural History of a Threatened Species

days and survival of adult female polar bears was only about 77%. When the survival rate of the adult females gets that low, the population will decline even without harvesting.

During population studies conducted on the sea ice in the spring from 2004 through 2006, following summer-fall seasons when the ice-free period was 135 days or more, we also found considerable evidence of polar bears suffering acute nutritional stress. Several instances each were seen of starvation, cannibalism, and bears hungry enough for seals that they clawed through sheets of solid ice in vain attempts to capture seals that might have breathing holes in the ice platform below. The average thickness of 14 holes clawed through solid ice sheets was 41 cm (16 in) with a range from 22-75 cm (9-30 in). Again, these events in themselves are not proof of climate warming. However, they are consistent with the kinds of things we would predict when bears become excessively hungry because of the possible negative effects of climate warming on their habitat and access to their primary diet species. In this context, it is worth noting that during our previous 30 years of field work in the Beaufort Sea, any of these individual events would have seemed unusual—that we saw several instances of each in only three years was dramatic.

Christine Hunter from the University of Alaska and her colleagues then used the data collected in the same coordinated population study in the southern Beaufort Sea from 2003 to 2006, along with climate modeling data, to predict the frequency of occurrence of years with extensive open water and little ice over the continental shelf for extended periods and assess the outlook for polar bears in the Southern Beaufort Sea. Their modeling projections indicated drastic declines in population size by the end of the 21st century. As noted earlier, 2007 set a new record for minimum amount of ice remaining in the Arctic Ocean at the end of summer. As of September 2010, three of the years of greatest ice retreat on record in the Arctic Ocean occurred in the last four summers.

available to be preyed upon were considerably lower than they are when the ice is over the continental shelf.

In 2001 and 2002, the ice-free period in the southern Beaufort Sea was relatively short (a mean of 92 days) and the annual survival of adult female polar bears was approximately 99 per cent. In 2004 and 2005 however, because of unusually warm summers, the ice-free period averaged 135

A ringed seal birth lair on which the roof has melted because of warm weather. The extreme fatness of the mother and the immature appearance of the pup suggest this event was premature.
(© Mats Forsberg)

A continuation of this trend will almost certainly have further negative effects on the bears.

Other polar bear populations in the Divergent Ice Ecoregion

For most of the polar bear populations in the Divergent Ice Ecoregion, there are no adequate long-term data with which to assess the possible effects of the lost sea ice cover on polar bears. However, from Figure 15, it is clear, that when compared to the long-term average from 1979-2000, the loss of sea ice in these areas has been catastrophic. This is especially true for the Chukchi Sea, Laptev Sea, and Kara Sea populations in the Russian Arctic. Although there have been anecdotal reports suggestive of difficulties being experienced by polar bears in Russia, these are the populations for which we have the least amount of either long-term or reliable recent scientific data. However, from a simple comparison of the enormous decline in sea ice along the Russ-

ian coast, to that in the Southern Beaufort Sea where significant negative impacts on polar bears have been confirmed, it seems highly probable the Russian polar bear populations are already experiencing severe negative impacts from climate warming.

Bear populations in the Archipelago and Convergent Ice Ecoregions

For the most part, we lack sufficient long-term information to be able to determine how much climate warming may be influencing long-term polar bear population trends in the Archipelago Ecoregion (M'Clintock Strait, Gulf of Boothia, Lancaster Sound, Viscount Melville Sound, and Norwegian Bay). Although it is known in general that increasing amounts of ice are melting, multiyear ice is being replaced by annual ice, and the duration of the open water season appears to be getting longer, we do not have sufficient data to be able to determine how such changes might be

affecting the population trends of polar bears in those areas. Overall, some of the effects of climate warming may be variable at the moment but, over the longer term, if the open water continues to become more extensive and long-lasting, the effects will almost certainly be negative.

Only in parts of the Convergent Ice Ecoregion along the northern coastline of the Canadian Arctic Islands and Greenland (southeastern border of the Arctic Ocean, Figure 16) is some ice predicted to remain into mid-century and beyond. This includes the present-day polar bear populations of the Northern Beaufort Sea, Norwegian Bay, East Greenland, and a currently

Side view of an adult female that was crushed when the roof of her maternity den collapsed on her during the winter. (© Peter Clarkson)

Front view of the same crushed female. One of her cubs is visible by her side. (© Peter Clarkson)

FIGURE 22A. MINIMUM ARCTIC SEA ICE IN 2000.

(© University Corporation for Atmospheric Research)

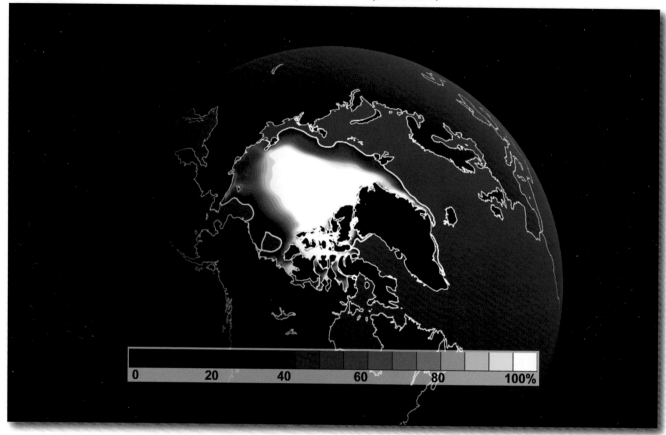

unnamed area along the most northerly coast of the Canadian Arctic Islands and northwestern Greenland. Because the Arctic tips away from the sun for an extended period each winter, cold weather will continue to cause ice to form, seasonally at least, in many areas, though it will be thinner than in the past and will melt earlier. However, because the prevailing directions of both wind and currents tend to move across the polar basin from the Russian side toward northern Canada and Greenland, they will continue to compress whatever ice remains in the polar basin in summer against the islands in this area (Figure 22). It seems possible that the continued compression of remaining areas of seasonal ice in the Convergent Ice Ecoregion will help to create what might, in time, be the last refugium for polar bears if climate warming continues unabated. At this point, it is impossible to speculate how many

bears such a northern refugium might be able to support, or for how long.

Effects of unseasonable warmer weather and rain in the arctic spring

The focus on polar bears as symbolic of the negative effects of climate warming in the Arctic tends to overlook that a whole ice-dependent marine ecosystem is being affected, from the algae and arctic cod that live on the underside of the ice to the bearded and ringed seals that depend on ice as a substrate upon which to give birth to their pups. As long ago as 1979, I witnessed the potentially devastating effects of warm spring weather and unseasonal rain on the subnivean birth lair habitat of the ringed seal. Tom Smith and I were camped on southeast Baffin Island, continuing our collaborative work on polar bears and ringed seal habitat in different areas of the Canadian

FIGURE 22B. MODEL PREDICTION OF MINIMUM ARCTIC SEA ICE IN 2040.

(© University Corporation for Atmospheric Research)

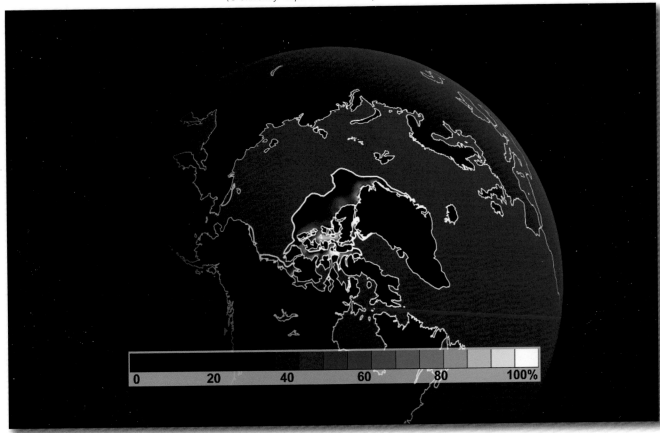

Arctic. Normally, the temperature in early April in that area is in the range of -15 to -20° C (+5 to -5° F). We were searching out seal lairs with Tom's dog and catching bears when we had a sudden warming and 24 hours of steady rain. It was another day or so before the weather improved enough to fly. We went back to the bay where we had been working before the rain started and found the downpour had been concentrated there and had simply washed away most of the snow-drifts. The seal pups were completely exposed when they were only a few days old, leaving them completely vulnerable to predation by arctic foxes and polar bears.

Female polar bears in their maternity dens in wind-drifted snow banks are also dependent upon cold weather to maintain the integrity of the snow at least until the family is ready to re-turn to the sea ice. In June 1989, Peter Clarkson and a colleague found an adult female with two cubs approximately a month old that had been crushed and suffocated when their den collapsed. From the age of the cubs, three to four weeks, it appeared the event must have occurred in mid- to late January. Exactly what the weather was like at the site of the den then is not known because there was no one in the area at the time. However, there had been at least one period during which the temperature went above freezing and there were at least two storms. Whether there might have been any rain is unknown. However, from the documentation of this incident, it is clear that unseasonally warm weather, especially with rain, in the future has the potential to have significant negative effects on polar bears in maternity dens.

Chapter 14

An adult female with three healthy
yearling cubs is an accomplished
mother and hunter.
(© Stefan Lundgren)

THE FUTURE

Concern that the polar bear might become endangered, because of excessive and unregulated hunting throughout much of its range, was the principal motivation for holding the First International Meeting on the Conservation of the Polar Bear in 1965. That meeting in Alaska provided the stimulus for negotiating the Agreement on the Conservation of Polar bears, signed in Oslo, Norway in 1973 (Appendix I), which in turn played a significant role in stimulating a huge international effort in research. Twenty

years later, the overall outlook had improved to the point that the circumpolar existence of the polar bear appeared secure into the foreseeable future, despite the continuation of a number of concerns. Now, more than 40 years later, it is clear the relative optimism that prevailed up to a decade or two ago may have been premature. In the following, I provide a personal view of some of the priority concerns, in ascending order of importance.

Management of hunting

As a result of total bans on hunting polar bears in the Soviet Union in 1956, and in Svalbard in 1973, the previously overharvested populations appeared to recover. Initially, there was some concern that the absence of hunting would result in the bears becoming less cautious about humans so that as their populations increased in size, so would the frequency of bear-human conflicts. To some degree, that concern appeared to have been borne out, at least initially. The experiences in both countries serve as a reminder that simply stopping hunting does not solve all the problems when one is dealing with conservation of large carnivores. More recently, the collapse of administrative structures in the Russian Federation appears to have resulted in reduced enforcement of wildlife conservation

Ecotourists in Svalbard observe an adult female and her lone cub as she travels along the coastline.
(© Ian Stirling)

clearly identified and that is always one of the most important tasks.

Contaminants

It now appears possible that increased levels of contaminants are capable of having significant effects on longevity, reproduction, and the immune systems of polar bears. Levels of different pollutants vary in different parts of the Arctic. Their levels and trends need to be quantified in relation to their sources, so they can be reduced. However, this is clearly a long-term problem and relates to many more elements of the arctic and global ecosystems than simply polar bears.

Making scientific studies and traditional ecological knowledge work together

Although scientifically-based estimates of population size guide the estimation of sustainable harvest for several of the hunted populations, the results from several of those studies are now dated and, for some areas are non-existent (see Table 1 p. 39). There are still no scientifically-based sustainable quotas for polar bears in Baffin Bay, a population shared by Greenland and Canada, despite concern that it has been overharvested for several years. In some areas where new studies have been completed, such as Davis Strait or the Southern and Northern Beaufort Sea populations, it appears that environmental circumstances may be changing in the foreseeable future, so it is uncertain how long projections of sustainable harvest may be relied upon.

A major difficulty at the moment in several regions, but particularly in Nunavut, Canada, has been a rejection of the value of scientific studies by Inuit hunters, especially when research indicates the possibility of a decline in population size which would in turn result in a lower estimate of sustainable harvest. Inuit who have hunted in particular areas for generations have a great deal of natural history knowledge of the bears there when it comes to things like identification of denning areas, important feeding areas, prey species

laws, giving rise to apparently significant, though not well documented, levels of poaching. Clearly, this is a priority problem that needs to be addressed.

In October 2000, the Bilateral Agreement between the United States and the Russian Federation on the Conservation and Management of the Alaska-Chukotka Polar Bear Population was signed by the governments of the Russian Federation and the United States. They have established a scientific committee and have begun to address the problem of establishing and maintaining sustainable harvest levels. There is still much work to do but the need for action has been

taken, areas of summer sanctuary, and so on. Although obviously a hunter's observations from his travels are reliable, it is generally not possible for individuals to be able to gauge accurately something like the size of a population or its trend (increasing, decreasing, stable), simply because the scale of the area inhabited by a polar bear population is so huge, relative to the tiny amount of it accessible to any group of hunters.

What one sees in one's local hunting area may, or may not, be reflective of the vast area occupied by the population as a whole. For example, as noted in the previous chapter, the fact that more bears have been seen in recent years in the fall in Arviat, north of Churchill in western Hudson Bay, does not indicate the population is increasing, as has been suggested locally. All the available scientific studies indicate the population is declining and the reason for seeing more bears around towns is that they are in poorer physical condition and looking for something to eat because of the negative effects of climate warming. On the basis of the most quantitative long-term study of polar bears done anywhere in the Arctic, it is clear that the size of the western Hudson Bay population has, in fact, declined by over 20% in the last 15 or more years. Even though every correlated metric, such as break-up dates, condition of bears, reduced survival, and the results of two additional surveys in areas requested by the hunters were all consistent with the scientific conclusion that the population is declining, this truism is still not currently accepted by many hunters. In Davis Strait, the hunters also reported seeing more bears and concluded that the population was increasing, an impression that was supported by the small amount of scientific data available at the time. Subsequently, an extensive and very expensive three-year scientific study provided some of the most reliable estimates ever obtained for a polar bear population anywhere and confirmed that the population had increased over the previous 20 year or so, the study also noted that the bear population may now be facing the possibility of future

decline because of the negative effects of climate warming on the sea ice. Although hunters suggested the polar bear population was increasing in both areas, a properly designed, large-scale population study spread over the entire region occupied by the bears at the time the survey was conducted, was required to determine whether or not the original hypothesis was correct.

I don't raise this example to say that one approach, science or Traditional Ecological Knowledge (TEK) is better than the other. They are different and each is more appropriate for some applications than the other. Also, Inuit hunters and scientists can work together on most projects and everyone will be the better for it. To me, the essential question to ask about anyone's conclusion about anything, whether from science or TEK, is simply, "What is your evidence, and does it withstand more broadly-based questioning?" For example, if the conclusion relates to where bears den, then seeing the den itself is incontrovertible evidence. Going to the same area in another year and finding no dens is also solid and reliable evidence. However, if the conclusion under discussion relates to where a bear goes in the winter on the sea ice on the edge of the polar basin or Baffin Bay, you need data from a satellite radio collar. If you want to know how many animals there are in a population, then you need to carry out a quantitative scientific study of some sort that covers the whole area. If you want to know the population trend, you have to conduct broad-scale population studies at long enough intervals and with large enough sample sizes to be able to detect change if it is occurring. However, one thing that is very clear is that the international community will not accept any country's claim to be managing polar bears in a sustainable fashion without seeing the results of scientific studies, the conclusions from which can be independently evaluated.

The new polar bear watchers
Undoubtedly, the most the most important fac-

tor helping to ensure the welfare of the polar bear is its enormous popularity. People who know they will never see a live polar bear are as interested in their conservation as those who have. The public as a whole has an insatiable desire to see and read about polar bears. Every year, film crews and writers come to Churchill, Manitoba, to do the same stories as their predecessors, and all seem to still be well received. In our lab, we always know when it is fall because the geese start to fly south, the leaves turn colour, and the photographers begin to phone for information about polar bears at Churchill.

Not too many years ago, polar bears were regarded as pests. Now they are seen as the most valuable attraction that Churchill has going for it. The town motto has become, "The Polar Bear Capital of the World." Every day in fall, specially built vehicles use designated routes to travel far out along the coast from Churchill so passengers can view and photograph the bears. Some visitors remain for a few days at special camps and hang out on the coast to watch bears in a more natural setting. Further down the coast at Nanuk Lodge smaller numbers of guests are taken out to see and photograph bears nearby and the bears come up to the protective fence to view the people at close distances. For hardier souls, Wat'chee Lodge near Churchill takes people out in the bitter cold of early spring to see female bears departing their dens with newborn cubs.

Meanwhile, in recent years, the use of ships to take people around the coastlines of Svalbard, Greenland, and Canada has expanded rapidly. In Svalbard alone, the number of individual eco-tourist visits to different parts of the archipelago

TABLE 5. CURRENT CLASSIFICATION OF STATUS OF POLAR BEARS BY INDIVIDUAL CIRCUMPOLAR ARCTIC NATIONS, THE CONVENTION ON INTERNATIONAL TRADE IN ENDANGERED SPECIES OF WILD FAUNA AND FLORA (CITES), AND THE POLAR BEAR SPECIALIST GROUP OF THE IUCN

Country (and Regions)	Classification	Legislative Authority	Year
International	Appendix II	Convention on International Trade in Endangered Species of Wild Fauna and Flora (UNEP)	1977
IUCN	Vulnerable	Polar Bear Specialist Group Assessment	2005
Canada (National)	Species of Special Concern	Species at Risk Act	1999
Canada (Newfoundland)	Vulnerable	Endangered Species Act	2002
Canada (Ontario)	Endangered	Endangered Species Act	2008
Canada (Manitoba)	Threatened	Endangered Species Act	2008
Denmark (Greenland)			
Norway (Svalbard)	Red List	Vulnerable	2006
Russian Federation		Red Data Book	2001
Russia (Kara-Barents Sea)	Category IV (uncertain status taxa and populations)	Red Data Book	2001
Russia (Laptev Sea)	Category III (rare taxa and populations)	Red Data Book	2001
Russia (Chukchi subpopulation)	Category V (recovering taxa and populations)	Red Data Book	2001
United States	Threatened	Endangered Species Act	2008
United States	Depleted	Marine Mammal Protection Act	2008

(Courtesy: Ian Stirling)

on expedition ships has increased from around 20,000 people ten years ago to almost 30,000 in 2009. One of the primary attractions is the polar bear and the opportunity to see them travelling and hunting on the pack ice. Many of these tours to Churchill and Svalbard are now booked a year or more in advance. Collectively, the ever-increasing number of people who see and become interested in polar bears has created a huge international constituency for their conservation. As a result, non-government organizations like Polar Bears International and the World Wildlife Fund have become incredibly important and have taken over much of the lead role in international polar bear conservation.

Hunting polar bears is still of significant cultural and economic importance to aboriginal hunters in Alaska, Canada, and Greenland. However, if climate warming continues unchecked, and the ice continues to disappear, population after population will follow the trajectory already illustrated in western Hudson Bay. It is not possible to have a sustainable harvest from a declining population. In time, the greater concern may become one of human safety in the presence of ever hungrier bears. However, today and for some time to come, there is a large potential for economic benefit to small northern communities from quality guiding of ecotourists, viewing polar bears, and experiencing arctic wilderness. You can still photograph bears in a population that may not be able to sustain a harvest and, with this kind of "use," each bear can be "recycled" many times.

Climate warming, loss of sea ice, and the future for polar bears

We are facing the previously unthinkable—the possible loss of summer sea ice throughout most of the Arctic in summer in a few decades (see Figure 22). During our study of over 30 years of the ecology of polar bears on the western coast of Hudson Bay, we have quantitatively measured things I can still hardly believe possible in a period as short as a human's working lifetime. The average date of break-up of the sea ice is now a full three weeks earlier than it was only 30 years ago! Freeze-up is getting later as well, thus prolonging the open water period. The overall effects on polar bears in Hudson Bay and elsewhere will be devastating, and mainly because of human-induced climate warming.

Table 5 summarizes the present classification of status of polar bears by and within individual arctic nations, the Convention on International

Trade in Endangered Species of Wild Fauna and Flora (CITES), and the Polar Bear Specialist Group of the IUCN. The great majority of these assessments have little to do with levels of harvest, contaminants, offshore exploration for hydrocarbons, or related issues. At the most fundamental level, the primary factor resulting in assessments such as "vulnerable," "threatened," or "endangered" are based on concerns about the predicted consequences of climate warming.

One sometimes hears the suggestion that climate warming will improve polar bear habitat in the far north. While that may be true for relatively short periods in those few areas where multiyear ice prevails at present, in the longer term a continuously warming climate will degrade and eliminate polar bear habitat everywhere.

Polar bears obtain almost all their annual energy requirements by hunting seals from the sea ice surface, not from other sources. Although they

A set of windblown polar bear tracks disappear into the distance.
(© Ian Stirling)

have been anecdotally reported to eat a wide range of things from berries and seaweed to birds, duck or goose eggs, and even the occasional small fish, the energetic intake from these sources is trivial in relation to the bears annual requirements. Speculations that polar bears might sustain themselves from alternate food sources on land are both fanciful and irresponsible.

Despite the enormous changes that have already been documented in the Arctic and elsewhere because of climate warming, humans still can and must respond. Several top climate scientists have indicated that if the world responds sufficiently in the next few decades, it is still possible to slow and stop the worst anthropogenic climate warming.

In 2007, following the record loss of perennial sea ice, the perception that nothing could be done to avoid catastrophe gained strength and the general media proclaimed polar bears were irreversibly doomed. However, Steve Amstrup and his colleagues from the US Geological Survey Alaska Science Centre provided new hope. In a paper published in the prestigious international science journal, *Nature*, they reported that if the global mean temperature rise could be kept below 1.25° C, combined with traditional wildlife management, it appeared polar bear numbers could be maintained in some parts of their present range at sustainable levels, though lower than present levels, throughout the century.

Carbon levels in the atmosphere and global temperatures could be stabilized, and hopefully reduced over time, if humankind is willing to act. For polar bears, time is critical. The sea ice that dominates the Arctic's marine ecosystem and provides the hunting platform that polar bears depend upon is rapidly disappearing. There are no quick fixes, either through technological developments or adaptations by the bears themselves to a terrestrial environment. Polar bears evolved into their existence as the supremely adapted predator of the sea ice because that large productive habitat was unoccupied. If that habitat disappears then, eventually, so will the bears that live and depend on it. It is vital that all humans and their respective governments use whatever time remains to help reduce global greenhouse gas emissions sufficiently quickly to ensure that both sea ice and polar bears persist for our children and grandchildren to marvel at.

A personal epilogue

The story of the polar bear through recent decades is both rewarding and worrisome. Starting from little knowledge and a deep concern about the survival of the species, scientists, Inuit hunters, and managers made a tremendous amount of progress, primarily by applying the knowledge gained from a great deal of basic research. Maybe, collectively, we can do that again. On a broader scale, even as humans continue to degrade the life systems of the planet, for some reason I continue to retain a certain amount of optimism. In particular, I hope the research on polar bears will help us to understand the critical importance of protecting tracts of habitat large enough to keep ecosystems intact because that is the only way to ensure the survival of large carnivores in general and with them, the biodiversity of the ecosystems they are a part of. We have limited time left in which to act, but the basic concept of what we have to do is not complicated. Humans must learn to be more of an integral part of the environment instead of fighting and destroying it. To the degree we still can, we need to leave an unspoiled Arctic behind us, like a wind-blown set of polar bear tracks across the drifting ice floes that remind us always of the ice hunter.

An adult female polar bear and her 4-month-old cub cautiously approach an unknown curiosity at the edge of the ice, unaware that it is "Icebergcam" documenting their behaviour, but also unaware yet that it is not good to eat. Note how the cub has picked up on the slight nervousness of its mother and stays as close as possible for protection, while still imitating her investigative behaviour (see pp. 152-153).
(© Philip Dalton/John Downer Productions)

GLOSSARY OF TERMS

activity budget documentation (or quantification) of how an animal allocates its time among daily or seasonal activities

Agreement on the Conservation of Polar Bears an international agreement signed in Oslo, Norway, November 15, 1973, by the five nations with resident polar bear populations: Canada, Denmark/Greenland, Norway, the United States, and the former U.S.S.R. The agreement holds member states accountable for taking appropriate actions to protect the ecosystems in which polar bears dwell, paying special attention to places where polar bears create dens, do a majority of their feeding, and where they migrate. Member states are required to manage polar bear populations in accordance with proper conservation practices based on the best available scientific data.

Allen's Rule a biological rule, first suggested by Joel Asaph Allen in 1877, which states that warm-blooded animals from colder climates should have shorter limbs or structures such as ears, than equivalent animals from warmer climates because shorter appendages help animals from colder areas to conserve heat.

altricial in mammals, altricial species are those whose newly-born young are relatively immobile, lack hair and must be cared for by adults; closed eyes are common, though not ubiquitous. Altricial young are born helpless and require care for a comparatively long time before they are able to be mobile on their own.

annual ice ice that forms at freeze-up in the fall and melts completely after break-up in the spring

anthropogenic caused by humans

aquatic stalk polar bear stalking a seal resting on the ice surface by swimming toward it, using water-filled channels in the ice, sometimes diving and swimming underwater and using ice floes for camouflage; suddenly exits the water in front of the seal and attempts to capture it before it can escape into the water

birth lair small cave dug into the bottom of a snow drift over a ringed seal's breathing hole in spring, by a pregnant female, to protect her newborn pup from cold weather and hide it from predators

break-up decay or melt of sea ice that begins in spring; some sea ice studies define "break-up" as the point where the ice and water each comprise one-half of the surface area

cannibalism the eating of an animal by another member of the same species

carnivore a "meat eater," an organism that derives its energy and nutrient requirements from a diet consisting mainly or exclusively of animal tissue, whether through predation or scavenging

circumpolar located or found throughout a polar region (Arctic or Antarctic)

climate change a change in the "average weather" that a given region experiences. **Global climate change** refers to changes in the climate of the Earth as a whole. The natural occurrence of a system of gases in the earth's atmosphere provides what is known as the "greenhouse effect" and it regulates the temperature on earth. However, as humans have adopted progressively more industrialized activities, the amounts of heat-trapping "**greenhouse gases**" in the atmosphere (e.g., carbon dioxide, methane) have increased. These human-caused increases in atmospheric levels of greenhouse gases, have enhanced the warming capability of the natural greenhouse effect. Most experts agree that average global temperatures could rise by 1-3.5°C over the next century, a rate that has never been experienced in human history. It is primarily human-caused unidirectional increase in greenhouse gases that is causing **climate warming** which will cause significant environmental change, especially in the Arctic.

continental shelf the extended perimetre of each continent and associated coastal plain which was part of the continent during the glacial periods, but is under relatively shallow seas during interglacial periods such as the present

co-management joint administration or cooperative management (co-management) of living resources by two or more groups, usually government-level (scientific-based) managers and local-level hunters with community-based systems of knowledge and goals in resource management

cub-of-the-year a polar bear cub less than one year of age, sometimes abbreviated to COY

dental formula the representation of the dentition of an animal. A dental formula consists of eight numbers, four above and four below a horizontal line. The numbers represent (from left to right) the numbers of incisors, canines, premolars, and molars in either half of the upper and lower jaws. The total number of teeth in both jaws is therefore obtained by adding up all the numbers in the dental formula and multiplying by two.

DLP an animal killed in Defense of human Life and Property

DNA Deoxyribonucleic acid which contains the genetic instructions used in the development and functioning of living organisms. Its primary role is the long-term storage of genetic information. In the rapidly developing field of studying **ancient DNA**, the genetic codes from fossil or subfossil specimens of a species, may be compared with its living descendants, to study their evolutionary history.

dominance hierarchy a system or set of relationships in animal groups that is based on a hierarchical ranking, usually established and maintained by behaviour in aggressive encounters: one or a few members hold the highest rank and the others are submissive to those ranking higher and dominant to those ranking lower.

ecoregion a large unit of land or water containing a geographically distinct assemblage of species, natural communities, and environmental conditions; the boundaries of an ecoregion are not fixed and sharp, but rather encompass an area within which important ecological and evolutionary processes most strongly interact.

ecosystem a holistic concept of the combination of all plants, associated animals and their interrelationships, combined with all the physical and chemical components of the environment or habitat, which together form a recognizable, self-contained, entity

ecotourism responsible travel to natural areas that conserves the environment; strives to be low impact and (often) small scale (as an alternative to mass tourism). Its purpose is to educate the traveller; provide funds for ecological conservation; directly benefit the economic development and political empowerment of local communities; and foster respect for different cultures and for human rights. Since the 1980s, ecotourism has been considered a critical endeavour by environmentalists, so that future generations may experience destinations relatively untouched by human intervention

epontic biological community attached to or associated with the under side of sea ice

euthanize the act of painlessly putting an animal to death to prevent suffering, because it is incurably sick or too injured to survive; term also applies to humane killing of problem or dangerous animals

fast ice sea ice which forms and remains fast along the coast, where it is attached to the shore; sometimes called **land-fast ice**

fatty acid analysis the identification of fatty acids from the fat of prey species, after they have been consumed and deposited in the fat of a predator, to trace or confirm what species of prey the predator has eaten and reconstruct the predator's recent dietary history (in the context of this book, using polar bear fat to determine what marine mammals it has been eating)

fidelity faithfulness to a particular location; **seasonal fidelity** is faithfulness to the same area at the same time each year

floe floating ice formed in a variably sized sheet on the surface of a body of water

freeze-up formation of sea ice, beginning in autumn and continuing to its maximum extent in winter

habitat ecological or other natural environmental area in which a particular species of animal, plant or other organism lives

haulout the behaviour associated with seals, of temporarily leaving the water between periods of foraging activity for sites on land or ice. Hauling-out is necessary in seals for giving birth, resting out of water, and moulting.

hybrid the offspring of mating between a male and female, each representing a different species; if the species are closely related, such as a polar and grizzly bear, the offspring can produce their own young fertile in a subsequent mating.

hibernation a state of inactivity and metabolic depression in animals, characterized by lower body temperature, slower breathing, and lower metabolic rate, to conserve energy, especially during winter. Hibernation may last several days or weeks depending on species, ambient temperature, and time of year.

herbivore an animal that gets its energy from eating only plants

home range the area within which an animal lives and travels and undertakes all its activities throughout the year

hydrophone a microphone designed to be used underwater for recording or listening to underwater sounds

implantation an event that occurs early in pregnancy in which the embryo adheres to the wall of uterus. At this stage, the embryo is called a blastocyst. After attach-

ment, the embryo receives oxygen and the nutrients from the mother to be able to grow. **Delayed implantation** is a reproductive strategy in which the fertilized egg (blastocyst) does not immediately implant in the uterus but is maintained in a state of dormancy for an extended period prior to implanting and beginning to grow. No development takes place as long as the embryo remains unattached to the uterine lining.

infanticide the killing of a newborn or young animal by an adult of the same species

Intergovernmental Panel on Climate Change (IPCC) the leading international body for the assessment of climate change; established by the United Nations Environment Programme (UNEP) and the World Meteorological Organization (WMO) to provide the world with a clear, scientific view on the current state of knowledge about climate change and its potential environmental and socio-economic impacts. The UN General Assembly endorsed the action by WMO and UNEP in jointly establishing the IPCC.

inter-island channel a water body between islands in an archipelago

Inuit simply means " the people"; usually refers to culturally similar indigenous peoples inhabiting the Arctic regions from Alaska to Greenland; known regionally as **Inupiat** (Alaska), **Inuvialuit** (Northwest Territories, Canada), **Inuit** (Nunavut, Canada), and **Greenlanders** or **Kalaallit** (Greenland)

Holocene a geological epoch which began 11,700 years ago; generally considered to continue to the present

IUCN International Union for Conservation of Nature is an international organization dedicated to natural resource conservation. The stated goal of the organization is to help the world find pragmatic solutions to the most pressing environment and development challenges. Groups of specialists on species, such as the **Polar Bear Specialist Group (PBSG)** advise the IUCN on conservation strategies and needs.

lead a linear crack in the ice, of variable size, with water in it

Marine Mammal Protection Act (MMPA) This legislation was enacted in the United States on October 21, 1972. All marine mammals are protected under the MMPA and it prohibits, with certain exceptions, the "take" of marine mammals in U.S. waters and by U.S. citizens on the high seas, and the importation of marine mammals and marine mammal products into the U.S.

maternity den the den in which a pregnant female polar bear gives birth to her cubs; most are dug into wind-blown snow drifts, but in southern and western Hudson Bay, maternity dens are dug into frozen peat banks in the permafrost; maternity dens are distinctly separate from temporary dens that a bear of any age and sex class may dig in drifted snow in which to rest for a brief period or to escape inclement weather

metabolism the set of chemical reactions that happen in living organisms to maintain life; these processes allow organisms to grow and reproduce, maintain their structures, and respond to their environment; **basal metabolic rate** is the amount of energy expended daily while at rest in a neutrally temperate environment, several hours after eating

myrmecophagic animals chiefly feeding on ants or termites, such as sloth bears in Asia

multiyear ice old ice up to 3 m (10 ft)or more thick which has survived at least two summers' melt. **Hummocks** (hillocks of broken ice that have been forced up by pressure) often form within it and the ice is almost salt-free.

negative stimulus any stimulus which is sufficiently unpleasant or negative that an organism learns to avoids the source, or situation, from which that stimulus originated

omnivore a species that eats both plants and animals

ovulation the release of an egg from the ovaries in order that it can be fertilized; **spontaneous ovulation** (such as in humans) the release of eggs automatically at some interval; **induced ovulation,** requires a period of active social interaction followed by copulation (such as in polar bears) before an egg is released from the ovary for fertilization

pack ice ice that formed both at sea and as landfast ice (originally attached to the shore but is no longer). It can be very flat (because the ocean is flat), but it is usually covered with very rough areas caused by the movement of sheets of ice against one other and buckling to form pressure ridges

PBSG Polar Bear Specialist Group, one of the species-specific specialist groups that operates under the auspices of the IUCN

pelagic living in open ocean water, anywhere from the low tide mark and including the entire oceanic water column

Pleistocene the epoch of geological time spanning from 2,588,000 to 12,000 years before present and which includes the world's recent periods of repeated glaciations.

polynya area of open water surrounded by ice; a recurring polynya is one that forms at the same place and at the same time each year

positive reinforcement receiving a reward in response to a behaviour, which in turn encourages the organism to repeat the same behaviour in the hope of being rewarded again

pressure ridges and rafting sea ice pressure ridges are the piles of ice rubble that criss-cross the ice pack. Ridges are created by opposing ice sheets buckling against each other and the subsequent piling of ice blocks on top of and beneath the two sheets. **Rafting** is the simple overriding of one sheet of ice by another.

primary productivity the process by which energy is converted by single-celled plants capable of synthesizing their own food from simple organic sources into organic compounds, principally through the process of photosynthesis. The total amount of productivity in a region or system is **gross primary productivity**. Almost all life on earth is directly or indirectly reliant on primary production

sassat modern Greenlandic word to describe an entrapment of whales in an opening in the water but surrounded by solid ice with no way to escape

still-hunting hunting by standing, sitting, or lying still and waiting for prey to come close enough to be captured

radio collar a neck collar with a radio attached that sends signals that can be used to relocate the animal wearing it, using an aircraft with antennae attached and tuned to receive a signal from the radio; **satellite radio collars** have a specialized radio capable of sending a signal to a satellite at a predetermined schedule which provides the location of the animal at that moment, and often additional associated data such as activity level, body temperature or outside temperature

scavenging feeding on an animal that is already dead of natural causes or that was previously killed, though not usually by the animal feeding on it; sometimes also used in reference to animals feeding on human garbage at a dump

sea ice any form of ice that is found at sea and originated from the freezing of seawater

sexual dimorphism the pattern of physical differences between male and female individuals that arise as a consequence of intrasexual (i.e., within the same sex) competition that determines eventual reproductive success; in bears, sexual dimorphism is most obvious in body size, with males being larger than females.

sexual maturity for a female polar bear, the age at which she is first capable of becoming pregnant and producing a cub; for a male, physiological maturity is the age at which he is capable of producing sperm and impregnating a female; however, **behavioural maturity** usually comes much later for a male polar bear because he has to become large enough to successfully compete with other males for access to a receptive female

sheltering digging of a temporary den in a snow drift by bears of any age or sex class, in which to escape cold or inclement weather while, for periods ranging from a few days up to several weeks; except for dependent cubs, while in such dens, polar bears metabolize their stored fat resources for survival

statistical significance the probability that an observed relationship (e.g., between variables) or a difference (e.g., between means) in a sample is real and did not occur simply by chance. The statistical significance of a result tells us about the degree to which the result is likely to be "true" (usually presented as the 0.05 level of confidence, meaning that in future tests, the same result would be expected 19 times out of 20).

subnivean in or beneath the snow layer

subpopulation a subset of the total population of a species, usually occurring within a defined area with limited mixing with other subpopulations, may have definitive genetic characteristics but still capable of breeding with animals from other subpopulations or groups of animals of the same species; in a management context often used interchangeably with **population**

terrestrial living predominantly or entirely on land

territoriality the aggressive behaviour by which an animal of a particular species consistently defends a geographic area against other animals of the same species and usually of the same sex and usually of the same sex. Animals that defend territories in this way are referred to as territorial.

thermister thermally sensitive resistors capable of recording temperatures over a wide temperature range to a remotely powered recording device. They are supplied in glass bead, disc, chips and probe formats.

Thule culture a maritime marine mammal hunting culture, originating in Alaska, that spread across the Canadian Arctic and into Greenland about 1000AD, resulting in the gradual displacement of the Dorset paleoeskimos who occupied the area previously. Thule culture declined after about 1600 AD from a combination of deteriorating climatic conditions and the introduction of diseases from contact with Europeans, but the Thule people continued to occupy arctic Canada and Greenland and are directly ancestral to the present-day Inuit.

Traditional Ecological Knowledge (TEK) sometimes also referred to as **Local Ecological Knowledge (LEK)**; a cumulative body of knowledge, practice, and belief, evolving by adaptive processes and handed down through generations by cultural transmission, about the relationship of living beings (including humans) with one another and with their environment; has some similarity to western ecological science in that it is based on an accumulation of observations, but usually not recorded and specific tests to validate or falsify hypotheses are not undertaken.

ulu a special crescent-shaped skinning knife, with the handle positioned like a "T" above the middle of its curve; used only by women

Wapusk the Cree Indian name for the polar bear; used to name Wapusk National Park in northeastern Manitoba, Canada, which was created in 1996 largely because of the high density of polar bear maternity dens in the area

weaning the process of gradually withdrawing the supply of the mother's milk from a mammal infant and introducing it to what will be its adult diet

yearling a cub between the ages of one and two years

LIST OF FIGURES

similar to 2007. (from Comiso et al. 2008 *Geophysical Research Letters* 35:L01703, doi:10.1029/2007GL031972)

Figure 16. Map of four polar bear ecoregions defined by grouping recognized subpopulations which share seasonal patterns of ice motion and distribution. The polar basin divergent ecoregion (yellow) includes Southern Beaufort Sea (SBS), Chukchi Sea (CS), Laptev Sea (LVS), Kara Sea (KS), and the Barents Sea (BS). The polar basin convergent ecoregion (PBCE) (green) includes East Greenland (EG), and Northern Beaufort Sea (NBS). The seasonal ice ecoregion (red) includes southern Hudson Bay (SHB), western Hudson Bay (WHB), Foxe Basin (FB), Davis Strait (DS), and Baffin Bay (BB). The archipelago ecoregion (orange) includes Gulf of Boothia (GB), M'Clintock Channel (MC), Lancaster Sound (LS), Viscount-Melville Sound (VM), Norwegian Bay (NW), and Kane Basin (KB) (Based on Amstrup et al. 2008 *Geophysical Monograph* 180, American Geophysical Union, Washington, DC) (Graphic: Evan Richardson)

Figure 17. Date of break-up of the sea ice used by the Western Hudson Bay polar bear population, from 1979-2007. (From Stirling and Lunn 1999 and Lunn and Stirling unpublished data).

Figure 18. Date of break-up in the area of sea ice where female polar bears with satellite collars spent at least 90% of their time each year (blue line) and the mean dates the bears came ashore in those years (red line). (From Stirling et al. 1999, *Arctic*, 52:294-306)

Figure 19. The relationship between the date of break-up and the physical condition of adult female (lower line) and adult male (upper line) polar bears when they come ashore to fast through the open water season. (From Stirling et al. 1999, *Arctic*, 52:294-306 and E. Richardson unpublished data)

Figure 20. Mean estimated mass of lone (and thus likely pregnant) adult female polar bears in the fall in Western Hudson Bay from 1980 through 2004 (dashed line indicates fit of linear regression) (from Stirling and Parkinson 2006. *Arctic* 59:261-275)

Figure 21. (a) The number of problem bears handled by the Conservation Officers in Churchill in Western Hudson Bay from 1984 through 2003, and **(b)** the relationship between the date of sea-ice break-up and the number of problem bears handled (solid line indicates the statistical fit of the correlation) (from Stirling and Parkinson 2006. *Arctic* 59:261-275)

Figure 22. (a) Minimum Arctic sea ice in 2000; **(b)** Model prediction of minimum Arctic sea ice in 2040. (© University Corporation for Atmospheric Research)

LIST OF TABLES

APPENDIX

THE GOVERNMENTS of Canada, Denmark, Norway, the Union of Soviet Socialist Republics, and the United States of America,

RECOGNIZING the special responsibilities and special interests of the States of the Arctic Region in relation to the protection of the fauna and flora of the Arctic Region;

RECOGNIZING that the polar bear is a significant resource of the Arctic Region which requires additional protection;

HAVING DECIDED that such proteciton should be achieved through coordinated nation measures taken by the States of the Arctic Region;

DESIRING to take immediate action to bring further conservation and management measures into effect;

HAVE AGREED AS FOLLOWS:

ARTICLE I

1. The taking of polar bears shall be prohibited except as provided in Article III.

2. For the purpose of this Agreement, the term "taking" includes hunting, killing and capturing.

ARTICLE II

Each Contracting Party shall take appropriate action to protect the ecosystems of which polar bears are a part, with special attention to habitat components such as denning and feeding sites and migration patterns, and shall manage polar bear populations in accordance with sound conservation practices based on the best available scientific data.

ARTICLE III

1. Subject to the provisions of Articles II and IV, any Contracting Party may allow the taking of polar bears when such taking is carried out:

(a) for bona fide scientific purposes; or
(b) by that Party for conservation purposes; or
(c) to prevent serious disturbance of the management of other living resources, subject to   forfeiture to that Party of the skins and other items of value resulting from such taking; or
(d) by local people using traditional methods in the exercise of their traditional rights and in accordance with the laws of that Party; or
(e) wherever polar bears have or might have been subject to taking by traditional means by its nationals.

2. The skins and other items of value resulting from taking under subparagraphs (b) and (c) of paragraph 1 of this Article shall not be available for commercial purposes.

ARTICLE IV

The use of aircraft and large motorized vessels for the purpose of taking polar bears shall be prohibited, except where the application of such prohibition would be inconsistent with domestic laws.

ARTICLE V

A Contracting Party shall prohibit the exportation from, the importation and delivery into, and traffic within, its territory of polar bears or any part or product thereof taken in violation of this Agreement.

ARTICLE VI

1. Each contracting Party shall enact and enforce such legislation and other measures as may be necessary for the purpose of giving effect to this Agreement.

2. Nothing in this Agreement shall prevent a Contracting Party from maintaining or amending existing legislation or other measures or establishing new measures on the taking of polar bears so as to provide more stringent controls that those required under the provisions of this Agreement.

ARTICLE VII

The Contracting Parties shall conduct national research programmes on polar bears, particularly research relating to the conservation and management of the species. They shall as appropriate coordinate such research with the research carried out by other Parties, consult with other Parties on the management of migrating polar bear populations, and exchange information on research and management programmes, research results and data on bears taken.

ARTICLE VIII

Each Contracting Party shall take actions as appropriate to promote compliance with the provisions of this Agreement by nationals of States not party to this Agreement.

ARTICLE IX

The Contracting Parties shall continue to consult with one another with the object of giving further protection to polar bears.

ARTICLE X

1. This Agreement shall be open for signature at Oslo by the Governments of Canada, Denmark, Norway, the Union of Soviet Socialist Republics and the United States of America until 31st March 1974.

2. This Agreement shall be subject to ratification or approval by the signatory Governments. Instruments of ratification or approval shall be deposited with the Government of Norway as soon as possible.

3. This Agreement shall be open for accession by the Governments referred to in paragraph 1 of this Article. Instruments of accession shall be deposited with the Depository Government.

4. This Agreement shall enter into force ninety days after the deposit of the third instrument of ratification, approval or accession. Thereafter, it shall enter into force for a signatory or acceding Government on the date of deposit of its instrument of ratification, approval or accession.

5. This Agreement shall remain in force initially for a period of five years from its date of entry into force, and unless any Contracting Party during that period requests the termination of the Agreement at the end of that period, it shall continue in force thereafter.

6. On the request addressed to the Depository Government by any of the Governments referred to in paragraph 1 of this Article, consultations shall be conducted with a view to convening a meeting of representatives of the five Governments to consider the revision or amendment of this Agreement.

7. Any Party may denounce this Agreement by written notification to the Depository Government at any time after five years from the date of entry into force of this Agreement. The denunciation shall take effect twelve months after the Depository Government has received this notification.

8. The Depository Government shall notify the Governments referred to in paragraph 1 of this Article of the deposit of instruments of ratification, approval or accession, for the entry into force of this Agreement and of the receipt of notifications of denunciation and any other communications from a Contracting Party specially provided for in this Agreement.

9. The original of this Agreement shall be deposited with the Government of Norway which shall deliver certified copies thereof to each of the Governments referred to in paragraph 1 of this Article.

10. The Depository Government shall transmit certified copies of this Agreement to the Secretary General of the United Nations for registration and publication in accordance with Article 102 of the Charter of the United Nations.

(Supplementary Note, not part of the Agreement: The Agreement came into effect in May 1976, three months after the third nation required to ratify did so in February 1976. All five nations ratified by 1978. After the initial period of five years, all five Contracting Parties met in Oslo, Norway, in January 1981, and unanimously reaffirmed the continuation of the Agreement in perpetuity.)

BIBLIOGRAPHY

Websites
The single most important web site is that of the IUCN Polar Bear Specialist Group (PBSG): www.pbsg.npolar.no

Note: This web site also has a large reference section (click on " Library"). There are three sections: past Proceedings of the PBSG, English language polar bear literature, and Russian language polar bear references. (PDFs of all PBSG Proceedings, back to 1970, can be downloaded free. These publications also have extensive information about management and research as well as references.)

Polar Bears International: *www.polarbearsinternational.org*

World Wildlife Fund Arctic:
wwf.panda.org/what_we_do/where_we_work/arctic/

Safety in Bear Country Society Polar Bear safety video *http://www.mace-canada.com/unitedstates/Products/polar_video2us.htm*

General overview
Amstrup, S.C. 2003. Polar bear, *Ursus maritimus*. pages 587-610, *in Wild Mammals of North America: Biology,Management, and Conservation*. Edited by G.A. Feldhamer, B.C. Thompson, and J.A. Chapman. John Hopkins University Press, Baltimore.

Born, E.W. 2008. *The White Bears of Greenland*. Ilinniusiorfik, Nuuk, Greenland. 128 pp.

Larsen, T. 1978. *The World of the Polar Bear*. Hamlyn, London. 96 pp.

Ovsyanikov, N. 1996. *Living with the White Bear*. Voyageur Press, Hong Kong. 144 pp.

Perry, R. 1966. *The World of the Polar Bear*. Cassell, London. 195 pp.

Stirling, I. 1988. *Polar Bears*. University of Michigan Press, Ann Arbor, Mich. 232 pp.

Stirling, I. 1993. *Bears: Majestic Creatures of the Wild* (Editor and contributor), Weldon Owens, Pty., Sydney, Australia. 240 pp.

Behaviour
Aars, J. and Plumb, A. 2010. Polar bear cubs may reduce chilling from icy water by sitting on mother's back. Polar Biology 33:557-559

Ames, A. 1994. Object Manipulation in Captive Polar Bears Ninth International Conference on Bear Research and Management, Missoula, Montana 9:443-449.

Amstrup, S.C. et al. 2006. Intraspecific predation and cannibalism among polar bears in the Southern Beaufort Sea. Polar Biology 29: 997-1002.

Belikov, S.E. 1976. Behavioural aspects of the polar bear, *Ursus maritimus*. International Conference on Bear Research and Management 3:37-40.

Canino, W. and Powell, D. 2010. Formal Behavioural Evaluation of Enrichment Programs on a Zookeeper's Schedule: A Case Study With a polar bear (*Ursus maritimus*) at the Bronx Zoo. Zoo Biology 29: 503-508.

Derocher, A.E., and Wiig. Ø.1999. Infanticide and cannibalism of juvenile polar bears (*Ursus maritimus*) in Svalbard. Arctic 52:307-10.

Derocher, A.E., and Stirling I. 1990. Aggregating behaviour of adult male polar bears (*Ursus maritimus*). Canadian Journal of Zoology 68:1390-1394.

Derocher A.E. et al. 2010. Nursing vocalization of a polar bear cub. Ursus 21: 189-191.

Furnell, D.J., and Oolooyuk, D. 1980. Polar bear predation on ringed seals in ice-free water. Canadian Field-Naturalist 94:88-89.

Kingsley, M.C.S., and Stirling, I. 1991. Haul-out behaviour of ringed seals in relation to defence against predation by polar bears. Canadian Journal of Zoology 69:1857-1861.

Lunn, N.J., and Stenhouse, G.B. 1985. An observation of possible cannibalism by polar bears (*Ursus maritimus*). Canadian Journal of Zoology 63: 1516-1517.

Ramsay, M.A., and Stirling, I. 1986. On the mating system of polar bears. Canadian Journal of Zoology 64:2142-51.

Stirling, I. 1974. Midsummer observations on the behaviour of wild polar bears (*Ursus maritimus*). Canadian Journal of Zoology 52:1191-1198.

Stirling, I. and Latour. P.B. 1978. Comparative hunting abilities of polar bear cubs of different ages. Canadian Journal of Zoology 56:1768-1772.

Taylor, M. et al. 1985. Observations of intraspecific aggression and cannibalism in polar bears (*Ursus maritimus*). Arctic 38:303-309.

Tumanov, I.L. 2001. Reproductive biology of captive polar bears. Ursus 12:107–108.

Zeyl, E. et al. 2009. Families in space: relatedness in the Barents Sea population of polar bears (*Ursus maritimus*). Molecular Ecology doi: 10.1111/j.1365-294X.2008.04049.x.

Zeyl, E. et al. 2009. The mating system of polar bears: a genetic approach. Canadian Journal of Zoology 87:1-15.

Climate warming, ice, and polar bears
Amstrup, S.C. et al. 2009. Rebuttal of "Polar bear polar bear population forecasts: a public-policy audit" Interfaces 39:353-369.

Amstrup, S.C. et al. 2010. Greenhouse gas mitigation can reduce sea-ice loss and increase polar bear persistence. Nature 468:955-958.

Amstrup, S.C. et al. 2008. A Bayesian network modeling approach to forecasting the 21st century worldwide status of polar bears, in Arctic Sea Ice Decline: Observations, Projections, Mechanisms, and Implications, Geophys. Monogr. Ser., vol. 180, edited by E. T. DeWeaver, C. M. Bitz, and L.-B. Tremblay, pp. 213-268, AGU, Washington, D. C. Mechanisms, and Implications. Geophysical Monograph 180. American Geophysical Union, Washington DC.

Amstrup, S.C. et al. 2006. Intraspecific predation and cannibalism among polar bears in the Southern Beaufort Sea. Polar Biology 29: 997-1002.

Comiso, J.C. 2002. Rapidly declining perennial sea ice cover in the Arctic. Geophysical Research Letters 29(20):1956-1959.

Comiso, J.C. et al. 2008. Accelerated decline in the Arctic sea ice cover. Geophysical Research Letters 35:L01703, doi:10.1029/2007GL031972.

Durner, G.M. et al. 2009. Predicting 21st century polar bear habitat distribution from global climate models. Ecological Monographs 79:25-58.

Derocher, A.E. et al. 2004. Polar bears in a warming climate. Integrative and Comparative Biology 44:163-176.

Ferguson, S.H. et al. 2005. Climate change and ringed seal (Phoca hispida) recruitment in western Hudson Bay. Marine Mammal Science 21:121-135.

Gagnon, A.S. and Gough, W.A. 2005. Trends in the dates of ice freeze-up and break-up over Hudson Bay, Canada. Arctic 58:370-382.

Gleason, J.S. and Rode, K.D. 2009. Polar Bear Distribution and Habitat Association Reflect Long-term Changes in Fall Sea Ice Conditions in the Alaskan Beaufort Sea. Arctic 62:405-417.

Gough, W.A. et al. 2004. Trends in seasonal sea ice duration in Southwestern Hudson Bay. Arctic 57: 299 305.

Hobson, K.A. et al. 2009. Isotopic homogeneity of breath CO_2 from fasting and berry-eating polar bears: implications for tracing reliance on terrestrial foods in a changing Arctic. Canadian Journal of Zoology 87:50-55.

Holland, M.M. et al. 2006. Future abrupt reductions in the summer Arctic sea ice. Geophysical Research Letters: 33: L23503, doi:10.1029/2006GL028024, doi:10.1029/2006GL028024.

Hunter, C.M. et al. 2010. Climate change threatens polar bear populations: a stochastic demographic analysis. Ecology 10:2883-2897.

Joly, S. et al. 2010. Sensitivity of Hudson Bay Sea ice and ocean climate to atmospheric temperature forcing. Climate Dynamics DOI 10.1007/s00382-009-0731-4.

Laidre, K.L. et al. 2008. Quantifying the sensitivity of arctic marine mammals to climate-induced habitat change. Ecological Applications, 18:S97-S125.

Mann, M.E. and Kump, L.R. 2008. Dire Predictions. D.K. Publishing, 208 pp.

Molnár, P.K. et al. 2010. Predicting survival, reproduction and abundance of polar bears under climate change. Biological Conservation 143:1612-1622.

Molnár, P.K. et al. 2011. Predicting climate change impacts on polar bear litter size.
Nature Communications 2:186 DOI: 10.1038/ncomms1183.

Obbard, M.E. et al. 2006. Temporal trends in the body condition of southern Hudson Bay polar bears. Climate Change Research Information Note 3:1-8. Available from http://sit.mnr.gov.on.ca.

Regehr, E.V. et al. 2007. Effects of earlier sea ice break-up on survival and population size of polar bears in western Hudson Bay. Journal of Wildlife Management 71:2673-2683.

Smith, P.A., et al. 2010. Has early ice clearance increased predation on breeding birds by polar bears? Polar Biology 33:1149-1153.

Stirling, I., and Parkinson, C.L. 2006. Possible Effects of Climate Warming on Selected Populations of Polar Bears (Ursus maritimus) in the Canadian Arctic. Arctic 59: 261-275.

Stirling, I. et al. 1999. Long-term trends in the population ecology of polar bears in western Hudson Bay in relation to climatic change. Arctic, 52:294-306.

Stirling, I. and Smith, T.G. Implications of Warm Temperatures and an Unusual Rain Event on the survival of Ringed Seals on the Coast of Southeastern Baffin Island. Arctic 57:59-67.

Stirling, I. et al. 2008.Unusual predation attempts of polar bears on ringed seals in the southern Beaufort Sea: Possible significance of changing spring ice conditions. Arctic 60:14-22.

Stroeve, J. et al. 2007. Arctic sea ice decline: Faster than forecast. Geophysical Research Letters. 34:L09501, doi: 10.1029/2007GL029703.

Towns, L. et al. 2010 Changes in Land Distribution of Polar Bears in Western Hudson Bay. Arctic 63:206-212.

Contaminants

Cardona-Marek, T. et al. 2009. Mercury concentrations in southern Beaufort Sea polar bears: variation based on stable isotopes of carbon and nitrogen. Environmental Toxicology and Chemistry 28:1416-1424.

Derocher, A. E. et al. 2003. Contaminants in Svalbard polar bear samples archived since 1967 and possible population level effects. Science of the Total Environment 301:163-174.

Haave, M. 2003. Polychlorinated biphenyls and reproductive hormones in female polar bears at Svalbard. Environment and Health Perspectives 111:431-436.

Muir, D.C.G. et al. 2006.Brominated flame retardants in Polar Bears (Ursus maritimus) from Alaska, the Canadian Arctic, East Greenland, and Svalbard. Environmental Science and Technology 40(2): 449-455.

Norstrom, R.J. et al. 1998.Chlorinated hydrocarbon contaminants in polar bears from eastern Russia, North America, Greenland and Svalbard: Biomonitoring of Arctic pollution. Archive of Environmental Contamination and Toxicology 1998:5:354-67.

Oskam, I.C. et al. 2003. Organochlorines affect the major androgenic hormone, testosterone, in male polar bears (Ursus maritimus) at Svalbard. Journal of Toxicology and Environmental Health, Part A, 66, 2119-2139.

Sonne, C. 2010. Health effects from long-range transported contaminants in Arctic top predators: An integrated review based on studies of polar bears and relevant model species. Environment International 36:461-491

Sonne, C. 2006. Xenoendocrine Pollutants may reduce size of sexual organs in east Greenland polar bears (*Ursus maritimus*). Environmental Science and Technology 40:5668-5674.

Wiig, Ø. 1998. Female pseudohermaphrodite polar bears at Svalbard. Journal of Wildlife Disease 34:792-796.

Dens and denning behaviour

Amstrup, S.C., and Gardner, C. 1994. Polar bear maternity denning in the Beaufort Sea. Journal of Wildlife Management 58:1-10.

Clarkson, P.L., and Irish, D. 1991. Den collapse kills female polar bear and two newborn cubs. Arctic 44:83-84.

Hansson, R., and Thomassen, J. 1983. Behaviour of polar bears with cubs in the denning area. International Conference on Bear Research and Management 5:246-254.

Kolenosky, G.B., and Prevett, J.P. 1983. Productivity and maternity denning of polar bears in Ontario. International Conference on Bear Research and Management 5:238-45.

Larsen, T. 1985. Polar bear denning and cub production in Svalbard, Norway. Journal of Wildlife Management 49:320-26.

Lunn, N.J. et al. 2004. Selection of maternity dens by female polar bears in western Hudson Bay. Polar Biology 28:350-356.

Messier, F. et al. 1994. Denning ecology of polar bears in the Canadian Arctic Archipelago. Journal of Mammalogy 75:420-30.

Ovsyanikov, N. 1998. Den use and social interactions of polar bears during spring in a dense denning area on Herald Island, Russia. International Conference on Bear Research and Management 10:251-258.

Ramsay, M.A., and Stirling, I. 1990. Fidelity of female polar bears to winter-den sites. Journal of Mammalogy 71:233-36.

Richardson, E. et al. 2005. Polar bear (*Ursus maritimus*) maternity denning habitat in western Hudson Bay: the importance of peat banks. Canadian Journal of Zoology 83:860-870.

Richardson, E. et al. 2006. The effects of forest fires on polar bear maternity denning habitat in western Hudson Bay. Polar Biology 30:369-378.

Rosing-Asvid, A. 2002. Age at sexual maturity of males and timing of the mating season of polar bears (*Ursus maritimus*) in Greenland. Polar Biology 25:878-883.

Scott, P.A., and Stirling, I. 2002. Chronology of terrestrial den use by polar bears in western Hudson Bay as indicated by tree growth anomalies. Arctic 55:151-166.

Schweinsburg, R.E. 1979. Summer snow dens used by polar bears in the Canadian High Arctic. Arctic 32:165-169.

Smith, T.S.et al. 2007. Post-den emergence behaviour of polar bears (Ursus maritimus) in northern Alaska. Arctic 60:187-194.

Uspenski, S.M., and Kistchinski, A.A. 1972. New data on the winter ecology of the polar bear (*Ursus maritimus*) on Wrangel Island. International Conference on Bear Research and Management 2:181–197.

Van de Velde, F. 2003. Polar Bear (*Ursus maritimus*) denning in the area of the Simpson Peninsula, Nunavut. Arctic 56:191-197.

Zeyl, E. et al. 2010. Denning-area fidelity and mitochondrial DNA diversity of female polar bears (*Ursus maritimus*) in the Barents Sea. Canadian Journal of Zoology 88:1139-1148.

Distribution and abundance

Aars, J. et al. 2009. Estimating the Barents Sea polar bear subpopulation size. Marine Mammal Science. 25:35-52.

Amstrup, S.C. et al. 2005. Using radiotelemetry to allocate harvests among polar bear stocks occupying the Beaufort Sea Region. Arctic 58:247-259.

Amstrup, S.C. et al. 1986. Past and present status of polar bears in Alaska. Wildlife Society Bulletin 14:241-54.

Amstrup, S.C. et al. 2001. Polar bears in the Beaufort Sea: A 30 year mark–recapture case history. Journal of Agricultural, Biological, and Environmental Statistics 6:221–34.

Derocher, A.E. and Stirling, I. 1995. Mark-recapture estimation of population size and survival rates for polar bears in western Hudson Bay. Journal of Wildlife Management 59:215-221.

Larsen, T. 1986. Population biology of the polar bear (*Ursus maritimus*) in the Svalbard area (Norsk Polarinstitutt Skrifter 184). Oslo, Norway.

Lønø, O. 1970. The polar bear (*Ursus maritimus* Phipps) in the Svalbard area (Norsk Polarinstitutt Skrifter 149. Oslo, Norway.

Larsen, T. 1985. Abundance, range and population biology of the polar bdear (Ursus maritimus) in the Svalbard Area. Ph.D. Thesis. University of Oslo, Norway.

Lunn, N.J. et al. 1997. Re-estimating the size of the polar bear population in Western Hudson Bay. Arctic 50:234-240.

Mauritzen, M. et al. 2001. Space-use strategies of female polar bears in a dynamic sea ice habitat. Canadian Journal of Zoology 79:1704-1713.

Taylor, M.K. et al. 2001. Delineation of Canadian and Greenland Polar Bear (*Ursus maritimus*) Populations Using Cluster Analysis of Movements. Canadian Journal of Zoology 79:690-709.

Taylor, M. K. et al. 2005. Demography and viability of a hunted population of polar bears. Arctic 58: 203-214.

Taylor, M.K. et al. 2006. Demographic parametres and harvest-explicit population viability analysis for polar bears in M'Clintock Channel, Nunavut. Journal of Wildlife Management 70:1667-1673.

Taylor, M.K. et al. 2009. Population demography and conservation of polar bears in Gulf of Boothia, Nunavut. Marine Mammal Science. 25:778-796.

Scott, R.F. et al. 1959. Status and management of the polar bear and Pacific walrus. Transactions of the North American Wildlife Conference 24: 366-374.

Wiig, Ø. 1995. Distribution of polar bears (*Ursus maritimus*) in the Svalbard area. Journal of Zoology 237: 515-529.

Wiig, Ø. 1998. Survival and reproductive rates for polar bears at Svalbard. Ursus 10:25–32.

Ecology

Derocher, A.E et al. 1993. Terrestrial foraging by polar bears during the ice–free period in western Hudson Bay. Arctic 46:251-54.

Derocher, A.E. 2005. Population ecology of polar bears at Svalbard, Norway. Population Ecology, 47: 267-275.

Derocher, A.E., and Stirling, I. 1990. Distribution of polar bears (*Ursus maritimus*) during the ice-free period in western Hudson Bay. Canadian Journal of Zoology 68:1395-1403.

Ferguson, S.H. et al. 1999. Determinants of home range size for polar bears (*Ursus maritimus*). Ecology Letters 2:311-18.

Hammill, M.O. and Smith, T.G. 1991. The role of predation in the ecology of the ringed seal in Barrow Strait, Northwest Territories, Canada. Marine Mammal Science 7:123-35.

Kingsley, M.C.S. et al. 1985. Distribution and abundance of seals in the Canadian High Arctic, 1980 1985. Canadian Journal of Fisheries and Aquatic Sciences. 42:1189-1210.

Lutziuk, O.B. 1978. Contribution to the biology of the polar bears (*Ursus maritimus*) on Wrangel Island during the summer-autumn period. Zoologischeskii Zhurnal 57:597-603.

Messier, F. 1992. Seasonal activity patterns of female polar bears (*Ursus maritimus*) in the Canadian Arctic as revealed by satellite telemetry. Journal of Zoology (London) 226:219-29.

Pomeroy, L.R. 1997. Primary production in the Arctic Ocean estimated from dissolved oxygen. Journal of Marine Systems 10:1-8.

Ramsay, M.A. and Andriashek, D.S. 1986. Long distance route orientation of female polar bears (*Ursus maritimus*) in spring. Journal of Zoology A (London) 208:63-72.

Ramsay, M. and Stirling, I. 1984. Interactions of wolves and polar bears in northern Manitoba. Journal of Mammalogy 65:693-694.

Stirling, I. et al. 1993. Habitat preferences of polar bears in the western Canadian Arctic in late winter and spring. Polar Record, 29:13-24.

Smith, T.G. 1980. Polar bear predation of ringed and bearded seals in the landfast sea ice habitat. Canadian Journal of Zoology 58:2201-2209.

Smith, T.G. 1985. Polar bears, *Ursus maritimus*, as predators of belugas, *Delphinapterus leucas*. Canadian Field-Naturalist 99:71–75.

Smith, T.G. and Stirling, I. 1978. Variation in the density of ringed seal (*Phoca hispida*) birth lairs in the Amundsen Gulf, Northwest Territories. Canadian Journal of Zoology 56:1066-1071.

Stirling, I. et al. 1977. The ecology of the polar bear (*Ursus maritimus*) along the western coast of Hudson Bay. Canadian Wildlife Service Occasional Paper 33. 62 pp.

Stirling, I. and McEwan, E.H. 1975. The caloric value of whole ringed seals (*Phoca hispida*) in relation to polar bear (*Ursus maritimus*) ecology and hunting behaviour. Canadian Journal of Zoology 53:1021–27.

Stirling, I., and Øritsland, N.A. 1995. Relationships between estimates of ringed seal (*Phoca hispida*) and polar bear (*Ursus maritimus*) populations in the Canadian Arctic. Canadian Journal of Fisheries and Aquatic Sciences 52:2594–2612.

Stirling, I. 1997. The importance of polynyas, ice edges, and leads to marine mammals and birds. Journal of Marine Systems 10:9-21.

Stirling, I. 2002. Polar Bears and Seals in the Eastern Beaufort Sea and Amundsen Gulf: A Synthesis of Population Trends and Ecological Relationships over Three Decades. Arctic 55, Supplement 1:59-76.

Uspenski, S.M., (Ed.) 1977. The polar bear and its conservation in the Soviet Arctic. A collection of scientific papers. Central Laboratory of Nature Conservation, Moscow

Zeyl, E. et al. 2009. Families in space: relatedness in the Barents Sea population of polar bears (*Ursus maritimus*). Molecular Ecology 18:735-749.

Evolution

Bahners, T. et al. 2008. Textile solar light collectors based on models for polar bear hair. Solar energy materials and solar cells. 92:1661-1667.

Cronin, M.A. 1993. Mitochondrial DNA in wildlife taxonomy and conservation
biology: Cautionary notes. Wildlife Society Bulletin 21:339-48.

Cronin, M.A. et al. 1991. Interspecific and intraspecific mitochondrial DNA variation in North American bears (*Ursus*). Canadian Journal of Zoology 69:2985-92.

Cronin, M.A. et al. 2009. Genetic variation, relatedness, and effective population size of polar bears (*Ursus maritimus*) in the southern Beaufort Sea, Alaska. Journal of Heredity 100:681-690.

Davison, J. et al. 2011. Late-Quaternary biogeographic scenarios for the brown bear (*Ursus arctos*), a wild mammal model species. Quaternary Science Reviews 30:418-430.

Hopkins, D.M. 1973. Sea level history in Beringia during the past 250,000 years. Quaternary Research 3:520-540.

Ingólfsson Ó. and Wiig, Ø. 2008. Late Pleistocene fossil find in Svalbard: The oldest remains of a polar bear (Ursus maritimus Phipps, 1744) ever discovered. Polar Research 28:455-462.

Kurtén, B. 1955. Sex dimorphism and size trends in the cave bear, *Ursus spelaeus*, Rosenmuller and Heinroth. Acta Zoologica Fennica 90:4-48.

Kurtén, B. 1964. The evolution of the polar bear, *Ursus maritimus* Phipps. Acta Zoologica Fennica 108:3-30.

Lindqvist, C. et al. 2010. Complete mitochondrial genome of a Pleistocene jawbone unveils the origin of polar bear. Proceedings of the National Academy of Sciences. doi/10.1073/pnas.0914266107.

Paetkau, D. et al. 1999. Genetic structure of the world's polar bear populations. Molecular Ecology 8:1571-84.

Scribner,K.T. et al. 1997. Population genetic studies of the polar bear (*Ursus maritimus*):A summary of available data and interpretation of results. Pages 185-196 *in* A.E. Dizon, S.J. Chivers, and W.F. Perrin, eds. *Molecular Genetics of Marine Mammals* (Special Publication No. 3). Society for Marine Mammalogy.

Stirling, I. 1977. Adaptations of Weddell and ringed seals to exploit the polar fast ice habitat in the absence or presence of surface predators. Pp. 741-748 *In*: G.A. Llano (Ed.) *Adaptations Within Antarctic Ecosystems.* Gulf Publishing Co., Houston.

Stirling, I., and Derocher, A.E. 1990. Factors affecting the evolution of the modern bears. International Conference on Bear Research and Management 8:189-205.

Human impact

Amstrup, S.C. 1993. Human disturbances of denning polar bears in Alaska. Arctic 46:246–250.

Blix, A.S. and Lentfer, J.W. 1992. Noise and vibration levels in artificial polar bear dens as related to selected petroleum exploration and developmental activities. Arctic 45:20-24.

Derocher, A.E. and Stirling, I. 1991. Oil contamination of polar bears. Polar Record, 27:56-57.

Honderich, J.E. 1991. Wildlife as a hazardous resource: An analysis of the historical interaction of humans and polar bears in the Canadian Arctic 2,000 B.C. to A.D. 1935. M.A. Thesis, University of Waterloo, Waterloo, Ontario.

Lunn, N.J. 2004. Selection of maternity dens by female polar bears in western Hudson Bay, Canada, and the effects of human disturbance. Polar Biology 7:359-356.

Øritsland, N.A. et al. 1981. Effect of Crude Oil on Polar Bears. Environmental Studies No. 24. Department of Indian and Northern Affairs, Ottawa. 268 pp.

Ramsay, M.A. and Stirling I. 1986. Long–term effects of drugging and handling free-ranging polar bears. Journal of Wildlife Management 50:619-26.

Stenhouse, G.B. et al. 1988. Some Characteristics of Polar Bears Killed during Conflicts with Humans in the Northwest Territories, 1976-86. Arctic 41:275-278.

Stirling, I. 1988. Attraction of polar bears *Ursus maritimus* to offshore drilling sites in the eastern Beaufort Sea. Polar Record 24:1-8.

Stirling, I. 1990. Polar bears and oil: Ecological perspectives. Pages 223-234 *in* J.R. Geraci and D.J. St. Aubin, eds. *Sea mammals and oil: Confronting the risks.* Academic Press, San Diego, CA.

Towns, L. et al. 2009. Spatial and temporal patterns of problem polar bears in Churchill, Manitoba. Polar Biology 32: 1529-1537.

Management and conservation

Bethke, R. et al. 1996. Population delineation of polar bears using satellite collar data. Ecological Applications 6:311-17.

Brower, C.D. et al. 2002. Polar bear management agreement for the Southern Beaufort Sea: An evaluation of the first ten years of a unique conservation agreement. Arctic 55:362-372.

Derocher, A.E. et al. 1997. Male-biased harvesting of polar bears in western Hudson Bay. Journal of Wildlife Management 61:1075-1082.

Lyster, S. 1985. *International Wildlife Law*. Cambridge: Grotius Publications. 470 pp.

Prestrud, P. and Stirling, I. 1994. The international polar bear agreement and the current status of polar bear conservation. Aquatic Mammals 20:113-24.

Regehr, E.V. et al. 2010. Survival and breeding of polar bears in the southern Beaufort Sea in relation to sea ice. Journal of Animal Ecology 79:117-127.

Regehr, E.V. et al. 2007. Survival and population size of polar bears in western Hudson Bay in relation to earlier sea ice break-up. Journal of Wildlife Management 71:2673-2683.

Taylor, M.K. et al. 1987. Modeling the sustainable harvest of female polar bears. Journal of Wildlife Management 51:811-20.

Towns, L. et al. 2009. Spatial and temporal patterns of problem polar bears in Churchill, Manitoba. Polar Biology 32:1529-1537.

Methods

Calvert, W., and Ramsay, M.A. 1998. Evaluation of age determination of polar bears by counts of cementum growth layer groups. Ursus 10:449-453.

Mauritzen, M. et al. 2002. Using satellite telemetry to define spatial population structure in polar bears in the Norwegian and western Russian Arctic. Journal of Applied Ecology, 39:79-90.

Medill, S. et al. 2009b. Estimating cementum annuli width in polar bears: Identifying sources of variation and error. Journal of Mammalogy 90:1256-1264.

Medill, S. et al. 2009. Reconstructing the reproductive history of female polar bears using cementum patterns of premolar teeth. Polar Biology DOI 10.1007/s00300-009-0689-z.

Ramsay, M.A. and Stirling, I. 1986. The long-term effects of drugging and handling free-ranging polar bears. Journal of Wildlife Management 50:619- 626.

Stirling, I. et al. 1989. Immobilization of polar bears (Ursus maritimus) with Telazol in the Canadian Arctic. Journal of Wildlife Diseases 25:159-168.

Thiemann, G.W. et al. 2009. Using fatty acids to study marine mammal foraging: The evidence from an extensive and growing literature. Marine Mammal Science 25: 243-249.

Movements

Amstrup, S.C. et al. 2000. Movements and distribution of polar bears in the Beaufort Sea. Canadian Journal of Zoology 78:948-66.

Amstrup, S.C. et al. 2001. Comparing movement patterns of satellite-tagged male and female polar bears. Canadian Journal of Zoology 79: 2147-2158.

Durner, G.M. and Amstrup, S.C. 1995. Movements of a polar bear from northern Alaska to northern Greenland. Arctic 48:338-341.

Ferguson, S.H. et al. 1997. Space use by polar bears in and around Auyuittuq National Park, Northwest Territories, during the ice-free period. Canadian Journal of Zoology 75:1585-94.

Garner, G.W. et al. 1990. Seasonal movements of adult female polar bears in the Bering and Chukchi Seas. Bears: Their Biology and Management, Vol. 8: 219-226.

Mauritzen, M. et al. 2003. Female polar bears, Ursus maritimus, on the Barents Sea drift ice: walking the treadmill. Animal Behaviour, 66:107-113

Messier, F. et al. 1992. Seasonal activity patterns of female polar bears (Ursus maritimus) in the Canadian Arctic as revealed by satellite teleme-

try. Journal of Zoology (London) 226:219-229.

Physiology, diet, and growth

Arnould,J.P.Y. and Ramsay, M.A. 1994. Milk production and milk consumption in polar bears during the ice-free period in western Hudson Bay. Canadian Journal of Zoology 72:1365-1370.

Atkinson, S.N. and Ramsay, M.A. 1995. The effects of prolonged fasting on the body composition and reproductive success of female polar bears. Functional Ecology 9:559-67.

Atkinson, S.N. et al. 1996. The effect of growth in early life on body size in polar bears (Ursus maritimus). Journal of Zoology (London) 239:225-234.

Baker, B.E. et al. 1963. Polar bear milk. 1. Gross composition and fat constitution. Canadian Journal of Zoology 41:1035-39.

Best, R.C. 1977. Ecological aspects of polar bear nutrition. Pp. 201-211, In, Phillips, P.L. and Jonkel, C. (Eds), Predator Symposium. Montana Experimental Station, University of Montana, Missoula.

Best, R.C. 1982. Thermoregulation in resting and active polar bears. Journal of Comparative Physiology B 146:63-73.

Best, R.C. 1985. Digestibility of ringed seals by the polar bear. Canadian Journal of Zoology 63:1033-1036.

Best, R.C. et al. 1981. Physiological indices of activity and metabolism in the polar bear. Comparative Biochemistry and Physiology 69A:177-185.

Cherry, S.G. et al. 2009. Fasting physiology of polar bears in relation to environmental change and breeding behaviour in the Beaufort Sea. Polar Biology (DOI 10.1007/s00300-008-0530-0.

Derocher, A.E. et al. 1993. Aspects of milk composition and lactation in polar bears. Canadian Journal of Zoology 71:561-567.

Derocher, A.E. and Stirling, I. 1998. Geographic variation in growth of polar bears (Ursus maritimus). Journal of Zoology (London) 245:65-72.

Derocher, A.E. and Wiig, Ø. 2002. Postnatal growth in body length and mass of polar bears (Ursus maritimus) at Svalbard. Journl of. Zoology (London) 256:343-349.

Derocher, A.E. et al. 2002. Diet composition of polar bears in Svalbard and the western Barents Sea. Polar Biology 25:448-452.

Derocher, A.E. et al. 1990. Effects of fasting and feeding on serum urea and serum creatinine levels in polar bears. Marine Mammal Science 6:196-203.

Hobson, K.A. and Stirling, I. 1997. Terrestrial foraging by polar bears during the ice free period in western Hudson Bay: metabolic pathways and limitations of the stable isotope method. Marine Mammal Science 13:359-367.

Hurst, R. et al. 1982a. Polar bear locomotion: body temperature and energetic cost. Canadian Journal of Zoology 60:40-44.

Hurst, R. et al. 1982b. Body mass, temperature and cost of walking in polar bears. Acta Physiologica Scandica 115: 391-395.

Iverson, S.J. et al. 2006. Spatial, temporal, and individual variation in the diets of polar bears across the Canadian Arctic: Links with and indicators of changes in prey populations. Pp. 98-117 *In*, Boyd I. (Ed), *Management of Marine Ecosystems: monitoring change in upper trophic levels*. Symposium of the Zoological Society of London.

Kingsley, M.C.S. 1979. Fitting the von Bertalanffy growth equation to polar bear age-weight data. Canadian Journal of Zoology 57:1020-1025.

Lunn, N.J. and Stirling, I. 1985. The significance of supplemental food to polar bears during the ice-free period of Hudson Bay. Canadian Journal of Zoology 63:191-297.

Nelson, R.A. et al. 1973. Metabolism of bears before, during, and after winter sleep. American Journal of Physiology 224:491-96.

Nelson, R.A. 1983. Behaviour, biochemistry, and hibernation in black, grizzly, and polar bears. International Conference on Bear Research and Management 5:284-90.

Øritsland, N.A. 1969. Deep body temperature of swimming and walking in polar bear cubs. Journal of Mammalogy 50:380-382.

Øritsland, N.A. 1970. Temperature regulation of the polar bear (*Thalarctos maritimus*). Comparative Biochemistry and Physiology 37:225-33.

Øritsland, N.A. and Lavigne, D.M. 1976. Radiative surface temperatures of exercising polar bears. Comparative Biochemistry and Physiology 53A:327-330.

Øritsland, N.A. and Ronald, K. 1978. Solar heating of mammals: Observations of hair transmittance. Journal of Biometeorology 22:197-201.

Øritsland, N.A. et al. 1976. A respiration chamber for exercising polar bears. Norwegian Journal of Zoology 24:65-67.

Ramsay, M.A. and Dunbrach, R.L. 1986. Physiological constraints on life history phenomena: the example of small bear cubs at birth. American Naturalist 127:735-743.

Rode, K. et al. 2010. Comments in response to "Estimating the energetic contribution of polar bear (*Ursus maritimus*) summer diets to the total energy budget". Journal of Mammalogy 91:1517-1523.

Russell, R.H. 1975. The food habits of polar bears of James Bay and southwest Hudson Bay in Summer and autumn, Arctic 28:117-129.

Stirling, I. and Archibald, W.R. 1977. Aspects of predation of seals by polar bears. Journal of the Fisheries Research Board of Canada 34:1126-1129.

Stirling, I. and Øritsland, N.A. 1995. Relationships between estimates of

ringed seal and polar bear populations in the Canadian Arctic. Canadian Journal of Fisheries and Aquatic Sciences 52:2594-2612.

Stirling, I. and McEwan, E.H. 1975. The caloric value of whole ringed seals (*Phoca hispida*) in relation to polar bear (*Ursus maritimus*) ecology and hunting behaviour. Canadian Journal of Zoology 53:1021-1026.

Thiemann, G.W. et al. 2006. Seasonal, sexual, and anatomical variability in the adipose tissue composition of polar bears (*Ursus maritimus*). Journal of Zoology 269:65-76.

Thiemann, G.W. et al. 2007. Variation in blubber fatty acid composition among marine mammals in the Canadian Arctic. Marine Mammal Science 23:241-261.

Thiemann, G.W. et al. 2007. Unusual fatty acid Biomarkers reveal age- and sex-specific foraging in polar bears (*Ursus maritimus*). Canadian Journal of Zoology 85:505-517.

Thiemann, G.W. et al. 2008. Polar bear diets and arctic marine food webs: insights from fatty acid analysis. Ecological Monographs, 78:591-613.

Watts, P.D., and Hansen, S.E. 1987. Cyclic starvation as a reproductive strategy in the polar bear. Symposium of the Zoological Society of London 57:306-18.

Wilson, D.E. 1976. Cranial variation in polar bears. International Conference on Bear Research and Management 3:447-53.

Reproduction

Atkinson, S.N. and Ramsay, M.A. 1995. The effects of prolonged fasting of the body composition and reproductive success of female Polar Bears (*Ursus maritimus*). Functional Ecology 9:559-567.

Derocher, A.E. and Stirling, I. 1994. Age-specific reproductive performance of female polar bears (*Ursus maritimus*). Journal of Zoology London 234:527-536.

Derocher, A.E. 1999. Latitudinal variation in litter size of polar bears: ecology or methodology? Polar Biology 22:350-356.

Derocher, A.E. and Stirling, I. 1998. Maternal investment and factors affecting offspring size in polar bears (*Ursus maritimus*). Journal of Zoology (London) 245:253-260.

Derocher, A.E. et al. 2010. **Sexual dimorphism and the mating ecology of polar bears (*Ursus maritimus*) at Svalbard. Behavioural Ecology and Sociobiology. DOI 10.1007/s00265-010-0909-0.**

Lønø, O. 1972. Polar bear fetuses found in Svalbard. Norsk Polarinstitutt-Arbok 1970:294–98.

Ramsay, M.A., and Stirling, I. 1986. On the mating system of polar bears. Canadian Journal of Zoology 64:2142–51.

Ramsay, M.A., and Stirling, I. 1988. Reproductive biology and ecology of female polar bears (*Ursus maritimus*). Journal of Zoology (London) 214:601-634.

Tumanov, I.L., 2001. Reproductive biology of captive polar bears. Ursus 12:107-108

Wiig, Ø. et al. 1992. Breeding behaviour of polar bears in Hornsund, Svalbard. Polar Record 28:157-159.

Zeyl, E. et al. 2009. Families in space: relatedness in the Barents Sea population of polar bears (*Ursus maritimus*). Molecular Ecology doi: 10.1111/j.1365-294X.2008.04049.x.

Zeyl, E. et al. 2009. The mating system of polar bears: a genetic approach. Canadian Journal of Zoology 87:1-15.

Traditional Knowledge and Anthropology

Berkes, F. et al. 2000. Rediscovery of traditional ecological knowledge as adaptive management. Ecological Applications 10:1251-1262.

Berkes, F. 1999. *Sacred Ecology: Traditional Ecological Knowledge and Resource Management*. Taylor and Francis, Philadelphia. 217 pp.

Boas, F. 1964. *The Central Eskimo*. Lincoln, Nebraska. Pp. Originally published in Washington, DC as part of the 6th Annual Report of the Bureau of Ethnology, Smithsonian Institution, 1888.

Born, E.W. et al. 2011. *Polar Bears in Northwest Greenland: An Interview Survey about the Catch and the Climate*. Museum Tusculanum Press, University of Copenhagen, Copenhagen. 232 pp.

Hallowell, C.R. 1926. Bear ceremonialism in the northern hemisphere. American Anthropologist 28:1-175.

Henri, D., Gilchrist, H.G. and Peacock, E. 2010. Understanding and Managing Wildlife in Hudson Bay under a Changing Climate: Recent Contributions from Cree and Inuit Ecological Knowledge. Pp. 267-90, *In*: Ferguson, S., Mallory, M. and Loseto, L. (Eds.). *A Little Less Arctic: Top Predators in the World's Largest Northern Inland Sea, Hudson Bay*. Springer. New York.

Huntington, H. P. 2000. Using Traditional Ecological Knowledge in Science: Methods and Applications. Ecological Applications 10:1270 1274.

Keith, D. et al. 2005. *Inuit Qaujimaningit: Inuit Knowledge of Polar Bears*. CCI Press. Edmonton: 242 pp.

Larsen, H. 1969-70. Some examples of bear cult among the Eskimo and other northern people. Folk 11-12:27-36.

Lewis, A.E. et al. 2009. Movement and aggregation of eastern Hudson Bay beluga whales (*Delphinapterus leucas*): A comparison of patterns found through satellite telemetry and Nunavik Traditional Ecological Knowledge. Arctic 62:13–24.

McGhee, R. 2001. *Ancient People of the Arctic*. UBC Press. Vancouver, B.C. 244 pp.

Randa, V. 1986. *L'Ours Polaire et les Inuit*. Société d'Etudes Linguistiques et Anthropologiques de France. Paris. 323 pp.

Rasmussen, K. 1921. The Netsilik Eskimos : Social Life and Spiritual Culture. Report of the Fifth Thule Expedition, vol. 8. Copenhagen.

INDEX